Good Kids

Why You Suffered in Silence and
How to Break the Cycle

MAGGIE NICK, LCSW

First published by Sheldon Press in 2025
An imprint of John Murray Press

1

Copyright © Maggie Nick 2025

The right of Maggie Nick to be identified as the Author of the Work has been asserted by her in accordance with the Copyright, Designs and Patents Act 1988.

All rights reserved. No part of this publication may be reproduced, stored in a retrieval system, or transmitted, in any form or by any means without the prior written permission of the publisher, nor be otherwise circulated in any form of binding or cover other than that in which it is published and without a similar condition being imposed on the subsequent purchaser.

This book is for information or educational purposes only and is not intended to act as a substitute for medical advice or treatment. Any person with a condition requiring medical attention should consult a qualified medical practitioner or suitable therapist.

A CIP catalogue record for this title is available from the British Library

Trade Paperback ISBN 9781399821254
ebook ISBN 9781399821261

Typeset by KnowledgeWorks Global Ltd.

Printed and bound in Great Britain by Clays Ltd, Elcograf S.p.A.

John Murray Press policy is to use papers that are natural, renewable and recyclable products and made from wood grown in sustainable forests. The logging and manufacturing processes are expected to conform to the environmental regulations of the country of origin.

John Murray Press	Sheldon Press
Carmelite House	Hachette Book Group
50 Victoria Embankment	123 South Broad Street
London EC4Y 0DZ	Ste 2750
	Philadelphia, PA 19109, USA

www.sheldonpress.co.uk

John Murray Press, part of Hodder & Stoughton Limited
An Hachette UK company

The authorised representative in the EEA is Hachette Ireland, 8 Castlecourt Centre, Dublin 15, D15 XTP3, Ireland (email: info@hbgi.ie)

Dedication

For Allie and Oliver:
Getting to love you and be your mom is the greatest honor and privilege of my life. May you always know your inherent worth. May you always be a soft, loving spot for yourself to land when you're struggling. And may you always feel at home in yourselves.

For Little Mags:
I dedicate this book as a love letter to you and your relentless, fierce, beautiful spirit. I'm sharing your story to help other "good" kids heal. I'm so proud of you and us.

Contents

About the author	ix
Foreword by Eli Harwood	xi
Introduction	xv

Part 1: Learning

1 The Good Kids Aren't Alright — 3
   What Is a Good Kid? — 4
   Meet Me: A Recovered Good Kid — 8

2 Good Kid Biology — 15
   Nervous System 101: Fight, Flight, Freeze, and Fawn — 16
   Good Kid Origins — 27
   Good Kids vs. "Bad" Kids — 28

3 "You Should Be Grateful." — 31
   Our Parents' Misguided Beliefs — 31
   Growing Up with Emotionally Reactive Parents — 48
   Growing up with a High-Needs Sibling or "Problem Child" Sibling — 56
   Our Parents Don't Get Their Impact — 59

4 The Voice That Says It's All Your Fault — 63
   What Is Shame? — 63
   Shame Hurts Most When It Comes From People We Love — 69
   The Unspoken Rules for Good Kids — 72

Part 2: Healing

5 You Didn't Want To Be "A Burden" — 99
   A Child Never Misbehaving Is A Red Flag — 100
   Kids Resist To Release To Regulate — 105

6 The Part Where You Stop Being Mad At Yourself — 109
   How To Regulate Your Nervous System — 110
   IFS/Parts Work — 127
   How To Feel Your Feelings — 137

7 You Carry Your Childhood Into Every Relationship — 141
   A Rescue Dog Who Didn't Know It Needed Rescuing — 141
   People Pleasing — 148

8 Giving Yourself What They Couldn't — 159
   Awakening Fight Response — 160
   You and Anger: It's Complicated — 163
   Good Kid Recovery — 167

Part 3: Parenting

9 Facing Your Stuff So Your Kids Don't Have To   177
    Parenting and Reparenting, Together   180
    How Kids Actually Develop   183
    The 6 Core Needs: What We Need Most   185

10 Seeing the Signs and Showing Up Differently   201
    Check Engine Lights for Good Kids   201
        Perfectionism and Debilitating Fear of Failure   201
        Chronic People Pleasing   203
        Bottling Their Emotions   207
        Anxiety and Hypervigilance   210
        Only Having Two Speeds: 150mph or Crashing and Burning   213
        Chronic Overachieving   219
        Overapologizing (Apologizing Excessively and Fearfully)   223
        Being Viciously Self-Critical   227
        Physical Complaints or Psychosomatic Symptoms   230
        Hidden Self-Soothing Behaviors   233
    The 5 Adjustments   239
        Shift From Critical To Curious   239
        Let Them Resist Without Shame   242
        Check Your Expectations   243
        Stand By Them, No Matter What   244
        Shift Your Focus   245

11 Raising Kids Who Don't Have To Recover   247
    Reality Checks for Our Parent's Misguided Beliefs and Expectations   249
    Breaking The Cycle of "I'm Not Mad, I'm Disappointed"   254
    Shame-Prone vs. Guilt-Prone Self-Talk   261

12 Big Feelings Shouldn't Equal Big Trouble   271
    Critical Steps Before Trying "Name It To Tame It"   276
    Meltdowns   279

13 When They Don't Push Back—And That's the Problem   287
    Time Out   289
    The Silent Treatment   290
    How People Pleasing Shows Up In Parenting   292
    Relational Colostrum: Why Circle Backs Are Liquid Gold   300
    Bringing It All Together: Disrespect and Refusing To Cooperate   304

Conclusion   309
Acknowledgments   311
References   313
Index   327

About the Author

Maggie Nick is a licensed clinical social worker, trauma therapist, parenting expert and Recovering Good Kid who finally, finally feels lovable as hell. She can't wait to help you get there, too.

For most of her life, Maggie was the one "nobody ever needed to worry about"—praised for being easy-going and the one everyone could always count on. Believing she had a "great childhood," she didn't realize until she was 25 and in therapy that her overachieving, people pleasing, perfectionism, and raging selflessness weren't her personality... they were lifelong relational trauma responses.

Her healing journey began as a fierce mission: to understand what the hell happened to her so she could break the cycle for her own kids. Relentlessly exploring and researching the stunning parallels she saw between her own healing and the experiences of her child and adult counseling clients led her to become a leading expert on Good Kid Trauma (Relational Shame Trauma) and a trusted voice for parents wanting to break generational cycles for their kids.

Maggie created her rebellious online community Camp Lovable to help Recovering Good Kids stop feeling like they have to be perfect all the damn time and learn how to say no and set boundaries without going into Fight/Flight. Maggie's "Good Girl" Rehab Membership connects women around the world in a safe, sacred space where they can stop needing to prove their goodness and finally feel worthy and good enough.

Maggie received her Masters in Social Work from Indiana University and her Bachelors in Sociology with a double major in Psychology from Virginia Tech. Her work is a fierce mix of hope and hard truths, guiding you back home to yourself. She's on a mission to help the world break cycles for our kids, and for the parts of ourselves that were never allowed to be messy and imperfect. Maggie lives near the beach in Florida with her husband, two kids and beloved dogs.

You can find her at maggienick.com.

For free resources and bonus material, scan this QR code.

Author photo © Lynn Tenille

Foreword by Eli Harwood

One of the most important things I have learned over the past two decades as a family therapist specializing in child development is that we cannot assess a child's emotional wellness by their behavior alone.

Emotionally healthy two-year-olds lose their marbles out of the blue, not because they are bad kids, but because their brains are growing new neural connections at warp speed. Emotionally healthy elementary school students say mean things when they are under peer pressure, not because they have cruel hearts, but because they are still learning how to respond to complicated social situations. Emotionally healthy teenagers disagree with their parents and may even sneak around in rebellion of rules, not because they are disrespectful, but because it is their developmental task to do whatever they can to gain independence and agency. Not all "bad behavior" is indicative of something wrong.

On the flip side, not all good behavior is indicative of things being right. Children who are being raised in deeply abusive and neglectful environments can be incredibly compliant and well-behaved on the outside, but riddled with trauma and anxiety on the inside. Children who appear to "go with the flow" and be "easy going," might actually suffer from deep insecurity and a fear of abandonment. The reasons behind a child's behavior are deeply relevant to whether or not that behavior emanates from a place of healthy development, or a place of trauma, fear, or concealment.

To truly understand a child's emotional health, we have to consider not only their behavior, but also the motivations behind their behavior, as well as the social environments influencing both of those things.

The antiquated notion that well-behaved kids are "good" and kids who act out or struggle to regulate their bodies are "bad," is not only a false understanding of behavior, it is a painful curse to kids on both sides of the labeling.

It is a curse to be called a bad kid because it creates a legacy of shame and low self-worth. It is also a curse to be called a Good Kid, because it creates a legacy of self-denial and the unfortunate trap of believing that one's self-worth is tied up in being "good" for other people.

Emotionally-well kids are not always well-behaved, and kids who are always well-behaved are not usually emotionally-well.

Instead, the markers of emotional wellness are rooted in authentic expression and connection. Children who feel securely attached to their caregivers, who know that they can rely on others for understanding, empathy, and soothing, are the most likely to grow up feeling worthy, connected, and resilient. As I wrote in my book, *Raising Securely Attached Kids*, "We can't control who our children are, but we can profoundly influence how they feel about who they are, and how they feel in relationship to us." As relational creatures we need permission to authentically express ourselves, and to mess up and feel messy and still feel loved, so that we can learn to see every part of us as worthy of connection.

You may have been labeled a "Good Kid" because of your capacity to bury your feelings to keep other people pleased. Or because of a survival instinct to keep your mouth shut and your hands obedient to avoid the wrath of a narcissistic parent. Or, perhaps, like me, you were labeled a Good Kid because you had a high sensitivity to other people's emotions, and so you learned to caretake and perform to help your parents keep their own heads above water.

If you didn't feel good in your childhood, then being labeled a "Good Kid" came with a high price to your own development journey.

Foreword by Eli Harwood

When I was young, my mother was struggling with severe depression, complex trauma, and very little social or emotional support. My father was decades into a dependence on alcohol that had been preceded by a dependence on cocaine. Neither of my parents were okay when I was a kid. Needless to say, neither was their marriage. Although I knew at my core that my parents loved me and wanted the best for me, I also knew that they were not reliable in emotional terms. Not because they didn't want to be there for me, or because they didn't care about what I felt, but because they were drowning in their own stuff.

So at a very young age I learned to caretake their emotional needs. I shrunk my own feelings and complaints. I regularly tried to encourage them and help them to feel worthy and loved, and when they were spiraling, I tried to soothe them and offer them emotional containment. I did everything in my power to regulate my parents, so that I could feel some semblance of security.

It's scary to be the most emotionally stable person in your childhood.

I remember the grownups in my life constantly telling me how mature I was; how articulate of a young woman I was; how impressed they were with my ability to make good choices, and what an old soul they thought I had. In a world of so much uncertainty, my achievements were a much needed life raft that kept my head above water.

I continued in this vein well into my 20s. I was given prestigious scholarships, leadership awards, and accolades for the Good Kid path. But underneath the water, I was unsure of myself, unclear about what really mattered to me, and afraid of being abandoned by the people close to me.

When we are good in order to cope with the bad in our childhoods, we never get the chance to be authentically ourselves. It takes a secure attachment relationship with our caregivers to feel permission to explore and express. While I may have given the impression of being self-assured in my childhood, deep down I was incredibly anxious about myself and my place in the world.

Luckily for me, my mother started going to therapy, and made healing a new family legacy.

I was able to find care from incredible therapists who chose to look underneath my Good Kid performance to help me uncover the real kid beneath it. They gently encouraged me to acknowledge the incredible responsibility and terror that I held in my growing up. And, piece by piece, to take care of my past and present self in ways that no one else had been able to up to that point. This processing and growing was emotionally challenging at times, but ultimately incredibly healing and freeing.

What Maggie has done in this book is to put together an incredible guide to help you do the same. To uncover the fullness of who you are beneath the "goodness" of who you had to be. To become wildly free, hopeful, and expressive without the pressure to hide your humanness.

It is a precious gift to truly know ourselves and to be authentically known and loved for being all of who we are. I hope these pages invite you to see that it was never your obedience, or your silence, or your service to others that made you good, it was your realness. You can't earn what you have always had inside of you: a worthiness to be seen, heard, and celebrated in your authentic self.

May these pages open you up to radically love and accept parts of yourself that haven't had that chance before, and may they also offer you determination to give your own kids the goodness of being secure enough with you to be their entire-messy-sacred-authentic self.

Introduction

One day in December 2020, on the way home from the store, I was hit with a lightning bolt of inspiration for an Instagram video. I pulled over, grabbed my phone, and started recording: "The price I paid to be the Good Kid, the easy-to-parent kid, the one 'nobody ever needed to worry about.'" I talked about my "personality"—a tangled mess of lifelong trauma responses disguised as strengths:

- Perfectionism
- People pleasing
- Needing to control everything
- Messed-up relationship with food.

I talked about how Good Kids suffer in silence—how they look like they're crushing life, but inside, they are not okay.

That video became my first viral post, and tens of thousands of people from all over the world flooded the comments, stunned. "This is my life," and, "How are you inside my head?" they said. Every little detail tracked for them. I had put words to something they had felt their whole lives but never knew how to name.

That was the first time I used the phrase Good Kid, but I had started having these profound, goosebumps moments with clients in my counseling practice. I'd have a session with an adult, then later that day, sit with a child or teen. And it would feel like I was talking to the *same person* at two different points in time. Sometimes it felt like I was with my adult client's younger self. Other times, like I was hearing from the grown-up version of my child client. The parallels were stunning.

Why did they struggle to ask for what they need and want?
They didn't want to feel like a burden.
What fear kept them in a chokehold?

That someone might be mad at them.
Which words consistently brought them to tears?
There is nothing wrong with you.
What was their deepest, most painful core belief?
That they're hard to love. Unlovable.
What was the connecting thread?
Shame.

What became clear to me is that we all struggle with different things on the surface, but underneath we are all carrying the crushing beliefs that no matter how much we succeed, achieve, and accomplish, we'll never outrun the fact that there is something fundamentally wrong with us. That we must be hypervigilant and make sure we only show the "good" side of ourselves because if people *found out* that we're actually unlovable... they would leave.

I wrote this book to *show you* how that happened and to walk you through the very mechanisms that ingrained those beliefs so deeply inside you. You deserve to understand what happened to you. You deserve to understand why you go into Fight/Flight trying to set boundaries. You deserve to understand why it feels like your life is in actual danger at the *thought* that someone might be mad at you.

I know your life experience keeps reinforcing these things. You do the math and keep coming back to the idea that you're the common denominator so it *must* be you. But this kind of hurt is sneaky. Quiet. Invisible. And it has a name: Relational Shame Trauma. Trauma that happened *inside* our relationships. It doesn't look, seem or feel like trauma or chaos. Sometimes, it looks like being praised for not having needs. Sometimes, shame hides under gold stars.

Relational Shame Trauma is the reason you keep ending up in the same kind of painful relationships. It's not because something's wrong with you, but because your brain and nervous system are being drawn like a magnet to familiar

Introduction

relationships... hoping this time it'll finally feel safe. Hoping that this time you'll finally be good enough. Hoping that this time, they'll stay. That pattern isn't proof that you're the problem. It's your brain and nervous system trying to heal.

You deserve to believe at the deepest level that you always were a story worth loving, exactly as you are. I wrote this book to help you understand all of this. Let these pages hold you the way you always deserved as you heal into believing these things for yourself. I'm proud of you and I'm cheering you on.

1
LEARNING

1
The Good Kids Aren't Alright

"A delight to have in class."
"An old soul."
"Never causes any trouble."
"So mature for their age."
"Such a Good Kid."

If you grew up as a Good Kid, you probably heard these words a lot. Said with pride. Said with relief. Said like they were the highest compliment a child could receive.

And you were good. Quiet. Easy. Mature beyond your years. So disciplined, you basically parented yourself. The one who made life easier just by existing. The one who was helpful without being asked. The one who never needed support.

While other kids whined, misbehaved, pushed back, or melted down, you were, "the one no one ever had to worry about." While other kids were emotional, demanding, or difficult, you were always "fine."

And when life got hard—when everyone else was crumbling—you were "the one they could count on."

Good Kids don't get checked on. No one asks if they're okay because they *seem* okay. They're self-sufficient, capable, and successful. Independent and seemingly *crushing* life. So no one—not even they themselves—realizes they're drowning in shame and suffering in silence.

But being "good" at surviving isn't the same as actually being okay. And if no one ever checked in on you, then let this be the moment you begin to check in on yourself now. Because Good Kids deserve to be cared for, too.

What Is a Good Kid?

The pressure to be "good" doesn't land the same way for every child. Some kids are naturally more easygoing, more attuned to others and more sensitive to approval and rejection. When a parent's love and care feels conditional—tied to performance, obedience, or making their life easier—the child doesn't just hear the message to "be good," they deeply internalize that their worth depends on it.

Good Kids are often naturally more easygoing and compliant rather than oppositional, making them especially vulnerable to that dynamic. Many also have a parent whose unhealed trauma, mental and physical health struggles, substance use and abuse, and/or a high-needs sibling, create an inconsistent and unpredictable environment. Sometimes, their parent is loving and warm... then suddenly they're dismissive and cold.

The phenomenon of the "good" kid is complex and deeply rooted in familial and cultural expectations of what we believe kids "should" be like. All kids are relentlessly told to "be good" and punished for "not being good." Yet, some kids are acutely aware of their fear of failure and disappointing others. This fear gets turned up to the max in the face of their parents' crushing expectations of excellence at all costs.

Their parent's emotional immaturity and discomfort with their own feelings means the Good Kid gets shut down, sent away and punished when they're emotional. Their parent withdraws *and withholds* love, attention, affection, and a willingness to care for them as a punishment, not understanding the devastating impact of the silent treatment on their child.

The Good Kid needs their parent to be emotionally attuned to *them*, but instead they are emotionally attuned to *their parent*—always watching, walking on eggshells for fear of setting off their parent's temper. This lack of emotional attunement from their caregiver means the Good Kid is left to deal with their own emotions without guidance, support, or soothing. The Good Kid will brilliantly adapt here and just try to never have emotions—by suppressing all emotion and figuring out a way to be *fine*, no matter what.

All kids try to be good—it's part of wanting to belong and be loved. But Good Kids don't just *try* to "be good"—they shapeshift into whatever the adults in the room need or want them to be. Good Kids suffer in silence and beat themselves up for falling short. Good Kids are praised for never needing the parent—for being so self-sufficient they basically parent themselves. And they don't need to be punished because they're constantly punishing themselves.

The Good Kid is that friend who *always* makes you feel so good about yourself. But inside, they feel like they'll never be good enough and they're viciously critical of themselves any time they're anything other than perfect.

They people please to avoid conflict and confrontation, going into Fight/Flight trying to say no.

Good Kids feel guilty about everything and apologize even when they haven't done anything wrong. They suppress their more unpleasant emotions and pretend they're fine. They numb their distress with food or substances that can escalate to an eating disorder or addiction.

Good Kids are relentlessly high achieving—driven, capable, and fueled by a debilitating fear of failure. They pile their plate with more than they can handle, chasing opportunities to prove their goodness, held hostage by the crushing fear of letting others down. They over function until their body forces them to stop and *crashes* with burnout.

Beneath it all they're haunted by a deep, unrelenting fear that something is wrong with them and they're only lovable when they're "being good."

"But I Had a Great Childhood."

If you've ever thought this, let me start by saying: you are not alone. Our brains are wired to focus on the good—it's a survival instinct. Parts of us push away and distract us from the hard stuff, convincing us that because our parent clearly loves us, worked hard to provide for us, and gave us so much, we don't deserve to feel hurt, sad, or resentful. "We should be more grateful."

I'm not here to convince you that you didn't have a good childhood. I'm here to help you find your way back to the Parts of you that *weren't* fine—but couldn't show that on the outside. The Parts who took one for the team again and again and pretended they were fine. The Parts that swallowed their pain, pushed aside their needs, performed calm and learned to "be good"—no matter what it cost you.

We believe that because our childhood *looked* good in many ways, it *was* good—no matter how we actually felt inside. That gap between how things looked and how they felt is what makes this kind of trauma so sneaky, confusing and insidious. It has a name: Relational Shame Trauma, and it's less about what happened on the outside and more about how we were made to feel about ourselves on the inside, in our relationships with our caregivers. For many of us, Parts of us hold onto the belief that it was good beyond logical reason and we end up carrying around these quiet, unseen wounds. But: love and harm can coexist. Your pain is real, even if your childhood wasn't "bad enough" by some invisible, made-up cultural standard.

Relational Shame Trauma often takes root in the quiet, invisible moments. It doesn't always come from outright neglect or abuse. More often, it grows in the subtle, wordless exchanges—how emotions were handled or, more often, ignored. It's in the unspoken rules that taught you to "be good," that not rocking the boat was more important than being real about how you felt. It's in the way you were praised for being responsible, agreeable, or helpful, but made to feel ashamed when you were needy, upset, or struggling. It's the unacknowledged expectation that love and approval had to be earned—through behavior, performance, and keeping everyone else happy.

You can have parents who loved you deeply but still left you carrying shame. Because for most of us, our parents truly didn't know any better. They were carrying their own internalized shame, unresolved trauma, and outdated ideas of what parenting "should" look like. They believed things like "kids should always, always, always behave," that "being 'good' means you respect your parents" and that "good kids don't cry or complain," and they raised us with those same beliefs—beliefs that made us feel like there was something wrong with us when we were emotional, messy, or just being kids.

The sneakiest part is that this kind of trauma doesn't look, seem or feel like trauma. It feels like you—who you are. It feels like the anxiety that keeps you up at night, the perfectionism that drives you, the voice in your head that says you're not good enough unless you prove yourself. You think that's who you are.

It feels like apologizing when you've done nothing wrong and avoiding conflict at all costs because, if you didn't, people wouldn't want to be around you. Your Inner Critic is always there, whispering: "If people really knew who you are, they wouldn't love you. They would be horrified." It cuts so freaking deep. I see you.

Here's the thing—you can love and appreciate your parents. You can honor the ways they tried to be the parent you needed. But your healing requires you to honor not just their *intent* but their actual *impact* on you, because that's the part that shaped how you see yourself, how you move through the world, and how you show up in your relationships. It's not about blaming them—it's about being honest with yourself about what actually happened, so you can start to heal and do things differently for yourself. And maybe for your own kids, too.

It can feel like betrayal, like you're being *disloyal* to your parents, to question the way they parented you. But you don't owe your parents the kind of "loyalty" that means ignoring your own pain or pretending things didn't hurt when they did. You deserve to have fierce loyalty to *yourself*—to your healing, to your well-being, and to the future you're trying to build. You are allowed to love your parents and still hold space for the ways their actions or patterns hurt you. Denying your own experience doesn't heal anything—it just keeps these freaking cycles going. And you, my friend, are here to break them.

You deserve to feel safe in your body, to believe in your inherent worth, and to live free from the weight of shame you were never meant to carry. You deserve to feel at home in your body and in your life—not constantly hustling for approval, not tiptoeing around conflict, not shrinking yourself to make others comfortable. You deserve to take up space, to show up messy and real, and to finally believe, deep down, that you were always enough, just as you are.

Meet Me: A Recovered Good Kid

I am still recovering from being a Good Kid.

Named "Most Likely to Succeed" in 5th grade, I was an Honor Roll student, successful in multiple sports and had lots of friends. I was always so happy and positive on the outside that when my boyfriend dumped me in high school, and I cried in front of my friends, they panicked because they had never seen me upset before. I was violating some secret agreement I had apparently made with life: I took care of other people emotionally. And... nobody took care of my emotional needs.

I remember proudly telling a friend in college that I was simultaneously double majoring, taking 18 credit hours, working 20 hours a week, volunteering as an on-call Victim Advocate with the local domestic and sexual violence shelter, *and* training for freaking a marathon.

I thought I was fine. I really did.

I was "fine," but stressed out all the time. I finally got myself into therapy, and we kept bumping into my desperate, frantic attempts to be perfect. All roads kept leading back to my deep desire to be good... enough.

My Therapist said it was anxiety. I didn't *feel* anxious. But then it hit me like a bolt of lightning—my anxiety was the energy I carried trying to never upset anyone; never disappoint anyone; never be a burden on anyone. It came from bottling up every feeling, people pleasing like it was my job, and obsessing over doing everything perfectly.

I was so proud of never making mistakes—but at what cost? Because, once I noticed my thoughts, I actually worried about *everything*. I watched everyone's moods like a hawk. I hustled and shapeshifted to make sure people liked me. I constantly checked in with others to make sure that we were "okay." I was so scared of conflict, scared of making people mad or disappointed, my default state was hypervigilance.

As I pulled harder on this thread, I reached a very scary conclusion: this wasn't me. This wasn't my personality; it was trauma. My "personality"—my anxiety, my people pleasing, my perfectionism—was a bunch of trauma responses. As a kid, I relied on them religiously to manage a mother who struggled with an emotional instability, volatility and would ice me out to tame me back into being "good." But I never grew out of them. And as an adult, I thought being "fine" was just how I was wired, but I was actually carrying all this unprocessed pain.

This was a total game changer and explained why looking at pictures of Little Me had started to feel like a gut punch.

In therapy, I finally was able to connect with her—my tender, hurting Inner Child that I had spent a lifetime ignoring. She was needy like I expected her to be, but my instinctual reaction to her neediness surprised even me: I wasn't annoyed; I wasn't disgusted. I felt understanding, tenderness, and endless patience. It was like I was gesturing to her to crawl up in my lap for a snuggle and asking her to let me take care of her.

But loving her didn't come easily at first. I met much more resistance than I expected—some Parts of me that struggled to see her as precious and lovable. Other Parts of me thought she was too much, too needy, too exhausting to be worthy of love and care. While other Parts of me needed her to be different than she was, to be lovable. Still, I felt this sacred responsibility to keep trying, to keep pushing through that resistance... for her. To not give up on her. To be someone who finally stayed and didn't leave her when she was struggling.

I started checking in with Little Me throughout the day to see how she was doing, to let her know that she mattered to me. I told her that taking care of her felt like a privilege and a delight, not a burden. I practiced staying with her when she was struggling.

Shifting the way I related to Little Me made me notice how others related to Today Me—I paid attention to the people who stayed with Today Me when I was struggling. No matter how many shameful truths I revealed to them about how I was actually not perfect, my husband, Matt, and my therapist just kept on supporting me, believing in me and showing up for me. They didn't flinch, they didn't pull away from me, they met me in my most vulnerable moments without rushing me to be okay. This changed something so deep for me—I started to believe that maybe Little Me deserved this, too. The more I practiced staying with her, the more I saw the truth that I had never been able to see before: I had always been lovable. I didn't have to be perfect to be chosen. I could support others *and* I was worthy of being supported by others. Love wasn't something I had to beg for and brace to lose.

I learned in therapy how to stop bottling up my feelings and pretending I was okay all the time. Pretending messed me up. I realized it was actually a privilege—not a right—for people to get to be in my life. I started telling my nervous system, "You are safe now, I've got you," and learned how to speak to my body in its own language (the language of regulation). And slowly, the people pleasing, perfectionism, hypervigilance, walking on eggshells—it all started to get better. I got better.

I finished graduate school. I opened my own therapy practice. And when I launched my Instagram account to share my insights, I was stunned to discover so many more like me around the world.

Over the years, I had not one but two different therapists tell me I am the most viciously self-critical client they have ever treated. And I clawed my way through the soul crushing shame that told me I was somehow "too much" and... not enough. I've healed more than I ever thought was possible and I really, truly love the hell out of Little Me and Today Me. I don't beat myself up about every little thing anymore; I cheer myself on so damn hard. No more going into Fight/Flight trying to stand up for myself, I set boundaries and speak my needs like a boss. People can like me or not like me—that's not my business. I don't need others to see me as "likeable" to know and feel I'm lovable. I know who I am.

That healing has made space for me to give my children the mother they deserve—who *apologizes* when I hurt them. A mother who *wants* to know when I've hurt them, so I can make it right. A mother who *doesn't* take their misbehavior and disrespect personally. A mother who *lets them feel safe being fully human*, with all their messy, developmentally appropriate struggles. A mother who *doesn't* make them feel like they have to earn love or like something's wrong with them. A mother who holds them accountable with love, not shame. So they'll never have to go through all of this like I have.

I know it might feel like healing is out of reach—because nothing's ever worked, right? But I'm living proof it can. And I've watched client after client walk themselves out of the same pain you're carrying now.

Take my hand and together, we're going to dismantle the ideas that you'll never be good enough, that there is something fundamentally wrong with you *and* that you need to be perfect and achieve huge things in order to be lovable. Then I'm going to teach you how to break these cycles for your kids. Let's go.

The Caterpillar's Burden: The Cost of Expectations

Imagine a caterpillar, munching on leaves, crawling around on the ground. Someday, it will be a butterfly soaring through the sky. But, for right now, it is just a caterpillar.

Imagine we demand that the caterpillar *fly*. We criticize the caterpillar for not even having wings. We borrow a phrase from our childhood, and sternly tell the caterpillar, "I expected more from you."

(Deep breath, I know that one cuts deep. Sorry.)

It would be ridiculous, right? We are being unreasonable. Caterpillars can't fly. But the caterpillar is young. It doesn't know that our expectations are impossible. It *believes us* that it should be able to fly. And because it doesn't want to disappoint or let us down and is deeply afraid of failure, the caterpillar climbs up a tree trunk, stretches over the open air, jumps—

And plummets to the ground.

A little bruised but undeterred, it climbs, jumps, and falls *again*. And *again*. And *again*. But the caterpillar keeps climbing the damn tree. It's now exhausted, terribly stressed and feeling ashamed from "failing" to meet our expectations. Because we said it "should" be able to do it. The problem isn't the caterpillar. The problem is the expectation that it "should" be able to fly... *without wings.*

Because no matter how much pressure we put on the caterpillar to prematurely transform, it can't speed up its metamorphosis, its transition into an adult.

Good Kids are the caterpillars made to believe they *should have been able* to be a butterfly. They stare down unrelenting pressure and expectations from parents, teachers, and society to be perfect, achieve everything, and always, always, always behave. It's too much—they shoulder the pressure to be mature beyond their years and somehow more emotionally stable than the adults raising them.

The caterpillar would need so, so much freaking therapy to let go of the idea that it *should* have been able to fly. And Good Kids need so, so much therapy to let go of the idea that they *must* perform, please and accomplish in order to be *lovable*.

Our parents too were made to feel like they should have been able to be a butterfly. They passed down those unreasonable expectations because nobody ever told them: you were never failing—you were still a caterpillar.

2
Good Kid Biology

Nervous System Development

Clients and followers often tell me they don't remember their parents actively shaming them—it felt more like they shamed *themselves*.

So here's the thing: kids typically start throwing tantrums around 18 months but don't form long-term memories until about age five... so that's a solid three and a half years of Big Feelings, boundary-pushing, tantrums, and misbehavior that our parents were woefully underprepared to handle in a loving, regulated way. During those years, even if we don't consciously remember it now, they likely yelled, shut us down, threatened, punished, spanked, or otherwise handled our emotions in ways that felt overwhelming and incredibly unsafe. By the time we were five years old and forming memories, they didn't need to say it anymore—*we already knew* how things went if we got too emotional, pushed back, misbehaved, or resisted. We had internalized their responses into a script that said to us, "It's not safe to act like that" or "Don't go there, or everything will get scary and fall apart."

So if you can't consciously recall those early years, remember that your body was there. Your brain and nervous system paid extremely close attention, and they remember. Their entire job was to keep you safe—both physically safe and safe within your relationships with your parents, because your survival depended on keeping that attachment with them intact. If, when you got mad, sad, or frustrated, this always led to yelling, punishments, or withdrawing love, your body learned quickly: *Not safe! Shut it down. Hide how you really feel. Be extra nice and agreeable. Whatever it takes to keep from making them mad.* Not fighting back wasn't weakness—it was survival. It was your body's brilliant way of protecting you from their anger, from being made to feel ashamed, from the terrifying sense that their love and care might be taken away.

Nervous System 101: Fight, Flight, Freeze, and Fawn

Before we go any deeper, it's time to pause for a quick refresher on your nervous system. Your nervous system's job is to detect threats and help you survive. When it perceives a threat—whether a physical danger or an emotional one (someone being mad or disappointed with you, being criticized, or feeling rejected)—your nervous system activates your survival response: Fight, Flight, Freeze, or Fawn. When the threat is the loss of your parent's love, approval, and willingness to care for you, your nervous system adapts to keep you as acceptable, likeable, and low maintenance as possible.

You might not have used the words "nervous system response" before, but you probably know the feeling: your heart starts pounding, your chest feels tight, your stomach flips, and you suddenly feel like you need to run away, shut down, or fix everything immediately. That's your nervous system going into survival mode. For so many of us, those reactions didn't just show up when something physically scary happened—they kicked in when we felt rejected, shamed, or like we were in trouble with someone we loved.

Our nervous system is primarily concerned with safety, and our caregivers are meant to be a source of safety. When that safety is compromised, our parent feels like a threat. And our brain and nervous system shift, often automatically and unconsciously, to prioritize short-term emotional safety with our caregiver over longer-term well-being. Our parent's impact on our nervous system was utterly profound in dictating how we react in the face of danger and threats. Let's quickly walk through all four responses as they relate to Good Kids.

Sympathetic Activation (Fight or Flight): "Do Something" to Survive

Fight

Fight Response protects us when we feel threatened, but when fighting back feels unsafe—where speaking up leads to punishment, frightening anger and disappointment, and emotional withdrawal—our nervous system adapts and shuts down Fight Response to preserve connection with our caregiver. Instead of fighting back, Good Kids turn their Fight Response inward, silencing themselves, blaming themselves, and turning their anger and aggression on themselves. When our bodies get tense, our jaw clenches up and our stomach is in knots—but we say we're "fine"—that's our Fight Response, trapped inside. Still trying to keep us safe.

Flight

Flight Response is designed to get us away from danger. But what happens when the "danger" is the very person the Good Kid depends on for care and love to survive? They can't physically run away so they emotionally check out and shut down, outrun their feelings, stay small and invisible, and avoid conflict at all costs. They're always, always busy and on the go, feeling deeply uncomfortable with stillness. They never slow down to feel any discomfort or, really, anything.

When we feel overwhelmed and reach for our phone to numb out on, that's our Flight Response still working to keep us safe.

Dorsal Vagal Shutdown (Freeze Response): "Do Nothing" to Survive

The dorsal vagal response, which governs both the Freeze and Fawn Responses, can lead to dissociation—a numbing of emotional expression—along with a physical shutdown that suppresses the Fight/Flight impulse. This response leaves the child feeling helpless and immobilized, but also, paradoxically, hyper-aware and hyper-attuned to the caregiver's needs, moods, and emotional state. In an attempt to stay emotionally safe, the child's nervous system shifts into overdrive, focusing all energy on reading the environment and caregiver's moods like a hawk and adjusting their behavior to avoid conflict or emotional rejection, at all costs.

You were deeply dependent on your parents for safety and connection, for your literal survival. Little You did the best they could with a brain that was underdeveloped and a nervous system finely tuned to detect any signs of disconnection from your parents because that could lead to a loss of support from them. Your survival *depended* on them being consistently loving and willing to care for you so when they got mad or disapproved of something you did and acted like they didn't love you, or gave you the silent treatment and acted like you didn't exist... it may have felt like your connection with them was in jeopardy, which your nervous system perceived as a threat to your survival.

Your prefrontal cortex—the part of your brain that helps you with regulating your emotions and logical reasoning—was underdeveloped and paralyzed by the potential shame. So it was not able to rationalize that "Mom is just upset right now, but I know she loves me." The amygdala, the part of the brain that processes fear and detects threats, becomes highly activated when we sense conflict or disconnection with our caregivers. It floods our body with stress hormones which makes the whole situation feel completely overwhelming and terrifying. So the nervous system shifts into Freeze or Fawn.

Freeze

In Freeze Response, we feel immobilized, shut down, and numb. This can include dissociation—our brain and nervous system's last line of defense is to take us offline consciously. We mentally check out or feel detached from the situation, as if watching it from a distance. When we grow up with emotionally unstable and emotionally unavailable caregivers, unable to help us with our Big Feelings, we spend a lot of time in Freeze Response, dissociating. When speaking up leads to being dominated into submission and mistakes feel catastrophic, our nervous system learns that the safest thing to do is... nothing. Dissociation becomes a survival skill.

Please be kind and gentle with yourself when you find yourself in Freeze Response—you are *not* lazy, there is nothing wrong with you. Your brain is taking care of you the best way it knows how to, when all else fails.

For Good Kids, dissociation can show up when the pressure to be perfect, please others, or suppress our true feelings becomes too much to bear. Instead of fighting back or running away, we might have learned to emotionally shut down to survive those moments of fear, shame, or overwhelm. Dissociation is the brain's way of saying, "This is too much, so I'm going to protect you by pulling you out of it."

Good Kids also commonly struggle with perfection-based procrastination, which is often a Freeze/Flight Response in disguise. When the fear of failure and making a mistake feels too overwhelming, their nervous system pumps the brakes and they get stuck in an overthinking, avoidance loop, procrastinating from a place of paralysis. Believing that they must do it perfectly, without any mistakes. But that feels completely overwhelming... so the safest thing to do is nothing at all.

Dissociation becomes a habit. Over time, it leaves us feeling disconnected—not just from difficult situations, but from our own needs, feelings, and even our sense of self. Reconnecting with ourselves requires patience, compassion, and a lot of practice listening to what our body and emotions are trying to tell us, without judgment.

Fawn Response: "Make Yourself Small" to Survive

Polyvagal Theory and Attachment Theory speak to the pivot a child makes when they perceive their parent as a threat but cannot escape or fight back—they enter Fawn Response. The child attempts to avoid conflict and gain back the parent's approval and willingness to care for them by appeasing them, and becoming hyper-attuned to the parent's emotional state and suppressing their own emotions and needs. Fawn Response looks like parent pleasing—we apologize, smooth things over, and do whatever we have to do to please our parents and keep that connection and attachment with them intact. Fawn Response means abandoning ourselves—letting things go that hurt us and apologizing to *them*... when they owe *us* an apology. It means pushing down our hurt and Big Feelings and prioritizing their feelings, making sure *they* feel better. It means that *our* ability to feel okay depends on *them* being okay.

These patterns have followed you into your adult life—it's why you have such a hard time knowing how *you* actually feel. It's why you apologize all the time, even when you have nothing to apologize for. And it's why you are so, so good at holding space for others when they're hurting... but have no idea how to give yourself that same love and care. Or receive love and care if someone's trying to support you. Please be gentle and kind with yourself when you people please (Fawn)—your brain and nervous system are in survival mode and have hijacked you to keep you safe. You can absolutely heal this—lots more to come on what healing looks like.

The Stress Cycle

The concept of Completing the Stress Cycle, developed by Drs. Emily and Amelia Nagoski, is all about helping your body physically process the stress responses it never got to complete. All those times our nervous systems activated Fight/Flight Response but then pivoted into Freeze (shut down) or

Fawn (people pleasing) Response to keep us safe and connected with our caregivers, all that stress didn't just go away—it got trapped in our body. Completing the Stress Cycle means giving our body the Fight/Flight movement it needed when it sensed danger but never got the chance to have.

We complete the Stress Cycle by gently moving our body and activating our muscles which helps communicate to our body in a language it understands (regulation) that we have moved away from the threat, we are now safe and it can stand down. You can do this with simple equipment-free movements like raising your knees, doing push-ups on the wall, air squats or walking around the building. It's like letting the steam out of a kettle—a quick, physical release of built-up tension that allows your nervous system to return to a calmer, regulated state.

Your body still carries the stress from all the times you wanted to run but stayed, wanted to stand up for yourself but silenced yourself instead. Consciously releasing that energy physically by recruiting your muscles to help isn't just stress relief—it's teaching your nervous system in its native language that you are safe *now*.

The Gut–Brain Axis

A dysregulated nervous system means constant physical tension. You're constantly on edge, stressed, and I bet you're not sleeping well either. Sometimes, our mind recruits the body to help process and release unresolved emotions and trauma in unexpected ways—with chronic upset stomach issues.

The connection between emotional stress and gastrointestinal issues is well-documented in scientific literature, particularly in the context of Somatic Trauma and the Gut–Brain Axis. Our nervous system, when dysregulated by unprocessed emotions, can trigger physical reactions in our gastrointestinal (GI) system, like stomach cramps, nausea, and suddenly evacuating our bowels. This happens because the body is responding to emotional triggers that may not have been fully processed or released, and the GI system acts as an outlet for that unresolved emotional energy.

I think this is a brilliant workaround by our body. It believes it must still suppress our emotions, and because it cannot release the emotional trauma stuck inside through our mind, it hands it off to the body to release it by physically purging. The body finds a physical mechanism—like our bowels—to offload the emotional trauma. We may not even be consciously aware of the specific emotions or memories driving the response.

This physical release can help to calm our nervous system and allow our body to "reset" after a stressful or triggering event. Endorphins, our body's natural painkillers, are released to help counteract the discomfort caused by the stress response and soothe the emotional turmoil that's been triggered. This can alleviate some of the physical discomfort and emotional pain that comes with the release of stored trauma or stress and is part of our body's attempt to self-regulate and restore emotional balance after a stressful or triggering event.

I had IBS symptoms for most of my childhood into adulthood. I kept a heating pad in my desk and Maalox in the office refrigerator. I hardly went a day without violent cramping, acid reflux, and indigestion. I'm pretty sure I spent the first 38ish years of my life in Fight/Flight (sympathetic mode) so my body was fighting for its life and hardly ever in parasympathetic mode where it could "rest and digest." So... of course my tummy was upset all the time.

I've worked with so, so many counseling and coaching clients who share a similar experience: for years, they've dealt with chronic stomach and bowel problems—bloating, diarrhea, constipation, and cramping. It's been nothing short of extraordinary watching these physical symptoms begin to dissipate as clients learn to stop suppressing their emotions, heal their Relational Shame Trauma and start regulating their nervous system to facilitate deeper emotional healing. The physical tension stored in their body—especially in the gut—begins to release *and* their nervous system is spending time in parasympathetic mode (rest and digest) so their body is getting opportunities to digest food properly, leading to a remarkable improvement in their GI symptoms.

Attachment Styles

Attachment Theory explains how our earliest relationships with caregivers shape how we connect with others, regulate emotions, and navigate the world throughout our lives. Our attachment figures—the people responsible for our safety and emotional needs—taught us, for better or worse, what love and connection felt like. When we brace for the silent treatment, assume someone is mad at us the second their tone shifts, or feel panicked at any sign of distance, that's not just an attachment wound, it's a trauma response. Our nervous system learned to expect rejection, withdrawal, or criticism based on past experiences, creating patterns and nervous system sequences we unconsciously carry into adulthood.

For anyone lucky enough to have emotionally attuned, consistent, and responsive parents, this created a secure attachment, allowing them to trust, express emotions freely, and feel inherently worthy of love. But for nearly all of us raised as Good Kids, our attachment was shaped by emotional neglect, fear-based, shame-laced discipline, and/or the expectation that we meet our parents' needs instead of the other way around. As a result, we developed insecure or disorganized attachment patterns.

Attachment patterns aren't random; they are survival strategies that we unconsciously chose to stay safe and maintain connection with others. Even now, our nervous system still runs the same playbook—whether it serves us or not, so let's look at the four main attachment patterns and how they show up for Good Kids.

Anxious / Preoccupied Attachment

This feels like constantly scanning for shifts in tone, body language, and energy—reading the room like your survival depended on it. You learned that love was conditional and staying connected meant anticipating moods, apologizing first, and working overtime to keep the peace. If someone was upset, your brain convinced you it was your fault and your job to fix it.

Now, the fear of disconnection still follows you. You have a hard time trusting that others will truly be there when you need them because support always felt uncertain or came with strings attached. In conflict, your nervous system braces for loss—not just of the argument, but of the relationship itself. You may feel overwhelming urgency to repair, even when you're the one who was hurt, because deep down, you believe that staying connected—making sure everything feels okay between you, making sure they're not mad at you—matters more than being right, being heard, or being true to yourself.

Avoidant / Dismissive Attachment

This feels like being self-sufficient, low-maintenance, and easy to raise. You learned that the best way to meet your needs was to act like you didn't have any. If you were struggling, you kept it to yourself. If you needed comfort, you figured out how to self-soothe in secret. You didn't stop needing connection and support—you just got really good at pretending you didn't. You stopped expecting your parents to be emotionally available because hoping for more just led to disappointment.

Now, you unconsciously keep emotional distance to feel safe. You crave connection but struggle to let people in. Vulnerability feels unbearable, like giving someone the power to hurt you. You rarely ask for help because depending on others feels dangerous or a set up up for rejection. It's confusing because you want intimacy, but when a partner tries to get close, they feel overwhelming or needy. You might withdraw emotionally or physically, needing space but not knowing how to explain it. When relationships get too intense, your instinct is to shut down, shut off, and handle it all alone—just like you've always done.

Disorganized Attachment

This feels like never knowing what version of your parent you were going to get. Sometimes, they were warm and loving. Other times, they were unpredictable, frightening, or distant with zero explanation for the sudden shift. You learned to be cautious, desperately trying to earn love while bracing for the next outburst or withdrawal.

You wanted to feel safe with them—you needed to—but sometimes, the closer you got, the more fear you felt. Even if you didn't feel consciously unsafe, your nervous system did. This is what fear without resolution looks like: when the person who is supposed to comfort you is also the one who sometimes scares you, your body stays stuck in high alert. Over time, your brain learned to associate love with unpredictability, leaving you caught in a push–pull dynamic. You crave connection but fear that getting too close means getting hurt.

Now, there are entire parts of your childhood you don't remember. And in relationships today, you might find yourself trapped between longing for closeness and fearing what happens when you let your guard down. Your nervous system doesn't trust stability; it's waiting for the other shoe to drop.

Secure Attachment

This feels like breathing easy in relationships, knowing that love isn't something you have to hustle for. It's trusting that you don't have to be perfect to be wanted, that you don't have to perform to belong. It's knowing, deep in your bones, that even when you mess up, even when you struggle, you are still good, still worthy, still loved. Secure attachment is having space for all of your emotions without fear of rejection or punishment—knowing you won't be shamed for being sad, dismissed for being angry, or made to feel like a burden for having needs. It's feeling safe enough to bring your full, messy self to the table and trust that you won't be abandoned for it. It's knowing that conflict doesn't mean disconnection, that repair is always possible, and that love is a safe place to land—not a test to pass.

Healing our attachment is so important because it rewires our emotional and relational muscle memory. It allows us to stop running on old survival patterns and start building the safety, trust, and connection we never had. It allows us to respond instead of react, hold steady instead of shutting down, and repair instead of resorting to shame. It's the foundation that makes it possible to become the person we've been searching for—someone fiercely devoted to us, for ourselves. The one who believes in us, who never loses faith in us, who refuses to abandon us, no matter what. It allows us to experience secure attachment with ourselves—the kind of love that stays and holds steady even when things are hard and the kind of relational safety that says: you don't have to earn this or prove anything because you are already enough. And to offer that same security to our kids, breaking cycles for good.

Because research is crystal clear: secure attachment is one of the most powerful protective factors for children. Kids with secure attachment have higher emotional intelligence, stronger resilience to stress, healthier relationships, and a deeper sense of self-worth. And when kids struggle—whether with anxiety, emotional outbursts, self-doubt, or low confidence—the single most impactful intervention we can offer them isn't a consequence, a reward system, or a script.

It's a secure attachment.

Good Kid Origins

The way a Good Kid responds to stress at a nervous system level is complex, profoundly impacted by:

- Their biological predispositions around natural temperament
- The relative chaos or safety and stability in their environment
- The relative chaos or safety and stability within their relationship with their caregiver
- The way the child is conditioned, particularly by their primary caregivers:
    - Being rewarded and praised for "being good"
    - Being harshly punished, rejected and having love, attention, affection and a willingness to care for you withdrawn and withheld for being "bad."

Some Good Kids start with a natural tendency toward Fight Response when under stress or threat, initially rising up and pushing back against their parent (the perceived threat). When the parent responds to the child in an intimidating way, the child can be conditioned to suppress Fight Response and adapt by shifting into Fawn Response for survival.

Intimidation is about frightening a child by sending a message of dominance, power, and control. This can happen physically or emotionally.

Physical intimidation can look like:

- Yelling at you, especially when close by—"I'll give you something to cry about!"
- Making threats about punishments
- Grabbing you aggressively
- Standing over you, taking over your personal space
- Slamming doors, slamming a hand down on furniture, throwing things, etc., to scare or startle you
- Spanking or threatening spanking or other violence.

Emotional intimidation can look like:

- "I'm not mad, I'm just disappointed"
- Making you feel responsible for your parent's emotions and well-being with guilt trips—"I can't believe this is how you repay me after all I've done for you!"
- The silent treatment—withdrawing *and* withholding love, attention, affection, and care for discipline, until you earn back the parent's approval
- Making you feel like you don't deserve love because of your behavior
- Threatening to leave.

Both types of intimidation can have a lasting and devastating impact on the parent–child relationship and attachment as well as the child's self-worth, emotional well-being and basic sense of safety which can lead to suppressing emotions, unresolved fear, anxiety, hypervigilance, and depression.

Good Kids vs. "Bad" Kids

Some kids have a naturally easygoing temperament and find it easier to "be good" than others. It has been theorized that Good Kids are more likely to naturally tend toward responding to stress and trauma in relationships, especially with their parent, using Fawn Response—meaning instead of naturally being confrontational (Fight Response), or running away (Flight Response), or shutting down emotionally (Freeze Response), Good Kids tend to people please their way to safety with their caregivers, being overly accommodating, suppressing needs and emotions to try to diffuse and avoid conflict and earn approval from their parent. When that natural tendency to Fawn meets fear-based, shame-laced discipline or withdrawal from a parent... it gets amplified. They learn that being accommodating and agreeable keeps them "safe" and earns approval—even if it means losing themselves in the process.

The Bad Kids (who, it's important to note, were never actually bad), on the other hand, naturally tend toward a Fight Response, meaning their brain and nervous system naturally tend toward pushing back, getting angry, being oppositional and aggressive and resisting authority. Instead of Fawning for approval, they fight for autonomy—and they are often punished for it. The literature shows that, psychologically, kids who respond to trauma with Fight instead of Fawn or Freeze tend to fare better in the long run because fighting back creates a sense of empowerment, while freezing and fawning reinforces a crippling sense of helplessness and powerlessness. A kid who fights back at least feels *some* sense of control, while a kid who fawns or freezes learns to disappear.

This whole book is about the shame carried by Good Kids. The shame carried by Bad Kids is believing their Fight Response is wrong and bad and makes them unlovable. But I see this so differently—kids who fight back aren't "bad," they're just wired differently to respond to stress. Their Fight Response isn't bad either—it's protective. I actually conceptualize healing for Good Kids and adults who are recovering as unearthing outward Fight Response—learning how to stand up for themselves, release anger instead of suppressing it, and reclaim the power they haven't been able to have. It's allowing them to feel empowered instead of helpless. When Big Feelings like anger rise, they've got to go somewhere—we want kids to release their anger out of their body instead of turning it inward and being angry and vicious with themselves.

3
"You Should Be Grateful."

Our Parents' Misguided Beliefs

Our parents had a whole bunch of misguided beliefs about what we as kids *should* have been capable of doing and how to be a "good" parent.

Any time we went against our parents' unspoken rules about how a child "should" behave, look, or feel, it triggered our fawn response—our instinct to shapeshift into whatever "lovable" version of ourselves would keep us connected to them and their love and care (and thus, safe). We weren't explicitly given this rulebook, but we felt it in every glare, every sigh, every punishment that told us, "This is not acceptable."

I suspect our parents never flat out told us any of this because, when you read them printed out here, you might get a sense of how ridiculous and unattainable they are.

A Parent's Worth is Tied to Their Child's Good Behavior and Achievements.

- Good parents have respectful, well-behaved kids who always, always, always behave.
- A parent's job is to raise a successful child because success equals happiness.
- A child's success reflects their parents' worth.
- What other people think of us matters above all else.

Respect is Earned Through Fear, Punishment, and Control.

- Punishments are necessary and not necessarily damaging, even when they hurt, humiliate, or shame a child.

- Punishments "build character" and "teach respect."
- Children behave *because* they respect their parent, and respect must be earned through punishing discipline.
- Children *should* be afraid of what will happen if they do something wrong again.

Emotions Should Be Suppressed to Maintain Control and Order.

- When a child has intense emotions, they should be able to calm down quickly and go right back to being cooperative and "fine" (like they can flip a switch and turn their feelings off.)
- A parent should teach their child to "control their emotions" by ignoring them or withholding love, attention, affection and a willingness to care for them (the silent treatment.)
- Expressing emotions like anger, frustration, or sadness is immature and burdensome to others.
- A child should never upset or provoke their parent because it's disrespectful and they need to learn their place. Children should be seen, not heard—especially when they're upset.

Independence, Selflessness, and Toughness Are Virtues. Vulnerability Is Weakness.

- Asking for help is a sign of weakness, and needing help makes the child a burden.
- Once kids "know better," they're expected to *be better*—and *never* need correction again.
- Children should handle their struggles on their own so they can become strong and independent because helping your kids makes them weak and dependent.
- If a parent apologizes to their child, they should make it clear it's still the child's fault because children should toughen up and learn to accept consequences.
- Focusing on your own needs is selfish and wrong.

Perfection Is the Standard. Mistakes Are Unacceptable.

- Children should be able to behave at all times, no matter the circumstances.
- Mistakes are a reflection of the child's laziness, carelessness, or lack of respect, and they deserve criticism or punishment.
- A parent should express their disappointment and make the child feel guilty for failing to meet their expectations with "I'm not mad, I'm just disappointed" to help teach them about right from wrong, the importance of making good choices and to motivate the child to try harder next time.

These misguided beliefs shaped our parents' ridiculous and unattainable expectations of us. Their impossibly high expectations shaped their disappointment and disapproval of us. Their crushing disappointment and disapproval shaped the fear and shame-laced discipline we received.

And that shame-laced discipline shaped our "personalities" made out of trauma responses and viciously painful core beliefs about how we had to be to be lovable. And the insane expectations we hold ourselves to. This is **Relational Shame Trauma**. It's not just a feeling—it's an entire identity built around *performing for love and safety*. And breaking free from it isn't just about thinking differently. It's about *unlearning the survival strategies we built to stay safe*.

The Way Our Parents Were Parented Shaped Them as Parents

The phenomenon of Good Kids—children who are highly compliant, excel academically, and often suppress their own emotions and needs in order to meet strict parental expectations—has roots that stretch back generations.

Behind every Good Kid is a parent navigating their own unmet emotional needs, fears of abandonment, deep sense of unworthiness, and struggle with their unresolved Relational Shame Trauma. These parents were raised to bottle and suppress their emotions so they struggle to regulate their emotions, often vacillating between bottling and exploding. Because they have no experience of healthily managing their own emotions, they have a low tolerance for their child's Big Feelings.

Generational Trauma

Your parents' beliefs about how to be a good parent and how to discipline their child were profoundly shaped by:

- Their attachment to their own parents
- The environment they grew up in
- The unspoken rules of their family.

For most of human history, parents didn't even recognize that kids had emotions beyond what was visible on the surface, let alone feel responsible for actually tending to those emotions. Emotional needs? That wasn't even on the radar. Kids were expected to be able to be rational all the time and never emotional, to "control" their emotions... all on their own, and to always, always behave. This really meant that kids were expected to make things easier for the adults around them and just parent themselves.

Our grandparents didn't understand that our parents had fundamental human and emotional needs for soothing and ongoing support in a nurturing environment. Instead, our grandparents raised our parents to be emotionless, self-controlled "mini adults," which was not only unfair but completely unrealistic—and developmentally *impossible*.

Our grandparents didn't know that their expectations set up our parents for failure. And this is where Relational Shame Trauma begins: the belief that your worth is tied to meeting standards, even when those standards make no sense for who you are or what you're capable of at any given age. It's the feeling that there's something wrong with you if you can't meet those expectations, and the real kicker—being punished in your relationships for failing to live up to them.

This strict, emotionally restrained parenting style often meant that our grandparents barely expressed any emotion themselves, and even less was allowed from their children. This reinforced our parents' belief that their feelings weren't safe and definitely weren't acceptable. Unsurprisingly, our parents had no chance to emotionally mature and develop emotional intelligence and self-regulation skills.

This kind of parenting gave our parents deep, unhealed emotional wounds, and left them feeling like something was inherently wrong with them for the messy parts of being a human. To navigate their own Big Feelings and struggles, they developed maladaptive coping mechanisms, which later shaped how they responded to *our* Big Feelings and struggles.

Emotions were something to be controlled—really, that meant suppressed—and definitely not allowed to cause any inconvenience. If a child was upset, they were usually told to "calm down" or "snap out of it," like their feelings could just be turned off with a flick of a switch. Parents sometimes took it even further, using threats like, "I'll give you something to cry about," or resorting to punishment like spanking or giving the child the silent treatment, sending them off to their room until they "pulled themselves together."

Trauma Passed Down

So often, parents have a deep, loving desire to protect their child from the pain and shame they experienced as kids. This instinct comes from a place of fierce love, but generational trauma is like muscle memory—you didn't build it yourself, but it still lives in your nervous system, ready to fire. Your brain absorbed the way your parents reacted to you and learned *this is how a parent is supposed to respond*. And unless we actively rewire those patterns, they take over in moments of stress. Without even realizing it, parents can unintentionally perpetuate the very patterns that shamed them and shaped their "good" kid identity. In trying to shield their child, they end up passing down the very same wounds they were trying to prevent. Healing isn't just about wanting better—it's about doing the work to override the old muscle memory and create something new.

Let's say your parent grew up in a household where being emotional and having Big Feelings set off their own parents' temper or led to getting the silent treatment. Your parents may have desperately wanted to help you feel safe with your emotions, but when that moment hit, their instincts and unresolved trauma got triggered and hijacked them. And they ended up shutting down your emotional outburst and making you feel ashamed for having it.

This is not because they didn't care—it was an instinctive reaction to try to "protect" you from the same pain they endured as a kid. They could have wanted to help you with the Big Feelings, but if the only way they ever saw big emotions handled was through shaming and shutting them down, they were going to shame and shut down your emotions. The yelling was like saying, "Oh my gosh, no! It's not safe to do that! Stop, I'm trying to protect you!" Because without realizing it, they were not just reacting to their child—they were reacting to their own unresolved hurt inside.

Parents tend to struggle most with the behaviors in their child that hit too close to home—the ones that remind them of the parts of themselves they were taught to feel ashamed of. This triggers the parent's unresolved shame. Unconsciously, they may shame or punish the child for expressing those needs—not out of lack of love or malice, but out of an instinctive effort to protect the child from the rejection, criticism and abandonment the parent once faced... by their parents. This cycle, while incredibly well-intentioned, teaches the child to suppress parts of themselves to avoid being shamed, reinforcing the Good Kid persona.

When parenting is driven by these unconscious fears and unresolved Relational Shame Trauma, the focus often shifts from *who* the child is to *how* the child behaves. The child becomes a reflection of the parent's success, and the parent resists, punishes, shuts down, and shames any behavior that disrupts that image... just like their parents did with them. The Good Kid learns to silence their needs, emotions, and individuality to maintain connection and avoid conflict, internalizing the message that their worth is tied to their behavior. That's Relational Trauma laced with Shame and when it comes from a parent, it impacts and fundamentally shapes their nervous system and creates deep emotional wounds. Children of emotionally immature parents may develop attachment issues, low self-worth, or chronic feelings of not being good enough.

How Our Parents Raised Us

For our parents, good parenting meant raising respectful, high-achieving kids who *never* stepped out of line. Success was everything, not just for the child but as a reflection of their worth as parents. We were raised with the same mindset of our grandparents and parents—behavior is everything. With an extreme and unrelenting focus on obedience, discipline, and making sure we knew our place. We heard things like, "Children should be seen and not heard," which really just meant, "Stay quiet, stay out of the way, and don't make a fuss."

The goal wasn't to nurture us as individuals, but to prepare us for the future by drilling in strict discipline and tough love. Our parents felt entitled to punish us as much as they needed to shape us into respectful, well-behaved children. But what they called "respect" was really instant, unquestioning obedience. That's not respect; that's dominating a child into submission. They also believed that punishment and humiliation "built character."

The idea was that children should "toughen up" and handle struggles on their own without help, because needing help was seen as weakness. Mistakes were unacceptable, and anything less than perfect behavior was met with criticism or punishment, often leaving us feeling unworthy and like a failure. In this environment, the constant fear of disappointing them or upsetting their control left us with deep-seated shame, unable to express vulnerability or emotion without fearing rejection or punishment.

Like their parents before them, our parents' goal was not to raise us to feel good about ourselves and enjoy our lives. Their job was to raise strong boys and prepare them for career stability and subservient girls whose worth was fundamentally tied to serving others and being good wives, mothers, and homemakers. We were expected to bottle up our emotions and act like little adults—always perfectly behaved and hiding any vulnerability or feelings.

Our emotional needs were completely ignored or treated like a problem to fix. The underlying message was clear: emotions were not to be trusted or shown—they were inconvenient, and people don't love you when you're like *that*. Our parents used fear and shame-laced discipline to crush those emotions and shape us into a child who didn't express anger, sadness, or frustration in ways that might be "too much" for our parents to handle.

The visceral feeling of shame we experienced in those moments was overwhelming—it wasn't just about being told to stop crying, it was about feeling like *we* were wrong, *we* were a problem, *we* were a disappointment and there was something wrong with *us* for having the emotions in the first place.

An unbelievable number of child and adult counseling clients have said some version of this to me: "It felt like my parent's willingness to love and care for me was tied directly to my ability to shut down my feelings" and, "It feels like my parent doesn't love me when I'm emotional." This makes a child feel and believe that love and approval are only available to them if they keep it together—if they don't show how hard things are for them on the outside. These patterns of suppression, shame, and punishment shaped so many of us to grow up believing that we have to hide our feelings to be lovable, that we are a burden when we're struggling, and that we are *hard* to love.

If you're nodding your head right now, I see you. You were made to feel like your emotional needs—really, any needs— were not valid or worthy of attention, support, and love. Growing up, your feelings were shut down, and worse, you were made to feel *ashamed* and like there was something *wrong* with you for having them. But here's the actual truth: your emotions and needs were always worthy of love and care. And so were you.

"Too Much" and "Not Good Enough"

This set the stage for lifelong beliefs that you were "too sensitive" and "too much" while simultaneously also feeling "not good enough" for others. You internalized that you should be able to handle everything on your own, that needing help or support makes you like a burden on others. These beliefs have become so deeply embedded in your sense of self that they keep you white-knuckling your way through life, trying to outrun your emotions and pretending they don't exist.

As a recovering Good Kid, you make sense, and your struggles make sense. The shame you internalized has done a number to you, as shame does. It has left you trapped in perfectionism, people pleasing, and a constant fear that someone will "find out" you're not enough and you're actually unlovable. That deep-seated fear that there's something wrong with you is exactly what Relational Shame does—it infiltrates every part of who you are and how you see others. It's incredibly hard to feel confident in yourself or believe you deserve love when you were made to feel like you weren't lovable, just for being yourself. When we live in shame, we don't just feel flawed—we expect others to reject or abandon us too. This warps our relationships, making us hyper-aware of any disapproval, disappointment, or rejection. And that white-knuckling through life? It's exhausting. You deserved so much more than that.

After all this, we become parents ourselves without *any* real modeling around how to express and manage our emotions in healthy ways or how to discipline kids in a way that doesn't dominate them into submission to us, crushing their self-worth in the process. We unconsciously repeat so many of our parent's mistakes because of course we do—that's how generational trauma works. Becoming the parent allows us to access our childhood trauma in ways that can't be replicated—we get smacked in the face when we respond to our kid with love instead of the fear and shame we got. We feel shaken when we are able to actually see the way we deserved to be treated compared with how we actually were treated. We're simultaneously gobsmacked, triggered, and proud when our kid is able to do the things we were never allowed to do. More on this coming in Part III!

Punishments Were the Norm

When we acted out, we were punished. Do something wrong... then something painful would follow. Because suffering wasn't just a consequence—suffering was the *lesson*. They believed we needed to *hurt* in order to learn. That we *deserved* to hurt because we messed up. That pain was how a "good" parent raised a "good" kid.

Punishments could take many forms:

- Physical harm
- Restriction of activities that we enjoyed
- Emotional withdrawal
- Shaming ("What is wrong with you?," "I'm not mad, I'm disappointed" or name calling)
- Isolation ("Go to your room!")
- Forced apologies
- Public humiliation.

Here, I need to focus for a moment on emotional withdrawal—aka the silent treatment—because you need to understand how devastating it is. When it's normalized for a kid, as it was for most of us, you really can't see its true impact.

The silent treatment is where a parent goes from emotionally warm to cold, withdrawing *and* withholding their love, attention, and affection from their child to punish and discipline them. Some parents give their child the silent treatment for minutes or hours, others for days, weeks or, in extreme cases, even years. At some point without explanation or discussion, the parent is not mad anymore and is willing to talk to the child again. There is no discussion and everything is swept under the rug by the parent. The parent might lecture the child about their behavior and drop their punishment. The child is to never bring up the parent's behavior.

The silent treatment is one of the most normalized forms of emotional abuse and—as a trauma therapist seeing the long-term impact every single day—I consider it one of the most damaging and destructive forms.

> **From Brittney**
>
> Apologies have never been a thing in my family. There was a pattern throughout my childhood where my mom would be mad at me for something that was usually unclear to me, and then she would stop talking to me for a while. During that time, she was very unlikely to meet my needs without some intense yelling. Usually, I would simply fend for myself until she got over it. This happened so much that I can't even think of a specific example from childhood. The silent treatment without resolve or apology was like breathing.
>
> In college, I got into an argument with her at Thanksgiving, and she got so mad (unbeknownst to me) that she cut off my phone and stopped talking to me until I broke the silence and wished her a Happy Mother's Day—half a year later.

When our parents iced us out and ignored our cries and pleas for support and reassurance, whether we realized it or not, we experienced this as emotional abandonment. I know that might sound extreme, but think about it: you have a child in emotional distress who is begging their parent for support, but the parent has suddenly revoked their access to them to "teach them a lesson." The silent treatment takes away the parent's attention, warmth, affection, and willingness to care. It punishes the child by ignoring their cries and pleas for support out of a misguided belief that kids need to suffer, alone, before they deserve to be forgiven.

When we were subjected to the silent treatment, we felt like we didn't deserve our parents' love, attention, and affection because we were *so bad*. Often, parents even make their kids feel like they don't deserve comfort or care when they're hurting because of *how bad* they were, so the child is left to fend for themselves until the parent stops ignoring them. Ultimately, the silent treatment taught us that we don't deserve love, and that we're actually unlovable. That there is something wrong with us, deep down. That we can't be trusted. That people would stop loving us if they "found out" *how bad* we actually are.

"Don't Come Home If" Discipline

I was out to breakfast with my family when I heard a Baby Boomer at the next table brag loudly, "and then I told my son, 'Don't come home if you get a tattoo!'"

All her friends laughed. They were so pleased with themselves, but my mind felt like a violently shaken snow globe as a flurry of similar stories from past clients blew through my mind.

Growing up, many of us were subjected to this "Don't come home if" discipline—where if we didn't meet our parents' expectations or if we stepped out of line in any way, we weren't just grounded or lectured for disobeying... we were threatened with being disowned, kicked out of the house, sent to military school, or even put into foster care.

Did you have similar rules? Maybe your parent had a strict intolerance for:

- experimenting with your appearance—hair, clothes, jewelry, tattoos, etc.;
- challenging their beliefs—religion, politics, etc.;
- dating someone they didn't approve of;
- getting bad grades.

The deeper truth here is that what our parents were really saying through all these threats and ultimatums was this: "If you displease me, I will revoke my love and care." Their love was conditional—that it could and would be withdrawn and withheld if we didn't meet their expectations.

As adults now, if we try to bring up these experiences, our parent gets angry, defensive, or they outright deny any wrong-doing. To them, this kind of discipline was just "how things were done." They might claim it was a joke and they weren't being serious. And not only do they not believe they owe us an apology, but they often believe *we owe them* an apology for not being more grateful for "all they did for us," like providing for our basic needs, like food and shelter, was enough. The problem is, meeting basic needs isn't enough, and a child is going to take it seriously if you "joke" about disowning them and kicking them out of the damn house.

From Katherine

From a young age, my mom pounded Bible verses into our heads on the way to school. My brother and I were only allowed to listen to Gospel music. But for all of the time we spent at church—in the building, at events, with congregants—my mother was still mean AF. Making her happy was all I wanted. But it never worked.

Early on, she let us know that if we made her too mad or didn't like her rules, we could "get out!" Once, when we were little, she made my brother pack a duffel bag. He had pissed her off somehow, and she told us she was kicking him out. She drove us to K-street in Tacoma, which was a place rife with homelessness and drug abuse. She told him that if he kept up his bad behavior, this is where he was going to live.

After that, I was afraid to make her even a little mad. Although I wasn't the one who misbehaved, she regularly told me, "Don't think I won't kick you out too!" I spent my childhood being perfect to survive.

Generational Trauma Stops Here

Healing the Good Kid persona starts with parents choosing to show up for and heal themselves, which allows parenting to shift from being all about controlling your child, punishing them into being "good" and respecting you and seeing their success as a reflection on you, to being about meeting your child where they are with love and accountability and being able to not just tolerate but encourage kids to show up as their authentic, messy, imperfect selves.

To break these cycles, we have to take a step back and sit with the child we once were. We need to allow ourselves to get curious and *remember what it felt like* when our own big emotions were met with annoyance, anger, disappointment, rejection, or disdain—when we were sent to our room or given the silent treatment. That little version of us learned to believe there was something wrong with being emotional and, worse, that there was something wrong with us for feeling that way. We were told, directly or indirectly, that we were "too sensitive" or "too much," and so we learned to hide our pain and push down our Big Feelings to stay safe and feel loved.

This means facing that pain we've been carrying for years. It's about sitting with those younger parts of ourselves that still hold onto the shame, fear, and loneliness we felt as kids. These Parts need to feel what they never got the chance to feel back then. This isn't about blaming our parents—it's about being honest about what wasn't okay and giving ourselves the love and support we so desperately needed but didn't get. When we can look at that little version of ourselves and say, "You weren't too much; you were just a kid who needed someone to be there for you," we start to rewrite the story. This healing helps us separate what happened to us from what's happening with our kids now. Instead of shutting down their Big Feelings because they trigger something in us, we can stay calm(ish) and present, showing them they're safe and loved no matter what. And in doing that, we don't just heal ourselves—we break the cycle and give our kids a whole new experience of what love can be.

Kids Have Needs—Shocker!

Thinking back to my own childhood, those moments when I needed comfort or attention from my mother were often met with "you're too sensitive" or "you need thicker skin."

Exasperation. Annoyance. For needing her. I remember feeling so ashamed and like such a burden.

For me as a parent, I struggled so much with my daughter being needy—the train went off the tracks instantly. I was completely blindsided by how triggered I felt. Something deep inside me lit up in an unexpected and painful way. I had always dreamed of being the soft, safe place where my kids could fall apart and feel completely accepted by their mama. But in those moments, my body took over, and I felt something I hadn't expected or really ever experienced before: rage.

When my daughter would get needy, my brain and body went into autopilot, reacting before I could even think. The rage wasn't about her—it was about the scared little girl I used to be and all the ways I'd been made to feel ashamed for needing comfort, needing soothing, needing my mom. It was like my nervous system thought her neediness was *dangerous* because when I was little, being needy didn't feel safe. Sometimes, it was as if I blacked out for a second and when I came back to the moment, I had shut her down, said something harsh, or made her feel like she was wrong for needing me. Just like I had felt when I was a kid.

The craziest part is what my brain and nervous system thought they were doing—trying to *protect* her. By reacting the way my mom had with me. As if shutting her down would save her from being rejected by anyone else. But… instead of protecting her, I was doing the very thing I'd promised myself I'd never do. I know that this is probably exactly what happened with my mother and why she was so vicious with me when I was needy.

The shame cut me so deep, slamming me into a paralyzing Shame Spiral that made me believe I was a terrible mother because I struggled with this. My mother probably felt that too, but didn't have the tools or knowledge to understand how to change.

I am really proud of myself for the way I was absolutely determined to heal this and break this damn cycle—for my daughter and for Little Me. I did intensive work with my trauma therapist to untangle this and work with the Parts of me trying to protect her from what happened to Little Me. It took time, but I learned to honor that rage my body was trying to release and let it explode out of me... but into a pillow instead of being directed at my daughter. That rage was actually anger and frustration I had bottled and suppressed in childhood toward my own mother for how she made me feel in these moments—pitiful, pathetic, worthless and unlovable. Most rage is just shame in survival mode—trying to hurt before it gets hurt, again. And maybe most importantly, I was able to see that both my daughter and that needy little version of me deserved the safety and softness I'd always wanted to give her.

My Circle Backs with her after to repair look like me saying:

- "You needed me to be there for you, but I got mad, and I think I scared you—was that scary for you? It's safe to tell me if it was."
- "I am still learning how to help you and be your mom and this is stirring up some Big Feelings for me that I need to take care of."
- "You deserve support and comfort when you need it, and I am going to figure this out, so I can be there for you when you need to fall apart."

See Chapter 13, Relational Colostrum: Why Circle Backs Are Liquid Gold, for an explanation of Circle Backs.

Emotionally Reactive Parents

An emotionally reactive parent goes from seemingly calm to raging. They are sometimes fine with your behavior. At other times, though, they get angry and punish you for that same behavior. They offer you no verbal explanation for this about-face, and you can't find any logical reason for it.

When your behavior sets them off, they blame you for their temper—"Now look what you've done, I'm yelling!"—or threaten you with an impending temper—"Well, then you can explain to your father what you did when he gets home. He will *not* be happy about this."

Emotionally immature and reactive parents bottle their feelings. They don't let on that something is bothering them until they explode like a volcano. Most of the time when people get triggered, they're not actually that mad about the thing that finally sets them off. It's the build-up: their bad night of sleep, their slacking colleague at work, the coffee they dribbled on their favorite shirt at lunch, the way their sleeve caught on the door knob just before *you* dropped a cheap water glass. But the sound of shattering glass ended up shattering their extremely strained patience, and because they cannot manage their emotions in a healthy manner, they blow up at you instead.

Growing Up with Emotionally Reactive Parents

When your parent has explosive anger and seems to go from zero to raging, you experience anxiety, fear, and potentially terror—both when your parent explodes *and* at the thought of them exploding. You don't know when it will happen, so you become hyper-attuned to them to try to anticipate when they might explode. You are hypervigilant and on edge, listening for angry footsteps or sudden changes in their breathing or tone of voice. You walk on eggshells to keep from setting them off and you go into Fight/Flight if your parent seems mad or about to be mad.

If you have a sibling, you monitor your sibling's behavior. You intervene when they're acting out to keep them from setting your parent off (which does a number on your relationship with your sibling).

Without a stable caregiver to co-regulate with, you learned to suppress your own needs, internalizing the belief that needing anything is an inconvenience. You figured out—consciously or not—that the less you needed, the less you asked for, the less trouble you caused, the better. If you could be easy, helpful, and self-sufficient, maybe—just maybe—you wouldn't add to your parent's stress. Maybe you could avoid the yelling, the disappointment, the neglect, and your parent will love you in a way that feels stable and safe. The home is chaotic, but showing emotion only adds to the instability—so you learned to bottle it all up, silently carrying the weight of it alone.

Your nervous system perceived your parent as both a source of safety and a threat to your survival. Because you depended on your parent for survival, your body instinctively shut down the Fight Response, and you moved into Fawn Response, scanning for signs of your parent's mood shifts, softening yourself to avoid conflict, and prioritizing your parent's emotions over your own. Over time, this becomes your default way of relating—not because you didn't have needs, but because your nervous system was trying to make sure the person you depended on the most didn't turn against you.

Growing up with an emotionally reactive parent can also drive a crushing fear of upsetting others, where any time someone seems quiet or "off," you're anxiously asking them, "Are you mad at me?"

After having an emotionally reactive parent, I did the "Are you mad at me?" thing with my husband for years. If he was quieter than usual or seemed the slightest bit annoyed, a tsunami of anxiety and fear would rise up in my body. First, I immediately assumed it was my fault, even when there was absolutely no reason or evidence to think I had done anything. Then, I would anxiously review every minute interaction we'd had recently to figure out what I had done to upset him.

People who haven't had an emotionally reactive parent don't understand this. They're very rational about it. But when you've had a parent slam into rage unexpectedly and blame you for it, you internalize that it's your fault. You caused it.

Over time, to protect ourselves, we generalized this hyper-attunement to everyone—watching the whole room for signs that we were in trouble or that someone might be upset or mad. I don't have to tell you how utterly exhausting this is.

Most likely, your childhood was less about exploring, learning and being cared for, and more about managing your parent's moods, responsibilities, and their emotional well-being. With an emotionally reactive parent, you grew up in a world where instead of being supported, you were the one providing support to your parent. Instead of being reassured, you were the one reassuring your parent. And instead of feeling like a child, you did what you needed to do to become the adult in the room, long before you were ready, and you were praised by everyone for being "so mature."

On the inside, your brain and nervous system developed around you, focusing *out* on *others* instead of focusing *inward* on *yourself*. Many, many of my clients have no idea what they like, want, and need. They feel like they "should" know these things but how could they? We were attuned to our parents' emotions and well-being instead of what we as a child actually needed: for our parents to be attuned to *our* emotions and well-being. We didn't get to consistently be the person being cared for. So how on earth could we know what we like, want and need?

Parents with Narcissistic and Borderline Traits and Substance Use Disorder

In my early days as a therapist, one thing that surprised me was just how similar the emotional and psychological impact was for people who grew up with a parent struggling with substance use and those who had a parent with a personality disorder—especially Narcissistic Personality Disorder or Borderline Personality Disorder. The patterns of instability, emotional unpredictability, and the child's desperate attempts to manage their parent's moods and maintain a sense of safety mirrored each other. I wasn't surprised to find research confirming what I was seeing firsthand: the effects of these experiences can show up in very similar ways. Both environments create a foundation of instability and chronic stress, hypervigilance, and Relational Shame Trauma, leaving the child navigating an unpredictable world where their own needs and emotions take a backseat to their parent's struggles. If this is you, I see you.

Narcissistic and Borderline Traits

For some parents, their unhealed trauma shows up as narcissistic traits, which often involve their deep need for validation, control, or admiration. Parents with these traits might fixate on their child's achievements or behavior, believing they are a reflection of *their* own worth. Their thinking doesn't follow a straight line—it looks more like a child's scribbles, jumping unpredictably between entitlement, blame, self-importance, and being the victim. Their extremely limited capacity for empathy leads to inability and unwillingness to even see how they've hurt their child. They chronically shift blame so they are always right and their child is always the problem. They control their children with the threat of their rage.

For other parents, their unhealed trauma may manifest as borderline traits, where the parent has intense and unpredictable emotional swings. Their paralyzing fear of abandonment can lead them to compulsively abandon their child—emotionally (silent treatment) or physically—to protect themselves from the pain of being abandoned by their child. This creates unstable and inconsistent dynamics in the parent–child relationship because the child gets caught in the emotional whiplash of the parent's splitting behavior—where they feel loved and idealized one moment then suddenly and coldly rejected the next. Never knowing which version of the parent they'll get.

How It Feels to Be the Child

The child becomes an emotional caretaker, absorbing the brunt of their parent's unstable moods. They become hyper-attuned to the shifting tides of their parent's emotions, learning to self-censor, tiptoe, and anticipate their parent's needs before their own. One wrong move—a disagreement, an emotional reaction, or even an expression of independence—can trigger rage, withdrawal, or an emotional storm that leaves the child scrambling, over-apologizing and fawning to their parent to get back in their good graces. Instead of feeling safe to explore who they are, they become stuck in a role where their only job is to keep their parent regulated. Over time, they learn that their safest bet is to suppress their own feelings, avoid conflict at all costs, and make themselves as easy and accommodating as possible.

Because many parents who struggle with personality disorders have not processed their own pain and trauma, they often lack the capacity to validate their child's experiences. When the child expresses hurt or confusion, the parent may minimize, deny, or shift blame—not because they don't love their child, but because their own shame blocks them from seeing their impact. The child, desperate to believe in their parent's goodness, internalizes that blame instead. They must be *too needy, too sensitive, too difficult*. Over time, this belief becomes their truth, teaching them that speaking up, having boundaries, or expressing emotions is dangerous and leads to rejection and abandonment.

Substance Use Disorder

Some parents turn to substance use and abuse as a way to cope with their pain, which can lead to emotional neglect, inconsistency, and chaos. Many parents struggling with substance use desperately want to be there for their children and never intended to cause harm. But when addiction takes hold, it profoundly undermines their capacity and ability to provide the stability, emotional presence, and reliability their child needs. Some moments, the parent is warm, affectionate, and attentive, making them hope that maybe things will be different now. Other days, the parent is volatile, emotionally absent, or completely incapacitated, leaving the child to fend for themselves. The only consistency is the *inconsistency*.

How It Feels to Be the Child

The Good Kid often becomes the reliable one—the one who makes sure their siblings are fed, the bills are paid on time, and the house stays in order. They learn to clean up the messes, both literal and emotional, left in the wake of their parent's addiction. They carry the weight of responsibilities no child should have to carry, all while pretending everything is fine. It feels like they have to figure things out alone because there is no one available to catch them if they fall.

They cover for their parent's mistakes—making excuses, hiding evidence, or pretending everything is fine so no one will know what's really happening at home. If the parent forgets something important, lashes out, or breaks a promise, the Good Kid convinces themselves that they must not have reminded them enough, they must have done something wrong to deserve it.

Their survival depends on staying hypervigilant—constantly scanning for their parent's mood, level of intoxication, and whether today will be stable or another day of chaos. This instability forces them into chronic stress, stripping them of the chance to just be a kid because they're too busy managing the emotions and responsibilities of an adult.

Being a Good Kid Is a Survival Strategy

The unpredictability of a parent struggling with substance use or a personality disorder doesn't just create anxiety—it shapes their *identity*. They learn that their best shot at stability is being easy, agreeable, and never a problem. The only consistency is that their parent is inconsistent—some days, their parent is warm, nurturing, and attentive, giving them hope that if they just try hard enough to be "good," things will finally be okay. Other days, their parent is distant, unpredictable, or outright cruel, leaving them scrambling to adjust, to anticipate, to smooth things over before anything can escalate.

A Good Kid survives by being hyper-aware of their parent's every move. They watch their tone, their facial expressions, their footsteps, even the way they set down their keys. When their parent struggles with substance use, the Good Kid learns to stay invisible, self-sufficient, and never ask for too much, because their parent may be too impaired or emotionally checked out to respond. When their parent struggles with NPD or BPD, they become an emotional caretaker, constantly scanning for ways to manage their parent's moods and avoid triggering their unpredictable reactions.

Either way, the Good Kid learns that safety comes at a cost: their needs, their emotions, and their sense of self all take a backseat to keeping the peace. They don't think of it as survival mode—this is just life. But their nervous system knows and remembers. And when they carry those survival strategies into adulthood, they call it perfectionism, people pleasing, codependency, and high achievement—never realizing it was never about being good. It was always about being safe.

Parentification

Good Kids often stepped into roles far beyond their developmental stage, managing household responsibilities, caring for their siblings, parenting themselves, or even trying to protect their parent from themselves. They took on far more than they should have, getting themselves and their siblings ready for school, making meals, even caring for their parent when they're too impaired to function. They were the family stabilizer, the one who "had it all together"... because someone freaking had to.

Academically and socially, the impact is profound. School might feel impossible when home life is chaotic and overwhelming. Some kids shut down, struggling to focus, falling behind, and skipping school altogether. Others go the opposite direction, becoming high-achieving, perfectionistic Good Kids who pour everything into school as a way to escape.

But no matter how well they perform, it never quite feels like enough—because their self-worth was built on shaky ground. Socially, they often struggle to connect with peers who haven't lived through the same level of responsibility and stress. They might withdraw, feeling ashamed of their home life, or they might seek out relationships where they have to earn love and care—mirroring the dynamics they grew up with. They develop PTSD-like symptoms—nightmares, flashbacks, emotional numbness—without realizing that's what it is. Their body holds onto stress in ways they don't understand, leading to chronic pain, digestive issues, headaches, and exhaustion.

In relationships, they struggle to trust; the first person who was supposed to protect them let them down over and over again. They might crave closeness but fear it at the same time, leading to self-sabotaging patterns of pushing people away before they can be abandoned. Or, they become overly attached—clinging to people, desperate for reassurance that they won't be left behind again.

Perhaps the most painful part? The shame. The deep, aching belief that if they had just been better—more obedient, more helpful, less of a burden—things would have been different.

And even as adults, long after they've left that chaotic home, the shame lingers. It shows up in their relationships, their self-worth, their ability to rest, to trust, to believe they are enough just as they are. Breaking free from these cycles isn't just about unlearning the damage—it's about learning, sometimes for the first time, that they were never the problem in the first place. And they were worthy of care—with a parent unable to give them what they needed.

Growing up with a High-Needs Sibling or "Problem Child" Sibling

If they grew up with a high-needs sibling—whether the sibling had chronic medical challenges, mental health challenges, struggled with explosive emotions, or were labeled the "problem child" because of their defiance and acting out—Good Kids probably figured out early on that their best bet was to not be another problem. They learned to take care of themselves, to keep quiet about their needs, and to do whatever they could to make life easier for their parents. And the Good Kid got rewarded for it—their sibling got attention for their struggles and they got praised for being the mature one, the resilient one, the one who never needed help.

> "You're my rock."
> "I don't know what I'd do without you."
> "I don't have to worry about you."

At first, it felt like a good thing. They felt proud of being dependable and self-sufficient. But there was deep loneliness underneath—parts of them that needed to feel seen, soothed, cared for by their parents. Not just for being "so good," but for simply existing. They learned that asking for support meant taking resources away from their sibling, who "obviously" needed it more.

And yet—somehow—it was never enough. No matter how well the Good Kid behaved, how much they helped, or how little they needed, the attention always went to their sibling. When the sibling messed up, there was understanding: *They can't help it. They're struggling.* When the Good Kid made a mistake, there was disappointment. Their sibling got away with things the Good Kid never would have. The sibling got their emotions soothed while the Good Kid was expected to be fine on their own. That double standard stings.

They loved their sibling. They understood, on some level, why the sibling needed more. But that didn't erase the resentment of always being held to a higher standard—of being the strong one while the sibling got to fall apart. The Good Kid was expected to be perfect, but even then, it wasn't enough to earn the same level of care.

Now they might struggle with feeling unseen in relationships. They might hold themselves to impossible standards, constantly chasing enough. They might feel guilty for even admitting that part of them is still angry about it. If this is you, I see you. The role you played to survive wasn't fair to you. You weren't supposed to be the easy one at your own expense. You deserved to need things, to have feelings, to make mistakes—just as much as anyone else. And you still do.

The Amplified Trauma of Good Kids

In these environments, the rules for being a Good Kid—don't upset anyone, never mess up, and always put others first—aren't just implicit; they become utter survival strategies. You learned that your parent's love, stability, and even presence were dependent on how well you conformed to these unspoken rules. The pressure to be perfect, selfless, and emotionally invisible was relentless. It leaves you with an identity built around performance and people pleasing, unable to trust your own feelings and unsure how to ask for the love and care you desperately need and deserve.

Breaking free from these patterns as adults is incredibly challenging but deeply healing. It starts with recognizing that these behaviors were never about your worth—they were brilliant survival strategies to get your needs met someway, somehow... born out of impossible circumstances. Learning to give yourself the unconditional love and support you never received as a kid is the first step toward breaking the cycle and healing the shame that's been passed down.

Here, I want to gently remind you that you deserved love and care that you didn't have to earn first. You deserved to have a parent you could count on to love and care for you simply because you existed—not because of what you achieved, how well you behaved, or how much you were able to keep the peace. You deserved to feel safe enough to express your needs, Big Feelings, and messy, imperfect moments *without* fear of rejection, abandonment, or shame. You deserved to be a kid—free to explore, make mistakes, and lean on the adults around you for stability and guidance. You shouldn't have had to figure out how to be the grown-up in the room while you were still a child yourself.

That love, stability, and nurturing you worked so hard to give to your parent were always supposed to be what *they* gave to *you*. You were not meant to carry *their* emotional burdens or make up for *their* struggles with consistency. You deserved so much better than to have to silence your own needs so theirs could take priority. The roles were reversed in a way that left you feeling responsible for things no child should have to carry.

But none of this was your fault. You were a caterpillar doing your best to survive in a world that expected you to already be a butterfly. Your parent was incapable of doing *their* job— nurturing you through the stages of growth. Instead, you were made to feel ashamed for not meeting expectations you were never developmentally ready for. You were doing your best to get your most basic needs met by a parent who was not capable of that. You were forced to shapeshift into whatever "lovable" version of you would keep the connection alive with those who were supposed to parent you.

But the caterpillar is not failing or broken for not being a butterfly yet. It's becoming. Your parent wanted you to be emotionally mature, independent, and never needy—without giving you the safety and support needed to *become* those things. The problem was never you. And despite all... you survived. And now you get to give yourself the nurturing, support, and love without conditions you always deserved so you can finally step into who you were always meant to be.

Our Parents Don't Get Their Impact

"I needed to jerk your chain and get your attention."
—My mother, more times than I could count, when I confronted her about how hurtful it was to get the silent treatment.

One of the most painful parts of healing isn't just facing what happened—it's facing the fact that our parents refuse to face it with us. When we bring up the ways we were impacted, they shut down, get defensive, and double down on "I didn't do it on purpose" and "I thought I was doing the right thing," as if intention is all that matters.

But we know better—we know that we are all accountable for our impact, not just our intention. Refusing to acknowledge the harm they caused—even unintentionally—is like pouring lemon juice on an already raw and open wound, agitating it and making it harder to heal. We aren't asking for perfection. We aren't asking for them to hate themselves or carry guilt forever. We're asking them to see us, to validate what we went through, and to take responsibility for their impact, so we don't have to keep carrying the burden of explaining why it hurt.

Imagine I spend months building a really thoughtful, intricate gift for you—something I truly believe will make you so happy. I put my whole heart into it, beaming with pride as I hand it to you. But as soon as you open it, you have a massive allergic reaction and you report tremendous discomfort and pain inside. I never meant for this to happen. My intention was purely to make you happy. But, the reality is, I hurt you. And now, how I respond matters. Do I say, "I didn't do it on purpose, so you shouldn't feel bad"? Do I insist that because I meant well, both of us should ignore the fact that you're struggling? Of course not. Because whether I meant to or not, the damage has been done. The right thing to do is to see what happened, take responsibility, and say, "I didn't know, but I see now the impact I had. I am so sorry." That's what we want from our parents. Not an apology drenched in guilt and self-hatred. Just ownership. Awareness. Acknowledgment. The simple human decency of saying, "I see how that hurt you. And I'm sorry."

Put your Perspectacles on with me and see this clearly: our parents struggle to acknowledge the hurtful impact they had because they have never processed the hurtful impact their parents had on them. They are stuck in a cycle where their own pain was never truly dealt with—so they unknowingly passed it down.

Because they never looked at it, they cannot see the ways they harmed us. Not because they don't care, but because their unhealed shame and Relational Shame Trauma blocks them from being able to face it. How do we know this? Because when people are in shame, it shows up as defensiveness. Lashing out. Dismissing. Blaming. Instead of sitting with the discomfort of "I hurt my child" and owning that impact, shame tells them: "You're a terrible parent. You failed." And because that shame is so unbearable, they fight back—they get mad. They shut the conversation down. They gaslight. They turn it around on us. Not because they don't love us, but because they never built the capacity to process their own shame. Instead of letting it in, they bury it. Fight it. Deny it. Throw it right back at us. And in doing so, they make us feel like we're the ones in the wrong for bringing it up in the first place.

But we are not trying to make them feel like the worst parent in the world. We are not trying to take away all the good things they did. We are simply trying to get them to see us, to acknowledge what happened, and show up for their impact. Instead of making us feel like we're crazy for feeling it. We don't want guilt. We don't want performative apologies dripping in self-hatred. We just want the basic human decency of: "I see how that hurt you. I'm sorry."

The heartbreaking part is that many of them just can't do it. Not because they don't care, but because they don't know how. You need to let yourself grieve this—this grief is deep and heavy and important. You need to keep reminding yourself—Today You and Little You—that you deserve to feel seen by parents in the ways they hurt you and it freaking sucks that your parents are unwilling and/or unable to do that. I see you.

If I could say anything to our parents, it would be this: "Yes. Your parents would have never apologized. So why should you have to? Here's the thing... wouldn't that have felt so good? For them to say they were sorry for hurting you? Didn't you deserve that? You can keep digging your heels in and being mad at your kid for trying to have this conversation. It would be uncomfortable, yes, but it would also bring you closer to each other. You can break this cycle and give your kid the thing you deserved but never got."

4

The Voice That Says It's All Your Fault

What Is Shame?

Shame is one of our fundamental human emotions. Like a built-in safety mechanism, shame makes sure we stay connected and fit in with our people to avoid rejection and abandonment. Guilt and embarrassment are tied to *things* we did, but shame is a deeply relational emotion—it's the feeling that something about *us* is fundamentally wrong, broken, or unworthy of love, belonging and connection. Shame is about our identity—who we are, deep down.

You might not think you know much about shame but it's running in the background of your life every single day, whether you realize it or not. The guilt you feel for resting is laced with shame—the belief that you "shouldn't" be tired or *don't deserve* rest. The panic you feel over disappointing someone is laced with shame. Shame profoundly impacts how you show up in the world and how much space you believe you're allowed to take up. It shapes how you see yourself and what you expect from others. It tells you what you deserve and demands you shapeshift into the most lovable version of yourself to be safe.

How Shame Makes Us Feel

Shame is wired into our brain and nervous system, hijacking our thoughts, tightening our chest, making our stomach drop.

Shame doesn't just feel bad—it feels life-threatening and dangerous. Shame is often accompanied by a sense of painful vulnerability and exposure, as if we've been seen in a bad way that makes us unsafe, triggering survival-level responses in our nervous system, like freezing, withdrawing, or shutting down. In the body, shame feels incredibly heavy, like a weight pressing down on our chest or gut. It's that feeling of wanting to shrink, disappear, or hide under your desk.

Unlike other emotions, shame creates a fundamental sense of disconnection—not just from others but from ourselves. It pulls us out of alignment with our instincts and shuts them down, making it harder to trust our inner signals or act on our needs. Where sadness might move us to seek comfort, or anger might push us to take action, shame often leaves us stuck, unable to do anything because it feels like *we* are the problem.

Shame has this sneaky, insidious way of embedding itself deep inside, shaping how you see yourself, how you show up in relationships, and how you believe you deserve to be treated. And shame doesn't stay isolated around one incident. It grows, taking over your inner world with beliefs like, "There is something wrong with me," "I'm a burden," "I'm hard to love," "I don't deserve love," "I'll never be good enough," and "If people really knew me, they'd leave." It eats away at your sense of self, making you doubt your worth at every turn.

How Is Shame Different from Other Emotions?

What sets shame apart is its profound connection to our deepest survival instincts. As social beings, our survival has historically depended on belonging to a group. Shame taps into this primal need for connection, creating a feeling of "survival terror" when we fear that we might be rejected, excluded, or abandoned. Unlike guilt, which focuses on what we've done ("I did something bad") shame focuses on who we are ("I am bad").

Shame is the ultimate and most profound dysregulator of our nervous system because it disrupts our fundamental ability to feel safe and grounded. It takes over our nervous system, pulling us into a state of hypervigilance (watching for rejection or judgment) or shutdown (disconnecting to avoid pain). This is especially true for Good Kids because Relational Shame Trauma taught our nervous system to equate vulnerability with danger.

Shame shuts down our instincts—those inner signals that guide us to care for ourselves or seek support. It silences the parts of us that might want to cry out, "I need help" or "This isn't okay," replacing them with, "Stay small," "Don't be a burden," or "It's safer to hide." This makes healing from shame particularly challenging because it requires us to do the very thing shame teaches us to avoid: reach out, reconnect, and let ourselves be seen.

Shame has a profoundly powerful impact on our nervous system. It can trigger Freeze Response—causing us to shut down, avoid eye contact, or retreat from social situations. Shame also activates Fawn Response, where we overcompensate by people pleasing and trying to make ourselves "acceptable" or "more lovable" to avoid conflict, disappointment, rejection, and abandonment. When we feel exposed or criticized, or sense the possibility of rejection or abandonment, shame can trigger Fight Response, showing up as defensiveness, anger, or lashing out as a way to regain control and protect ourselves from deeper vulnerability. Shame can also trigger Flight Response, driving us to isolate, avoid, or even abandon relationships to escape feelings of inadequacy or rejection.

Ironically, these responses are all our nervous system's attempts to keep us safe and help us survive—but they often create the opposite effect. Whether we're shutting down, over-apologizing, lashing out, or pulling away, shame reinforces the very disconnection we're wired to avoid. Noticing and getting curious about how shame shows up in your nervous system is an important step to interrupting these patterns and creating space for healing and connection.

Impact of Shame-Laced Discipline

When our messy humanity and clumsy development "failed" to meet our parents' beliefs about themselves and about parenting, we were punished with shame-laced discipline. There is extensive emotional and psychological fallout when children are subjected to discipline that is laced with shame and fear—particularly when the discipline happens because of unrealistic, impossible expectations of the child. Children are still developing in every way, and expecting them to be well-behaved at all times and to have better emotional regulation and impulse control than their parents, without the tools to manage their feelings, is a set-up for failure.

However, it is possible to push a child into constant "good" behavior, and if you were a Good Kid, you get it. This major personality change requires an extensive amount of shame-laced discipline to "teach them to behave better" at a great cost to the child's sense of self, self-worth and nervous system.

Disciplining a child by:
- sending them away in shame "for what they did" (Time Out);
- withholding words or signs of affection (the silent treatment);
- saying thing like:
    - "What is wrong with you?"
    - "You should be ashamed of yourself."
    - "I'm not mad. I'm disappointed."
    - "I expected more from you."

This discipline is *based* in shame and fear. It's giving then abruptly withdrawing and withholding love, connection, and care from the child to control them and their behavior. It's going from warm and caring one minute… to cold and punishing the next.

This embedded shame into your identity and beliefs about who you are, what other people think about you, and what you deserve. This made you feel like you had to constantly prove your worth to avoid being "found out" as flawed and unlovable. If you made a mistake as a child, it wasn't seen as something to learn from. It felt like evidence that there was something wrong *with you* and you weren't lovable when you were *like that*.

It sends a very, very harmful message to the child: that their behavior is not only wrong, but there is something wrong with them, as a person, for doing that. They are bad. They are a disappointment. They are not worthy of love, attention, or care because of it. Children need consistent, nurturing support from their caregivers to develop a reliable sense of safety, self-worth, and emotional resilience. When their caregiver withdraws and withholds support in response to mistakes and misbehavior, the child's nervous system becomes dysregulated, activating our stress responses.

In Fight/Flight, our body activates to either confront or escape the perceived threat. But when the threat is our caregiver—whether through shame-laced discipline, emotional abuse, neglect, inconsistency, overwhelming dominance, or actual physically hurtful and threatening behavior—*the child's nervous system cannot safely fight or flee.* The child's nervous system knows the parent represents their primary source of survival and care, so fighting or fleeing from them endangers their ability to survive and get their needs met. Their nervous system might suppress Fight/Flight and the natural impulses to fight back or protect themselves and push them into Fawn (appeasing and avoiding conflict) or Freeze/Dorsal Vagal Shutdown (dissociation, physical shutdown, going numb). But at the same time, the child becomes hyper-aware and hyper-attuned to their caregiver's energy and mood, because it feels like their survival depends on their ability to scan and read every shift in tone and every expression keeps their caregiver emotionally regulated, at all costs.

As a kid, you learned to be extremely cautious, terrified of making mistakes, and feeling like failure was a reflection of who you were deep down inside. Now, you might struggle with vicious self-criticism, perfectionism, people pleasing, and a paralyzing fear of being vulnerable, all rooted in the belief that mistakes and not being perfect make you unlovable.

"No One Expected Perfection From Me—I Expected It From Myself."

This is one of the most common things I hear from adults who are recovering Good Kids. We insist that *we* were the ones holding ourselves to impossible standards. That *we* were the ones disappointed in ourselves. That our parents didn't have to be hard on us—because we were already doing it for them. And we're not wrong. This is exactly how Relational Shame Trauma works.

And here's the kicker: when shame-laced discipline happens over and over, you don't even need your parents to step in anymore. By the time you're old enough to remember, you've already been trained to do the work for them. Because we were desperate to see our parents as good, loving, and well-intentioned— and because admitting otherwise felt scary and unbearable—we turned the blame on ourselves. Instead of questioning whether their standards and expectations were fair or realistic, we told ourselves:

- "I just need to try harder."
- "I should have known better."
- "I can't believe I let that happen."

You shame yourself, judge yourself, and cut yourself off at the knees, all to keep their approval and avoid the unbearable sense that something is wrong with you. What you're wrestling with now isn't just your own shame—it's the shame they couldn't hold or handle in themselves, that they put onto you. Again, we keep coming back to their misguided beliefs about how children should always, always behave and be respectful. And what a "good" parent *must do* to punish kids into respecting them.

Shame Hurts Most When It Comes From People We Love

Relational Shame is unique because it's not just about what happens to us—it's about how those experiences were interpreted in the context of our relationships. For example, if our parents shamed us for expressing emotions or having needs, we interpreted that those parts of ourselves are unacceptable or unlovable. Over time, with consistent experiences like that, those beliefs become internalized at a deep level. This shapes not only how we see ourselves but also how we show up in relationships, often hiding or shutting down parts of who we are to avoid further criticism, rejection or judgment.

We become Good Kids as a response to **Relational Trauma**—repeated, everyday experiences inside the relationships in childhood that are *supposed to be safe*, where we experienced chronic disconnection, inconsistency, or harm. It's feeling criticized, unsafe, unloved, unseen, and like we had to earn love by being "good" or perfect. Where our parents did not consistently care for or respond to us—sometimes loving us when we were struggling and other times telling us to "Stop being so dramatic" and "Pull yourself together"—we are left feeling uncertain about whether we even *deserved* to be cared for. We were constantly unsure whether our basic emotional needs would be met, which fostered deep insecurity and self-doubt, not to mention stress.

Relational Trauma is also about feeling like we had to shrink ourselves—our needs, emotions, and struggles—to belong, be accepted, and earn approval and love. Always mindful that if we weren't "good," love and approval would be revoked.

Relational Shame Trauma is the deepest wound at the root of *all* Relational Trauma. We experience Relational *Shame* Trauma when these experiences come with the spoken or unspoken message that there's something fundamentally wrong, bad, unlovable, "too much," or "not enough" about us. Shame is so gnarly and devastating because it isn't just a surface wound that heals with time or distance—it's like a staph infection. On the outside, everything might look healed up and just fine, but underneath, it spreads like wildfire, impacting everything it touches.

From Mikaela

When I got home from practice at 6:30, I felt heavy. My day had been so upsetting, and I really just needed to be seen and heard. I went to my room and waited for my mom to arrive home from work. The anticipation was building and I was fidgety and couldn't concentrate on anything.

At 6:45, the door opened. My body relaxed and relief flooded me. Finally, I could fall into her arms and fall apart. I raced to the door, to my mom.

But before I could say anything, she started complaining about how everything in life was stressful and how she couldn't handle one more thing. She lectured about how the kitchen wasn't clean. She berated me for how I didn't care about my family. She reminded me I should have been cleaning because I had been home long enough to do it.

As she disappeared upstairs, I walked back to my room slowly. Head bowed, with a sore neck and shoulders, my heart sank. I felt defeated. I was too much. I was unlovable. I wasn't worth it. I would just be adding to my mom's already stressful day. Alone, I choked back my tears, pulled myself together, and left to clean the kitchen.

With Relational Shame Trauma, you feel like your worth and inherent lovability depends on meeting impossible, ever-shifting standards that don't match who you are or what you're capable of, especially at different stages of your life. You are punished within your relationships and made to feel like a disappointment, like you are unlovable, or like you are unworthy of care and connection. The people around you—whether it's a parent, partner, or friend—don't even need to say it out loud. You just feel it in how people pull away, withdraw their warmth, or give you the silent treatment. Those patterns of emotional withdrawal teach you that you're only worthy of love and care if you meet certain, often unrealistic, expectations—and there must be something wrong with you because you *can't* meet those expectations to even be deserving in the first place.

"I Don't Even Remember That."

Another common experience for Good Kids is chronic dissociation from the shame. So many of us struggle to remember our childhoods and the specifics of what hurt us—only that we feel a deep, unshakable sense of not being enough. That's because Relational Shame Trauma is insidious. It doesn't just hurt us in the moment—it buries itself so deep that we lose access to the why. This is a nervous system response. When shame is too overwhelming to process, we detach. We convince ourselves it wasn't that bad. We minimize and justify. We focus on all the ways our parents meant well and did their best because facing the full weight of their impact feels too scary and too much.

This is why so many Good Kids struggle to hold their parents accountable. We protect them, excuse them, and insist that *we* were the ones who expected too much from ourselves. Because if our parents did this to us, if they made us feel like we were never enough, then we have to grieve the truth. And grief is messy. It makes sense that parts of us work hard to keep us from seeing the truth.

The Unspoken Rules for Good Kids

Relational Trauma drives us to be that Good Kid, so let's talk about what that actually feels like. So often, in situations of shame-based discipline, the rules go unsaid until we mess up. This interplay between spoken and unspoken rules from our parents created a deeply ingrained set of expectations for us. Spoken rules provide the framework. Unspoken rules fill in the emotional and relational subtext that kept us stuck in compliance, self-suppression, and shame.

- Unspoken Rule 1—Be "good," agreeable, polite and grateful.
- Unspoken Rule 2—Success = Worth
- Unspoken Rule 3—Don't mess up.
- Unspoken Rule 4—Don't have big emotions.
- Unspoken Rule 5—Don't upset anyone.
- Unspoken Rule 6—Be my "easy" kid.
- Unspoken Rule 7—Need Less. Focus On Me.
- Unspoken Rule 8—Don't ask for help.
- Unspoken Rule 9—Don't make me look bad.
- Unspoken Rule 10—Take care of everyone else before yourself.

1. Be "Good," Agreeable, Polite and Grateful

You felt like you couldn't make mistakes and had to always, always "be good" with constant obedience and politeness, no matter how you felt inside. Speaking up, saying no, or showing emotions was labeled "bad," "disrespectful," and "ungrateful." You were expected to put on a constant performance to please and delight everyone with your perfect behavior and accomplishments, meet impossible expectations, and never, ever challenge authority… as a kid. You were also expected to be "easy to get along with."

Misguided Beliefs That Created This Rule
- Good parents have respectful, well-behaved kids who always, always behave.
- A parent's most important job is to raise a respectful, well-behaved child (and provide basic needs like a roof over their head).
- What other people think of us matters above all else.

What Parents Say to Reinforce This Rule
- "Good Kids don't talk back."
- "If you don't have anything nice to say, don't say anything at all."
- "Stop being disrespectful and do as you're told."

How It Felt
It wasn't just about following the rules. It was about always putting on a "good" face. You had to act like everything was fine, even when it wasn't, because being good wasn't just about what you did—it was about how you looked doing it. It might have felt like your worth was tied to how agreeable or easygoing you could be. Your parents' pride depended on your perfection, and any misstep on your part undermined their identity as a "good" parent.

The Impact
You felt constant pressure to suppress your true thoughts, feelings, and needs to meet impossible and unrelenting standards of politeness and agreeability. Over time, this taught you that challenging authority, speaking up, or prioritizing yourself was disrespectful and shameful. Your behavior must align with what others expect of you, no matter how you feel inside.

2. Success = Worth
It felt like love had a performance review where love and approval were only granted when you succeeded, achieved,

or made your parents proud. You learned to hustle for praise like it was oxygen. When your parent was upset, they ignored you, withheld affection, or made you feel invisible until you "earned" their approval back. Whether it came through outright rejection, emotional withdrawal and withholding (the silent treatment), them going away or sending you away (their physical absence), you were left feeling like you didn't matter and weren't loved because of what happened.

Misguided Beliefs That Created This Rule

- A parent's job is to raise a successful child because success equals happiness.
- A child's success reflects their parents' worth.
- What other people think of us matters above all else.

What Parents Say to Reinforce This Rule

- "I expected more from you because I know you're better than this."
- "Do you want people to think you're a failure?"
- "You did great, but next time aim for first place."

How It Felt

Love and approval in your family felt like something you had to earn. Maybe you were praised when you brought home straight A's, excelled at sports, or behaved perfectly, but affection was harder to come by if you made mistakes, upset them, or didn't meet expectations.

It wasn't about who you were—it was about what you could achieve and how you could behave. Every success brought temporary relief, but the pressure to keep performing never went away. This left you anxious, hyper-focused on how others perceived you, and created a relentless drive to achieve more to feel worthy of approval. You were terrified of failure, stuck chasing perfection, and feeling like falling short wasn't just a disappointment—it felt like you were letting them down in a way that made you question your worth.

The Impact
You internalized the belief that love, connection, and belonging were conditional and could disappear if someone "found out"—if you made a mistake, let someone down or showed your real, imperfect self. This left you feeling deeply unlovable and ashamed for needing connection, always fearing that stepping out of line would lead to rejection or abandonment.

You view love, pride, and acceptance as conditional on your success and perfection, leaving you feeling like your worth was tied to your accomplishments and that anything less than being the best was a failure. The only thing that mattered was the outcome—effort didn't matter unless it led to success. This drives your struggle with perfectionism, fear of failure, self-criticism and self-punishment (to "motivate" yourself), overachieving and overfunctioning, and a constant drive for external validation.

3. Don't Mess Up
You felt crushing pressure to get everything right because one mistake felt like it would disappoint and let everyone down. It wasn't just about doing your best—it was about never letting anyone down.

Misguided Beliefs That Created This Rule
- A child's success reflects their parents' worth.
- Punishments teach kids lessons, and kids need to suffer consequences to learn.
- Children should be afraid of what will happen if they fail.
- Mistakes are a reflection of the child's laziness, carelessness, or lack of respect, and they deserve criticism or punishment.

What Parents Say to Reinforce This Rule
- "I'm not mad, I'm just disappointed."
- "I thought you knew better."
- "I can't believe you messed this up."

How It Felt
Failure felt like the end of the world. You developed an intense fear of failure because a mistake wasn't seen as something to learn from—it was forbidden and proof that you weren't good enough.

The Impact
This created and nurtured an intense and paralyzing fear of failure that led you to strive for unattainable perfection. It made you feel like struggling and making mistakes was a personal failure that made *you* a disappointment, resulting in emotional withdrawal or rejection from your parents.

4. Don't Have Big Emotions
Your feelings weren't acknowledged, supported, or taken seriously. Your parent dismissed what you were going through and shut you down. Other times, they ignored your emotions altogether—no one asked how you were feeling or tried to comfort you when you were upset. They had no idea you were struggling and assumed you were fine because you were, "the one they never needed to worry about."

Misguided Beliefs That Created This Rule
- When a child has intense emotions, they should be able to calm down instantly.
- A parent should teach emotional control by ignoring the child or withholding affection.
- Expressing emotions like anger, frustration, or sadness is immature and burdensome to others.
- Children should be seen, not heard—especially when they're upset.

What Parents Say to Reinforce This Rule
- "Stop crying—it's not a big deal."
- "You're being so dramatic right now."
- "You're old enough to know better than to act like this."

How It Felt
You felt like your emotions made you "too sensitive" and "too much" for others, so you learned to push them down, keep them to yourself and pretend you were fine no matter what. Whenever you got sad, angry, or upset, you were made to feel like you were overreacting or being dramatic. Instead of feeling like it was okay to share what you were going through and still be loved, you learned that showing your feelings could lead to rejection, abandonment, scolding, and making your parent mad. It felt like there wasn't room for your feelings. You learned that the less emotional you were, the easier it was for everyone else... and the more they liked you. This left you feeling invisible, like your inner world didn't exist to others or wasn't worth their time or attention.

The Impact
You learned to see your feelings and emotional reactions as immature, inconvenient, unnecessary, and something that makes you a burden. You "controlled" them by suppressing them and, over time, this left you disconnected from your emotions, anxious, and stuck in a cycle of bottling everything up. The thought of being vulnerable about your needs and emotions makes your skin crawl, and you don't really know how to trust others will be there for you. You may find yourself turning to chronically distracting and numbing behaviors because facing your emotions feels overwhelming or unsafe.

5. Don't Upset Anyone

You were expected to keep the peace at all costs, even though it meant staying silent, suppressing your needs, and pretending you were okay when you weren't.

Misguided Beliefs That Created This Rule
- Children should behave at all times and avoid upsetting or disappointing their parents.
- Children are responsible for not setting off their parent's temper.
- What other people think of us is all that matters.

What Parents Say to Reinforce This Rule
- "Talk back to me again and see what happens."
- "You're lucky I still love you after what you just did."
- "Do what you're told and don't make it harder than it needs to be."

How It Felt
It wasn't just about avoiding fights—it was about making sure everyone stayed happy, no matter what it cost you. It taught you to prioritize harmony over honesty and connection over your own needs.

The Impact
Conflict or "misbehavior" (standing up for yourself) results in connection being severed, fostering a fear of conflict and confrontation. You learned to avoid asserting yourself, speaking up, and standing up for yourself to maintain family harmony at all cost.

6. Be My "Easy" Kid

You were expected to handle everything without "causing trouble" or adding stress because your parent *counted on you* to make their life easier. When you struggled or made a mistake, your parent acted like it was a personal betrayal, as though you'd broken some silent agreement to always be the one they could "count on" to basically parent yourself. It's the energy of "How could you do this to me?"—where "this" was struggling, needing them and not holding it all together *for them*.

Misguided Beliefs That Created This Rule
- Good parents have "easy" kids who don't create problems and always, always behave.
- Asking for help is a sign of weakness, and needing help makes the child a burden.
- Children should handle their struggles on their own so they can become strong and independent because helping your kids makes them weak and dependent.
- A parent should express their disappointment and make the child feel guilty for failing to meet their expectations with "I'm not mad, I'm just disappointed" to help teach them about right from wrong, the importance of making good choices and to motivate the child to try harder next time.

What Parents Say to Reinforce This Rule
- "I love that I never have to worry about you!"
- "I know you'll figure it out—you always do."
- "I can always count on you to do the right thing."

How It Felt
You were expected to take on adult responsibilities, whether that meant caring for your parent's emotions, managing household tasks, or being the "mature" one in the family. In some ways, it felt like you were the parent, while your parent acted more like the child.

You had to be the "low-maintenance" kid who basically raised themselves. It felt like the "most lovable" version of you was easy to deal with, so you tried to keep quiet when you needed something and figured it out on your own. It felt like your job was to be helpful *without even being asked* and not add to your parent's stress. Asking for help and needing support felt like you were letting them down.

Psst! Their disappointment wasn't really about you—it was about them. About how your feelings, mistakes, and struggles made their life harder. But carrying that weight was never supposed to be your job. It was *theirs*.

> **From Brittney**
> As a child, I was consistently shamed for needing anything, whether it was spilling something, making a mess, or simply wanting attention. As the youngest of three sisters, I learned early that my needs were an inconvenience and that work came before everything else. My mother, often overwhelmed with her work and responsibilities, would react to my needs with frustration—loud noises, yelling, and even physical reprimands. I became quiet and self-sufficient, avoiding asking for help or attention, as it was easier than facing her anger.

The Impact

Like Brittney, you learned to suppress your needs and emotions, avoid asking for help, and handle everything on your own. You saw needing support as failure. Over time, it started to feel like your worth came from being self-sufficient and never needing anyone—even when it left you feeling alone or overwhelmed. This left you disconnected from your own vulnerability and overwhelmed by a constant pressure to perform. It feels like everyone is counting on you to hold it together. And if you can't… you're letting them down. Goodness… those are such heavy burdens to place on a child. Or anyone, really.

7. Need Less. Focus On Me

In your family, you may have experienced enmeshment—you were the kid and they were the parent but *their* emotions, needs, and well-being were *your* responsibility. You needed your parent to be attuned to you—your emotions, your needs, your wellbeing. To notice when you weren't okay and check in. But you were attuned *to them*.

Misguided Beliefs That Created This Rule
- Children are mini-adults who have the emotional capacity of an adult.
- Children are responsible for not setting off their parent's temper.

What Parents Say to Reinforce This Rule
- "You're so mature for your age."
- "You're our family's rock."
- "I don't know what I would've done without you."

How It Felt
You may have been expected to soothe your parent's feelings, make sure they were okay, manage their problems and anticipate their needs. You needed all of that from them, but you worked hard to meet those expectations of you. If you expressed your own needs or tried to set boundaries, it might have been met with guilt, anger, or feeling dismissed and made to feel ashamed. It felt like there was no room for you to just be a kid.

The Impact
You grew up believing that your role was to keep others happy and take care of everyone else, even when you were not okay. Having needs or boundaries might still feel selfish or wrong, and you might struggle with feelings of guilt ("having needs is bad") and shame ("I am bad for having needs") when you try to prioritize yourself. You might struggle with people pleasing, emotional suppression and exhaustion, and difficulty knowing how on earth you're supposed to take care of yourself when so much of your life is fixated on ignoring your own needs

and emotions so you can take care of others. You stay stuck in cycles of burnout from always giving support while struggling to receive it. The core struggle to receive support? Concluding and still believing that you don't deserve support when you didn't receive it in childhood.

8. Don't Ask for Help

You felt like you had to handle everything alone because seeking support would mean you were incapable, lazy, or selfish. Your parents were trained to be afraid of "spoiling" you, so instead of supporting you through challenges, they pushed you toward independence before you were ready. Maybe way before you were ready. They praised you when you did things on your own and showed disappointment when you struggled or needed help. Over time, you learned to avoid ever asking for help or showing your struggle on the outside, because that meant failure. So you stopped asking, even when you really needed it.

Misguided Beliefs That Created This Rule
- Children should learn independence by figuring things out on their own.
- Parents should avoid doing things for their kids because it will make them weak or dependent.
- Asking for help is a sign of weakness, and needing help makes the child a burden.

What Parents Say to Reinforce This Rule
- "You're old enough to handle this on your own without me holding your hand."
- "Figure it out—I can't do everything for you."
- "If I do it for you, how will you ever learn?"

How It Felt
Independence was everything. You learned to keep your struggles private because you didn't want to risk being seen as a burden to others. Even when you felt overwhelmed—you had to figure it out for yourself, by yourself.

The Impact
You learned to associate vulnerability and needing help with weakness and shame, making it really difficult to rely on others or ask for support. This fostered a tendency to isolate when you're struggling (I call it "Turtling"—I pull into my shell and struggle to reach out to anyone). You also feel inadequate when you can't do something without struggle—instead of realizing that expecting yourself to be naturally good at everything and never need any help is and was a ridiculous, impossible expectation of you.

9. Don't Make Me Look Bad
Your job wasn't just to always, always behave—it was your job to protect your parent's image and show the world they were a good parent by being perfect. Your achievements, your manners, your "goodness" weren't about you—they were proof to the world that they were a good parent. Being anything less than perfect wasn't just disappointing—it was a threat to their image.

Misguided Beliefs That Created This Rule
- What other people think of us is all that matters.
- Children behave because they respect their parent, and misbehavior reflects a failure of parenting.

What Parents Say to Reinforce This Rule
- "I never have to worry about you. You always make me look good."
- "What will people think if they see you acting like this?"
- "You're embarrassing me. Pull it together."

How It Felt

It felt like you were carrying your parent's reputation on your back. Every decision you made felt like it had to be perfect, not just for you, but for them, too.

The Impact

You had to "be good" because your parent's reputation depended on it. You were the one who made them proud. Being around others felt like a performance, where your actions determined whether they were proud of you—or disappointed. This blurred the line between your parent's need for approval from others and your responsibility for maintaining their image by being "good."

On the other end, making them "look bad" meant judgment, shame, rejection, emotional withdrawal, or abandonment, leaving you hypervigilant and burdened with the belief that your worth was tied to how well you upheld their image. The pressure to "be good" and make your parent look good was crushing.

10. Take Care of Everyone Else Before Thinking About Yourself

You felt guilty anytime you put yourself first, believing your worth came from making others happy. Taking care of yourself felt wrong, no matter how exhausted or overwhelmed you were.

Misguided Beliefs That Created This Rule

- Good Kids think of others before themselves.
- Selflessness is a virtue; focusing on your own needs is selfish and wrong.

What Parents Say to Reinforce This Rule

- "Stop being selfish—think about other people for once."
- "Your sister needs you right now. Be the bigger person."
- "We don't have time for your drama right now—just be a team player."

How It Felt
It felt like being "good" meant putting yourself last. You learned that other people's happiness was your responsibility, no matter how much it cost you.

The Impact
You grew up believing that your needs were less important than everyone else's and taking care of yourself was selfish, bad, and wrong. This led you to chronically overextend yourself for others without considering your own well-being and capacity, creating a cycle of burnout, self-neglect, shame, and guilt whenever you tried to focus on your own well-being. As a result, you've likely struggled with people pleasing, feeling unappreciated, or losing sight of who you are beyond what you can do for others.

Let Me Tell You A Story
In 2008, I was 26, and I finally got myself into therapy about a year before.

"My mother has always called me 'Poor Little Pitiful Pearl,'" I say. "Anytime I didn't look pulled together, she would call me that."

"Wow." My therapist's eyebrows rise in shock then confusion. "You say that like you're talking about the weather. Those words are heavy and loaded, and not in a good way. I would expect it to feel painful to think about. But you just say them... without any emotion."

Our conversation moved on, and Poor Little Pitiful Pearl didn't come up again except in passing. Three years later, I moved out of state. My new therapist was deeply interested in seeing what Inner Child work could do to help.

"I'm ready to try," I say.

"Okay," my therapist says. "Imagine little you is sitting in that chair. Picture it, feel it like it's actually happening. Tell me what happens."

I imagine a six-year-old me sitting in that big office chair, her little feet kicking the air above the floor. She looks at me nervously, waiting to see how I'm going to react. I am overwhelmed with how precious she is.

I smile at her, like saying, "Hi, you."

She smiles back, seeming deeply relieved.
I ask her what she needs.
She climbs down from the chair, walks across the room and up into my lap. She cries into my shoulders.
I imagined holding her tight. I rub her back. I tell her she's safe now.
"Finally," she says.

Excuses and Accountability

Healing requires finding the courage to gently question your beliefs about your parents, seeing them for what they are: a child's attempt to make sense of their adult caregiver's behaviors that were never really about them. Children blame themselves to keep the illusion that the people they depended on were trustworthy, capable, and safe.

"My Parents Never Physically Hurt Me, So Why Does My Body Overreact?"

This is such a common question, and I feel it so deeply. Let's start here: just because you weren't physically hurt doesn't mean your body didn't experience those moments as terrifying. Relational Trauma is just as impactful as physical trauma because, as children, we depend on our parents for everything—love, safety, food, belonging, stability. When the parent you need is screaming at you, emotionally unhinged, or exploding with anger, your brain and nervous system perceive that as a threat to your survival. You were not overreacting, even if it feels that way now. Your body was doing exactly what it was designed to do: protect you in an environment that didn't feel fully safe.

As a child, your brain wasn't fully developed. You didn't have the tools to understand that your parent's anger wasn't about you or that their yelling was a reflection of their inability to regulate themselves. All you knew was that the person you needed the most was scary and unpredictable at that moment, and your nervous system kicked into high alert.

Even as adults now, when someone is yelling at us in a way that feels out of control, our bodies react. Our hearts race, our muscles tense, and we brace ourselves for danger. Imagine experiencing that as a child from the person you depend on to take care of you—with no way to escape, no way to make sense of it, and no reassurance afterward that you were still loved and safe. It wasn't just "how parents parented back then," it was your whole world feeling shaky, and your brain and body doing their best to adapt.

Looking back on those moments with your adult brain, it's easy to rationalize what happened. You might think, "Well, they were just trying to teach me an important lesson," or, "I probably deserved it because I wasn't behaving." But that perspective isn't fair to your Little You.

It *was* scary, maybe even legitimately terrifying for you at that moment. As kids, we don't have hindsight or critical thinking skills to see the bigger picture. What we do have is an intense and unrelenting need to feel safe, stable, cared for, loved, and connected to our caregivers. When that connection feels threatened—when someone we depend on acts like *we're* a problem or a disappointment—it shakes us to our core. And when there's no Circling Back together to reflect on the moment, no apology, no reassurance that they love us, and no saying that you didn't deserve to be yelled at like that, we internalize that we deserved it.

But here's the truth: you didn't deserve to be yelled at like that. You didn't deserve to carry the weight of your parent's inability to regulate themselves. When your parent blamed you for "setting them off," they placed the responsibility for their emotions on you, and that's a devastating burden for a child to carry. Let alone chronically. That's why it feels so complicated now—because you're still holding that blame, even though it was never yours to hold.

Also, that compulsive need to dismiss yourself, to downplay your pain and act like you're being ridiculous for "overreacting"—that's not just a habit. That's a survival strategy you learned in childhood. It was what you had to do to stay connected to your parent. You were not allowed to take your own pain seriously. If you had a Big Feeling, if you were overwhelmed, if you needed comfort, they responded with frustration, exasperation, mockery, irritation, or emotional withdrawal. So you learned to do it for them—to walk away from your hurting self inside, to silence, belittle, or even mock the parts of you that were struggling. That was how you kept belonging. That was how you kept the connection alive.

But you don't have to do that anymore. And I need you to hear this: it is keeping your nervous system stuck in Fight/Flight when the threat you're battling *is coming from inside of you.* When a part of you is hurting and another part immediately jumps in to shame, dismiss, or abandon it, your body is stuck fighting itself—trapped in an endless internal war.

I need you to stop abandoning yourself when you're hurting and when you're struggling. Stop calling your pain "ridiculous." So many of us grew up feeling like nobody wanted to be around us when we weren't happy, when we weren't easy, when we weren't "fine." But that can't be the way you treat yourself anymore. This is where you stand by your own side. Become the fierce, protective Mama or Papa Bear you always needed. Hold those hurting parts of yourself like they are sacred and let them know they are not a burden, not a nuisance, not too much. Meet them with the energy of deep, unwavering love—the kind that says: "It is a privilege to be with you when you show me how you're really feeling inside. You can fall apart with me—I still love you, and I still want to be here with you."

That's the safety your nervous system has been searching for all along. This safety facilitates deep healing at the cellular level by shifting the way your body holds and processes stress at a physiological level. Healing means being able to look back and tell your child self, "You weren't overreacting. That really was scary, and you didn't deserve that. I'm sorry you didn't have anyone to help you. I am here to support you now and I will not leave you." Let go of the idea that your parent's anger taught you a necessary lesson and instead see it for what it was: a misguided failure on their part to regulate their temper when you needed them most. You deserved better then, and you deserve to heal this now.

"But Punishments and Tough Love Made Me Better"

I hear this a lot from clients so let's go through them together.

"I needed those consequences to learn respect and responsibility."

First of all, let's acknowledge that consequences *do* help you learn. But a consequence delivered in a way that was intended to make you feel scared and not loved is a... punishment. Punishments teach submission and shame. They instill a fear of making mistakes, fear of disappointing others, fear of not being enough and fear of people "finding out" some deep truth about you, so horrified they leave.

Respect and responsibility don't come from shame or fear. Instead, they grow when a caregiver consistently treats *you* with respect and shows you what it looks like to take responsibility for their own hurtful actions *without* tearing you down. Did those "consequences" (punishments) actually leave you feeling worthy and capable—or ashamed and afraid of failure?

"I needed strict rules and tough love to learn how to behave."

Strict rules and "tough love" might have forced us to behave on the surface, but behavior doesn't even come close to telling the whole story for a child. We learned how to "be good" and "act right," but do you know what else it taught us? To brace ourselves for relationships to end whenever there's conflict, which is why we avoid conflict at all costs. And tough love taught us to suppress our big emotions to keep the peace instead of how to release emotions in a healthy way. It's hard to believe we can do better next time when we are made to believe that *we* are fundamentally bad.

Tough love might have looked like strength, but real love doesn't need to be tough to guide a child. Kids deserve gentle love that supports them, encourages them, and helps them feel connected with their caregivers—even when they mess up. Tough love taught you survival, but at what cost? Did it teach you to thrive, or did it leave you exhausted from trying to be "good" all the time?

"If they hadn't been so hard on me, I wouldn't have achieved what I have."

It's easy to look at our accomplishments and give credit to the strictness or harshness, but I would argue we succeeded *despite it*, not because of it. That drive to achieve often comes from a desperate need to prove our worth—a need rooted in shame. It's the fear of falling short, fear of letting others down, fear of not meeting expectations.

You've accomplished so much, but at what cost? Does the voice in your head cheer you on or criticize you for not doing more? Is your Inner Critic ever actually satisfied and proud? True achievement is not about desperately outrunning a fear of inadequacy. It's fueled by knowing you're inherently worthy no matter what. You deserved to feel loved and supported on your journey—not like you had to earn that love through success.

"It was hard, but their tough love made me strong."

It's true—we are incredibly strong. But I'd argue that tough love didn't make us strong in the way we deserved. It taught us to toughen up and act like we didn't need support when we really did. It taught us to "be tough" by swallowing our feelings and pretending we weren't hurting. Tough love didn't build the kind of strength that would allow us to feel safe resting with guilt... or ask for help without apologizing and feeling inadequate and like a "burden" for needing the help.

We deserved the kind of strength where we could trust that our worth isn't tied to how much we can endure. What we really needed was the strength that grows from being nurtured, supported, and loved unconditionally, the kind of strength that comes from knowing it's okay to be vulnerable, to fall apart, and to be seen in your messiest human moments without fear of abandonment, criticism, rejection, or punishment. Tough love might have taught us how to survive, but what we deserved was love that taught us how to truly live.

Tough love teaches kids that mistakes, struggles, or vulnerability will be met with harshness rather than compassion. While the intention might have been to "build character" or "make them strong," the reality is that it often builds walls of shame and fear instead of resilience. True strength and resilience doesn't come from being hardened by criticism or punishment—it comes from feeling safe to take risks, make mistakes, and still know you will be loved and belong.

Here's what the research tells us: kids not only don't need shame, fear, and punishment to learn and grow—kids *struggle to learn anything* under those conditions. Kids need consistent connection and compassion from their caregivers. They need to feel safe enough to make mistakes and be able to trust they'll still be loved by their caregiver. Harsh discipline fosters fear of failure, fear of conflict, and fear of abandonment... not resilience. Tough love doesn't build a child's self-worth— they learn to earn their self-worth through achievements, in perfection, in external validation. That's not thriving. That's surviving.

And... you deserved softness. You deserved a parent who could say, "You made a mistake, and it's okay. Let's figure this out together." You deserved to feel loved, not just when you were excelling but *also* when you were struggling and falling apart. Imagine who you could've been if you hadn't been carrying the weight of proving your worth every day. Imagine what it would've been like to grow up feeling inherently enough, no matter what.

I'm not here to blame your parents—they did the best they could with what they knew. But we *do* know better now. The idea that punishment is what makes us strong is a lie our culture has been passing down for generations. It's time to break that damn cycle. Because here's what I know for sure: your worth is not something you should have to *earn*. It should have been yours all along. You deserved care, softness, and love as a kid. You still deserve that today—and so do our kids.

It can be terrifying to allow ourselves to see and truly feel that our parents... hurt us. Even when we know intellectually they were doing their best with what they had, that they didn't mean to harm us or act out of malice—there are parts of us that will do everything to shield us from the overwhelming, scary truth: our parents hurt us. Sometimes on purpose. Sometimes through neglect. Sometimes through their inability to regulate themselves. And sometimes by failing to protect us from harm caused by another parent or caregiver. These parts of us have spent years trying to convince us that it wasn't really our parents' fault—that they didn't mean it, or worse, that *we* deserved it because we had misbehaved, disappointed them, or been "too much." And when that story became too scary and painful to hold, we turned on ourselves.

It makes sense that we kept blaming ourselves—because that felt safer than believing the people we needed most were the ones hurting us. As kids, our attachment to our parents was critical for our survival, so our brain and nervous system did the math: if the relationship feels safe, I'm safe. If the relationship feels dangerous, I'm in danger. The way to make the relationship "safe" was to twist the story around every time, convincing ourselves that *we* were the problem:

- "They got mad because I wasn't behaving. If I had just done what they asked, it wouldn't have happened."
- "I wasn't thinking about how my actions were impacting others, so I deserved to be punished."
- "They didn't step in because I should have been able to handle it on my own. It's my fault for not being stronger."
- "They didn't say, "I love you" because I hadn't proven I deserved it yet."
- "I made them look bad, so I deserved to be punished."

That's Shame Talking

That's not your voice... it's the voice of the shame you felt every time you got in trouble. It's the voice you picked up when being "good" felt like the only way to be loved. It is still convincing us that we were the problem, that we were too much, or not enough. It's how we protected ourselves as kids and felt safe with our parents—believing that if we just fixed ourselves, we were safe, we were stable and we could keep their love and approval.

You still blame yourself because they blamed you first, acting like their anger, their outbursts, their coldness were somehow your fault. Maybe your parents told you that you were "too sensitive," too "difficult," or "too much" to handle. If I showed on the outside that my parent hurt my feelings as a kid, I was told that I "needed to get thicker skin." Maybe your parents expected you to manage their emotions, to tiptoe around their temper, to shrink yourself to keep the peace.

> **From Cassidy**
>
> Shortly before I went no-contact with my mother, she casually asked me twice to go shopping and play pickleball with her. It would be hard to pick two activities I disliked more, so I declined. I was already busy during her shopping trip, and I loathed pickleball because exercise has always felt like punishment for being overweight. At the time, it didn't seem like a big deal.
>
> Fast-forward to the last conversation we had. As I was arguing that she wasn't respecting my boundaries, she countered by bringing up the times I declined shopping and pickleball with her. She concluded with, "I'm lonely, and you're not even doing anything about it."
>
> In that moment, I felt the familiar guilt I'd known my whole life when I did something she didn't like. I didn't know she was lonely—she never told me. I instantly regretted saying no, now understanding it was a problem for her. It became another silent, shameful entry on my "terrible daughter" list.

Gentle reminder: you were the child and that should have never been your job. It was their job to be the parent, to regulate their own emotions, to guide you with love instead of fear and shame.

And—our parents didn't know how. Their parents (our grandparents) didn't do that for them either; they have probably never seen anyone parent that way until maybe recently. I think most of them were also drowning in their own unhealed shame-laced wounds, bottled up emotions and unmet needs.

However, that doesn't change what you needed and deserved (and what they as a child needed and deserved, too). A child should never have to be the emotional adult in the relationship. You should have never been put in a position of feeling responsible for keeping them from yelling at you by being respectful and "good." You were not responsible for their inability and/or unwillingness to hold space for your emotions. And you absolutely were not responsible for the way they made you feel like you had to earn their love and approval just to feel safe.

When we were kids, we had no choice but to accept their version of the story—the one where their anger was our fault, where their reactions were something we "caused." When they snapped, punished, or withdrew, they often made it clear that we were the problem, that *we owed them* an apology just for existing in a way that inconvenienced or frustrated them.

That kind of messaging doesn't just fade away. It embeds itself deep in our nervous system, shaping the way we see ourselves and our relationships. It teaches us that love is conditional, that safety depends on keeping others happy, and that if someone is upset, we must have done something wrong. That may have been true and how it felt for you in childhood—but you deserved love you didn't have to earn, relational safety whether others were happy with you or not, and to know that other people's emotions and reactions are theirs to manage, not a personal failure on your part. They were the adults, and it was always their job to manage their own emotions. You were the child, and you deserved to be guided, supported, and loved through your messy, imperfect, emotional moments—not blamed for them.

This belief system became our survival strategy, a way to make sense of the painful experiences of being punished, yelled at, ignored, dismissed, and shamed. We built core beliefs around this that are still active today, telling us that we must be quieter, easier, less emotional, better behaved, and more perfect *in order to deserve love*. These beliefs are rooted in Relational Shame Trauma, where we learned to equate our worth and inherent lovability with how well we could meet others' expectations and avoid upsetting them. Over time, this creates a deep fear that we are unlovable as we are, that we must constantly perform to prove and earn our worth. These patterns don't just disappear when we grow up—they show up in our relationships, in our relentless Inner Critic, and in the way we question our own needs and dismiss our feelings to this day.

Listen to me: You've been bitch-slapped by shame long enough. You're allowed to put that shit *down*. You deserve to stop living like you're the problem and everything is your fault. You've carried that weight for way too long and you deserve to feel lovable in every single version of you—in your "too-much-ness," your messy tenderness and your awkward trying-so-hard-to-get-it-right self.

2
HEALING

5
You Didn't Want To Be "A Burden"

I know your parents felt like they "never needed to worry about you." But I wish they had. I wish they had been able to realize that you actually weren't *fine* all the time. I wish they had known how it made you feel when they bragged about how you "practically raised yourself." I wish they had been able to hold more reasonable expectations of you that allowed for your very human needs and very human struggles without making you feel like a disappointment. I would have told them that you needed their support even though it didn't seem like you did, that you needed them to ask you how you were really doing *and* make it feel safe for you to answer honestly.

Your parents thought that being a good parent meant having a Good Kid who was always well behaved, never disrespectful, high achieving and made the family proud. They did not know about the Good Kid to Burned Out Overachiever Pipeline. They did not know you'd spend the rest of your life recovering from this. They were raised this same way by parents who had absolutely no idea they had emotions or emotional needs either. They became your parents, completely unprepared to raise complex emotional beings. Their shame and fear-based, compliance-driven discipline did a number on you.

I see you. I believe that most parents did their best with what they had, so many of them utterly hijacked by their own Relational Shame Trauma and neglect. Unknowingly participating in and perpetuating these damaging cycles of generational trauma. I know they said, "You'll understand when you're a parent." I get goosebumps at how spectacularly that backfired for them because we are now parents and we do not understand at all.

A Child Never Misbehaving Is a Red Flag

Kids misbehave instinctively, sometimes against their own will and desire, for good reasons:

- To explore their environment, discover their limits and learn how things work.
- To release suppressed emotions and stress.
- To assert their autonomy and independence to build their sense of self.
- To test and confirm they are safe and secure with a stable caregiver capable of leading them.

Our parents took our misbehavior personally, like it was an insult to them and to their parenting. Our parents believed we should never misbehave, that their job as our parent was to roll up their sleeves and punish us as much as we needed until we "respected" them and did not misbehave.

They shut our misbehavior *down* with their anger, with the threat of their anger, with their disapproval, with their disappointment. So what happens when a child never misbehaves? It's a huge red flag for me as a Trauma Therapist.

A child who never misbehaves is overriding their natural survival responses—because their body has learned that misbehavior, protest, push back and anything that even looks like disrespect puts them at risk of emotional or physical threat.

A threat? Surely, Maggie, you can't be serious.

Yep, the inherent shame within a parent's disappointment and disapproval are perceived as a threat by a child's brain and nervous system. A parent's anger and rage are perceived as a threat by a child's brain and nervous system. When a child perceives their parent as a threat, their nervous system may initially trigger the Fight Stress Response, part of the body's natural reaction to perceived danger, preparing the child to resist and rise up to the threat. Think: pushing back against their parents with assertiveness or defiance (some might call that… "misbehaving").

When the child's Fight Response could harm their attachment bond with their parent—by enraging them or disappointing them so they withdraw support, love, and care from the child—the nervous system will *protect* the child by overriding Fight Stress Response and shift into Fawn or Freeze Stress Response—part of the body's natural reaction to ensure safety and survival by either pleasing, appeasing, and catering to the threat (Fawn) or shutting down completely (Freeze). Their nervous system will prioritize *connection with their Attachment Figure* over resistance, self-protection, or releasing stress in the name of *maintaining belonging to ensure survival*. Even when it has a devastating impact on the child's emotional well-being, their brain and nervous system will continue to choose safety over all else.

Childhood Is Supposed to Be Messy

You didn't really act out, did you? You didn't get in trouble a lot or need to be disciplined. Maybe your parents bragged about how easy you were to parent and how they never really even needed to discipline you. On the surface, that might sound like something to be proud of… but when you really understand what a healthy childhood looks like, those are massive red flags.

Here's what I wish I could go back in time and tell our parents, and their parents before them: childhood is supposed to be messy. Kids are supposed to burst into tears over seemingly nothing and fall to the ground in frustration because they didn't get their way. They're supposed to get overwhelmed by their Big Feelings and pick fights with their siblings. Kids are supposed to say things like "You're the worst" to their parent when their frustration boils over. This is not bad. I repeat, *this is not bad.*

Too many cultures celebrate a Good Kid who never misbehaves as the ultimate sign of successful parenting. It's seen as proof that the parent has done everything right—raised a polite, respectful, and obedient child. But a child who never pushes back, never misbehaves and never needs to be disciplined is *not okay*. On the surface, they might look like they are thriving, but that child has learned to overpower their natural instincts to express emotions, release stress, and advocate for themselves, often out of fear of the consequences. Instead of being a reflection of "good" parenting, it points to a dynamic where the child feels unsafe to be their messy, imperfect, and fully human self—and that's a big problem.

Childhood was supposed to be a time where we misbehaved as a way of figuring out our emotions, our relationships, and our place in the world. We were not born knowing how to regulate Big Feelings or navigate conflict—it's something we needed to learn through experience. I wish I could tell our parents that a child who was melting down was not being "bad"—they were demonstrating where they were in their development and saying, "This is too big for me right now, I need your help."

When we learned to never push back, to always obey, to bury our frustrations and silence our needs, it meant something important inside us had been shut down. Our natural, biological mechanisms for releasing stress had been overridden—because we feared what would happen if we dared to let it out.

If only our parents could have seen these moments as our cries for connection rather than evidence they were failing as parents, maybe they could have offered us the calm, steady presence we needed instead of reacting with punishments to make us respect them again. But because they *also* feared failing and being seen as "failing parents," this blinded them to the real reasons why we were being "bad" and "acting out."

Messiness is part of the growing process. We needed to be able to push back sometimes because that's how kids learn how to self-regulate and build their sense of self by standing up for themselves. We needed to feel safe to misbehave sometimes because misbehavior is a messy, beautiful, necessary process that would have given us crucial opportunities to test the world around us, learn what's okay and what isn't, and figure out how to identify, speak up and advocate for our needs. It's also how we would have learned to self-regulate.

When kids push back, cry, or even explode emotionally, they're not "choosing" or trying to be difficult—they're releasing the stress and emotions that have built up in their little bodies. And that release is essential to offload that bottled-up stress so they can regulate their nervous system and calm back down.

When a child is afraid to stand up for themselves or push back against their parents, it's not a sign of respect. It's a sign of fear. It means they've learned that any hint of resistance—whether it's a frustrated tone, a slammed door, or even just breaking eye contact—will result in anger, punishment, forced isolation and maybe also the withdrawal of love, attention, affection and a willingness to care for them. What our parents and all parents before them called "respect" requires *dominating a child into submission*. Over time, the child moves into submission—the child's nervous system will shut down their access to Fight Response to preserve connection with their caregiver, moving them into Fawn/Freeze Response and "respectful" submission to their parent. I know this has been long seen as the benchmark of "Good Parenting" but this is not a good thing. It's a cause for concern.

I wish I could go back and tell our parents that we were not "choosing" to be disrespectful... we were dysregulated and our impulse control was undermined. That our resistance was our way of trying to tell them we needed to release some bottled-up stress. And that shutting down every single sign of disrespect—every eye roll, sigh, or frustrated word—meant we had no way to let out the stress that was building inside our body. When they shut down our "backtalk" or told us to "stop being dramatic," they didn't realize they were shutting down the only way we knew how to handle overwhelming emotions. Instead of releasing all that bottled-up tension, we pushed our feelings down, deeper and deeper, until they had nowhere to go.

The trouble with feelings is that we can push and push and push them down but they don't just disappear because we ignore them. Our bodies are wired to get that stress out somehow. When, despite our best efforts to keep everything inside, our feelings finally bubbled over for us—maybe with tears, frustration, or snapping at someone—we felt like we'd failed. We thought there was something wrong with us for not being able to hold it all together, for not being the "good" kid we were supposed to be. But that was just the natural way our bodies were begging for help to offload all the pressure. That there's nothing wrong with having Big Feelings and there's nothing wrong with being human.

These patterns don't just "go away" as we grow older—they shape how we see ourselves and how we navigate relationships for the rest of our lives. When you hear about a kid who never needed discipline, who was so "easy" they basically raised themselves, it's not a badge of honor. It's a warning sign that the child wasn't allowed to have a full childhood, complete with the messiness, Big Feelings, and boundary-pushing that are vital to their emotional health and development. If our parents had understood that, maybe they would have been able to respond with patience, instead of trying to shut it all down. Maybe they could have seen that those messy moments were actually opportunities to help us feel better and grow.

What a difference it might have made for us if they had known that the goal should have never been perfection and looking shiny from the outside. We needed the goal to be: connection and feeling good on the inside.

Kids Resist to Release to Regulate

Children's behavior is a reflection of their internal emotional and nervous system state and reactions to external pressures. Misbehavior is born out of an internal struggle. A parent's reaction to a child's misbehavior determines if that internal struggle can become an external struggle the child releases... or if it's further suppressed, reinforced, and turned inward.

So, a disrespectful child is really just a dysregulated child who needs an emotional release to help them calm down (think: a balloon that's about to *pop*). When kids reach this point, they move into what I call *The Resistance* and what Dr. Gordon Neufeld and Dr. Gabor Maté refer to as *Counterwill*. Essentially, when a child's stress level gets too high, their body tries to help them release that pressure by pushing back—resisting their parents and the rules. It's like their nervous system is desperately trying to let off steam before they hit their breaking point. In this moment, they might seem defiant or oppositional, but really, they're trying to manage the overwhelming emotions inside. It's not a "bad" behavior; it's a sign they need help to release and regulate their emotions before they can find calm again. This is how it goes:

> Children resist to release to regulate:
> Children resist their parents
> to release stress
> to regulate their bodies.

But this is how it went for us: our parents, like their parents before them, saw resistance as disrespect and something they needed to punish out of us, so they shut down any and all resistance. This accidentally and unintentionally also shut down our ability to release stress and regulate our body. When they punished us for being dysregulated and needing an emotional release, they further reinforced the way we suppressed and bottled our feelings and pretended to be *fine*.

We lived our lives like a balloon about to pop, keeping everything inside. More stress and emotions kept coming, so the air kept on inflating the balloon, without any way to let it out.

Just as the balloon can only hold so much air before it starts to strain to keep itself together... a child can only suppress their emotions so much before it becomes too much to handle.

No matter how hard it tried, the balloon would eventually reach a point where it couldn't hold itself together anymore. And... *pop*.

And no matter how hard you tried to keep them in, you eventually reached a point where you couldn't hold all of your emotions inside anymore. And... *pop*.

I bet you remember that look of bewilderment and disappointment on your parent's face.

That shame cut so deep. It was so awful. You felt so anxious after that. You kept an eye out for any warning sign that history would be repeating itself. You promised you'd do everything to keep a tighter lid on yourself next time.

But eventually, when all of the emotions you bottled and suppressed came exploding out of you again at some point... you didn't even need your parent to say it. *You* were already so disappointed in yourself.

> **You Launched Right Into It All On Your Own:**
> "I know it's wrong to do that."
> "Why do I keep doing that?"
> "What the hell is wrong with me?"

You Didn't Want To Be "A Burden"

I just want to lovingly point out: you're beating yourself up and feeling like something is wrong with you because, despite your relentless efforts to suppress every feeling, to never "burden" anyone with your messy emotions… sometimes, your body couldn't hold everything in. Sometimes, everything overflowed or exploded out. That wasn't a failure on your part. All balloons pop eventually if they keep getting more air, with no way to let the air out.

6
The Part Where You Stop Being Mad at Yourself

Being a Good Kid meant strictly following a set of spoken and unspoken rules that prioritized your obedience, emotional "control," and the ability to meet others' expectations to earn approval and love, both within the family and beyond.

Research on Relational Trauma shows that Good Kids in these dynamics often internalize the belief that their worth is tied to their performance and ability to avoid conflict. Culturally, "good girls" are taught to prioritize selflessness and taking care of others' needs and emotions, while "good boys" are expected to be confident, strong, laser focused on success and achievements... and never, ever, ever be vulnerable or show weakness.

Healing from this is a lot like getting deep tissue work from a massage therapist—when they press into tight, knotted muscles, it hurts before it feels better. They're not creating that pain, they're releasing tension and stress that's been stored in our body for years. The same thing happens when we get triggered and have what feels like an *overreaction*—our body isn't just responding to *this* moment, it's bracing because what's happening right now feels familiar in a way that's painful. Which triggers years of suppressed shame and stress that has been compounding over time.

If we avoid the release, our body has to hold onto it again, making space for even more unprocessed stress. It's like getting that deep tissue massage and then *not* drinking enough water after—those toxins settle right back where they were. When we resist our emotions and shove them back down, we're just demanding that our body continue to carry that heavy weight. Healing means allowing ourselves to get triggered and learning how to let those emotions move through and out of us. Instead of keeping them trapped inside. It's not overreacting—it's finally unburdening ourselves by showing up to release what we were never allowed to release before.

When you grow up bracing and scanning for signs that someone's mad—walking on eggshells to keep the peace—your body gets stuck in survival mode. That's your sympathetic nervous system (fight/flight) trying to protect you—and it's why you still feel anxious, on edge, or like something bad is about to happen, even when everything seems "fine."

Feeling better doesn't come from talking yourself out of it. It comes from showing your body, in the language it understands (nervous system regulation), that *you're safe now*. That there's no threat and it can finally stand down.

How to Regulate Your Nervous System

These simple practices can be done on-the-go to help you shift your body out of its hypervigilant state, allowing you to reclaim restful sleep and, in turn, begin the deeper process of healing.

Completing the Stress Cycle with Air Squats, Wall Push-ups, Lunges, Tiny Jumps or Walking

Activate your musculoskeletal system with gentle movement. It doesn't have to be anything like CrossFit—the magic is in contracting your muscles. Though I do find that the resistance from lifting heavy things helps me regulate faster—I keep a kettlebell and a set of dumbbells at my office for this reason. Try to turn toward the discomfort in your body and mind, asking your body to help you release that tension, stress and Big Feelings.

Moving your body engages your limbic system, especially the amygdala and hypothalamus, which are deeply involved in threat detection and emotional processing. Movement and contracting your muscles helps you complete the stress cycle with bilateral stimulation so your body understands that you have moved away from the threat/perceived threat and you are now safe. So you can move out of Fight/Flight (sympathetic) into your parasympathetic nervous system.

Physiological Sigh

Take two inhales through your nose, then a long, somewhat forceful exhale out your mouth. Towards the end of the exhale, close your mouth and hum.

Controlled breathing and humming activates your vagus nerve which in turn, activates your parasympathetic nervous system, which helps your body calm down and regulate out of Fight/Flight.

Butterfly Tapping

Cross your arms over your chest so that your fingertips rest just below your collarbones. Your arms should resemble butterfly wings. Begin tapping; gently tap one hand, then the other, in an alternating rhythm on your chest. This bilateral tapping mimics the sensation of wings fluttering, which is why it's called Butterfly Tapping. Keep the taps light and soothing. While you tap, breathe deeply and slowly. Do this for 3–5 minutes. These practices help re-engage the ventral vagal system, which is responsible for social connection, calm, and relaxation.

Grounding by Holding Something to Regulate

Rubbing a soft blanket, stuffy, or hugging a pillow can help calm your nervous system by engaging your sense of touch. If you push whatever you're snuggling into your chest, it will activate pressure receptors that tell your brain you're getting a hug!

Grounding techniques bring your prefrontal cortex (the part of your brain responsible for logical thinking) back online, reducing the intensity of emotions.

When Our Mind Recruits Our Body to Release Trauma

Galit Atlas's brilliant work on and book *Emotional Inheritance* explores how unresolved trauma and emotions from our past, particularly with our caregivers, can be passed down through generations—and these inherited emotional patterns are not just carried in our mind but also in our body. When we have emotions and trauma that hasn't been fully processed or released at a cognitive level, our mind will sometimes recruit our body to release it through physical responses.

When dysregulated, the gastrointestinal (GI) system can provide an outlet for that unresolved emotional energy. Our nervous system triggers physical GI reactions, like stomach cramps, nausea, and suddenly evacuating our bowels.

I've worked with so, so many counseling and coaching clients who dealt with chronic GI problems. But as my clients learned to stop suppressing their emotions and start regulating their nervous system to facilitate deeper emotional healing, the physical tension stored in their body—especially in the gut—begins to release, leading to a remarkable improvement in their GI symptoms.

We need to stop feeling mad and disappointed in our body for what has felt like chronically letting us down with these GI symptoms... and shift into thanking our body for taking care of us. I made this shift and so many things suddenly shifted in such a positive and healing direction. I went from an instant fear response at the first sign of an upset stomach or headache—"Damnit, body, here you go again. Pull yourself together!"—to "Body, I see you. I'm listening. What can I do to care for you right now? What do you need?"

When we nurture the parts of ourselves that were once neglected, our body starts to feel safer and perhaps for the first time in our lives... at ease. Instead of on high alert all the time. Relational safety and connection—with a therapist, coach, or loved one—can help regulate our nervous system and calm physical symptoms including GI distress.

Healing from Relational Shame Trauma

Shame is like a staph infection—it might look healed on the outside, but underneath, it's raging. And if you don't treat it, it spreads: into your self-worth, your relationships, your ability to feel safe in your own skin. That's the thing about shame—it hides in the shadows. But your body remembers. Just like a staph infection needs intentional care and treatment to heal, shame requires attention, compassion, and deliberate work to release its hold unconsciously. It's not easy, and it can feel deeply uncomfortable to face what's festering inside. But healing shame doesn't mean ripping yourself apart—it means gently treating the wounds, layer by layer, with understanding, radical acceptance, and the love you needed throughout your life. Over time, what once felt like an infection that would consume you can become a scar—a reminder of what you've survived and a testament to the healing you've fought so hard for.

Shame's Impact on Our Nervous System

Over time, repeated experiences of shame become embedded in the nervous system, creating pathways that make us hypervigilant and hyper-attuned to criticism, rejection, perceived failure, and the possibility of abandonment. These pathways lead to compulsive behaviors like avoiding vulnerability, never being needy or a "burden" on others, suppressing emotions, feeling terrified of making anyone mad, and overperforming to avoid criticism and earn acceptance.

Shame signals to our brain and nervous system that our actual survival is in jeopardy—that continuing to be emotional, needy or "too much" will result in rejection, abandonment, and our belonging being revoked. Parts of you paid very, very close attention to all of this, all led by your Inner Critic who took detailed notes of all the times you were made to feel unlovable, unacceptable, worthless, like a disappointment, and not deserving of love, especially in environments where love felt conditional or where criticism and shame were used to control behavior.

Rewrite Your Story

First, we need to acknowledge that our parents hurt us or failed to protect us, whether because of deliberate malice, absentminded neglect, or, most commonly, simple ignorance. As adults, continuing to carry that blame keeps us stuck in damaging and destructive cycles of shame, unable to see the ways our childhood experiences shaped our nervous system, our relationships, and how we see ourselves.

Sitting with the truth of this can feel like our entire foundation is shaking. It requires our brains to reconfigure the story we've told ourselves for years. And that's heavy work. But here's the thing: we can honor that our parents were doing their best *and* still hold them accountable for their impact. Intention and impact are not the same thing. Yes, they may not have known any better, but that doesn't erase the pain and impact of their actions or the ways their behavior shaped us. Our healing depends on being brave enough to separate out the story they tried to write for us from the reality of how their actions affected us.

> **From Cassidy**
>
> I was never really allowed to say "no" to my mother. In the moment, I might get away with it, but later it would become leverage—justification for why she was mistreating me now.
>
> I've carried the shame of being a "terrible daughter" for so long—it's a dark secret I've never shared, fearing others would discover it. For a long time, my fear of being a "bad daughter" kept me from seeking help, preventing me from questioning whether that belief was even true.

Healing means learning to separate what happened to us from who we are, deep down inside.

Holding Our Parents Accountable with Compassion

We can remind ourselves that a disrespectful child is a dysregulated child, who is struggling and needing guidance, support and help getting regulated. And when a child is struggling, they deserve *more* care, *more* love, *more* support—not less. By challenging these old scripts, we can begin to rewrite the story—not as one where we were the problem, but as one where we were doing our best to survive in an environment with caregivers that did not have the resources or regulation to parent us the way we now know kids need and deserve.

The responsibility for their anger, their reactions, and their emotional needs should have *never* been put on us... the child. When we face these truths, we make space for a deeper, more honest healing. We can hold compassion for the struggles our parents faced while finally letting go of the burden of blaming *ourselves* for their actions, mistakes and shortcomings. There is grief work here—grieving the ways we weren't protected, cared for, and soothed the way we deserved. This allows us to build a relationship with ourselves rooted in relentless self-compassion, clarity about the pain and shame we carry, and the courage to heal Today Us and Little Us from what happened.

The truth is, most of our parents weren't given the tools to process their own pain, and without healing, that pain got passed down. They weren't withholding love on purpose—their capacity and ability to love in the way we needed was profoundly impaired. Their own shame may prevent them from recognizing their impact, making them defensive or dismissive when we tried to express our hurt.

We Never Agreed to This

One of the most insidious, lingering wounds from the way we were parented is this unspoken rule—one that still shapes our relationships with our parents today—*We are not allowed to make them feel bad for hurting us.* We were raised to believe that only bad, ungrateful people do that. Bringing up our pain is actually a betrayal of "everything they did for us." In fact, we should be so grateful for the roof they put over our heads, the food they put on the table, the sacrifices they made—that we should just let everything else go.

However, we never actually agreed to this deal. We never agreed to carry the weight of our pain alone, so they never have to feel bad about causing it. And yet, we still feel that deep gut punch any time we try to acknowledge the ways we were hurt. They see our pain as an attack, our truth as an accusation, and our healing as an act of disloyalty. They believe that keeping the peace is more important than telling the truth.

But their comfort is not more important than our pain.

Intention doesn't erase impact. Even if they never meant to harm their child, the harm still happened. Even if they were "doing their best," their best still left deep wounds. That's why breaking these cycles starts with acknowledging the reality of what happened, holding space for the grief of what was missing, and learning how to give ourselves the love, safety, and attunement we didn't receive. And healing into a version of ourselves who doesn't have to "be good" to deserve that love and safety.

Reality check coming in hot: we are not responsible for protecting the people who hurt us from the reality of their impact. Love isn't pretending we weren't hurt or protecting them from the reality of their mistakes. Gratitude does not erase harm. Acknowledging the ways we got hurt does not erase their effort. And holding them accountable for their impact is not making them the villain.

If your parent's unhealed trauma shows up in one of these ways, the dynamics that create Good Kids were amplified in ways that were deeply confusing and painful for you. The environment revolved around your parent's unmet emotional needs and unhealed trauma, leaving you in the impossible position of trying to fill those gaps while suppressing your own needs and emotions. For so many of us, this meant living in a constant state of hyper-awareness, hypervigilance, and self-monitoring to avoid rocking the boat. And being attuned to our parent's needs, emotions and well-being instead of them being attuned to ours.

Let Go of the Struggle

Healing from the deep, sticky layers of Relational Shame Trauma isn't about fighting harder, pushing through, or trying to control everything. It's about surrender; about loosening the freaking stranglehold that shame has had on our lives that has kept us hustling for control, hiding every imperfection at all cost, and trying to force everything to feel okay. All in the name of avoiding anyone ever *finding out*—that *there is* something wrong with us and we're actually unlovable.

The truth is, healing happens when we stop resisting the very things that make us human—our emotions, our needs, and the parts of us that feel broken or unworthy. When we stop shaming ourselves for our reactions, when we *trust* that our feelings make sense, and when we allow ourselves the space to feel everything, that's when the real healing begins. Surrender doesn't mean giving up; it means accepting that it's okay to not have all the answers, it's okay to be vulnerable, and it's okay to trust ourselves again. Letting go of the struggle and trusting the process is where the magic happens. This is how we heal—and this is how we learn to trust ourselves again. You deserve both.

Shame Resilience

Shame thrives in secrecy and isolation, but it loses its grip when we bring it into the light of connection and compassion. Healing Relational Shame involves creating safe spaces—whether in relationships, therapy, or community with others who get it—where you can practice being seen and have the experience of feeling loved and valued just as you are. For who you are, the real you, instead of how you look to other people. Shame tells us we're unworthy of love and belonging, but the truth is, those feelings of unworthiness were learned. And what's learned can be unlearned, one loving, compassionate step at a time.

Healing from Relational Shame Trauma isn't about fixing yourself—you were never broken. It's about learning to feel safe being fully you.

The parts of you that feel hardest to love are not problems to solve; they are storytellers of your experiences. When you meet them with as much patience, care, and gentleness as you can, you're doing more than healing shame—you're creating a new, more compassionate relationship with yourself.

You're giving yourself the gift of being fully seen and loved—just as you are. Like you always deserved.

Inner Dialogue

When you talk to yourself—whether it's Today You, Little You, different Parts of you, or your body—think of it as showing up for yourself the way you show up for everyone else, namely with patience, encouragement, and relentless support. Because healing Relational Trauma happens in relationships, we heal in relationships. We need to experience what it feels like when someone responds with curiosity instead of criticism, when someone doesn't ignore or punish us for struggling, when someone apologizes after they've hurt us instead of pretending it didn't happen. And while finding safe, supportive people is an essential part of this process, the most constant relationship in your life is the one you have with *yourself*. So what would it look like to start showing up for yourself the way you've always needed? To be the one who stays, who listens, who offers kindness and steadiness no matter what?

I used to resist this because, honestly, it felt kind of… pathetic that I even needed to do this for myself. Back then, I had no idea that it was shame talking. It felt embarrassing, like I should just be able to handle life without this level of care. Then I realized something: everyone deserves this. It wasn't my fault that I didn't get it growing up. But now I have the opportunity to give myself this kind of relentless support for the rest of my life. And when I show up for myself like this, it feels like the hug I have waited for for decades. It feels so deeply healing and like one of the greatest privileges of my life to give myself, little me and my body this kind of relentless support, encouragement, and care.

Talking to ourselves can feel awkward, I get it. If you've ever tried to talk to yourself, saying things like "We're safe" or "I'm safe", maybe it didn't change anything. It didn't for me. Every time, my nervous system would immediately fire back with, "No, we're not!" So, instead, try "*You* are safe." That shift matters. It's *you* in relationship with *you*.

Imagine a scared child; you wouldn't say, "We're fine," and expect them to believe it. You'd kneel down, look them in the eyes, and gently say, "You are safe. I'm right here. I've got you." That's the energy we need to bring to ourselves. Be that loving, steady presence who sees you struggling, who has your back, who holds your hand through the hard moments. Be the one who doesn't gaslight your fear but acknowledges it with warmth and reassurance. The more you do this, the more your nervous system will start to believe it. Not because you force yourself to "just get over it," but because, for the first time, you're truly being held the way you deserve.

Your Inner Critic

You know that mean, critical voice in your head? The one that tells you you're not good enough, that viciously criticizes every mistake, and tells you that nobody could possibly love you if they "found out?" That's your Inner Critic, and it's the voice of your Relational Shame. It's the echo of those early experiences, where your survival felt like it depended on pleasing others, doing everything perfectly, accomplishing and achieving, avoiding disappointing anyone and conflict at all costs and constantly shapeshifting into the "most lovable version" of you in that moment for that person.

I know it seems impossible, but your Inner Critic is actually working its ass off to protect you every minute of every day. I absolutely thought my Inner Critic voice was my highest self until I was… 35 years old. But our Inner Critic isn't the voice of truth—but the voice of fear and shame. Every time you were made to feel ashamed, abandoned, rejected, and punished, it built what I call your Code of How to Be Valuable—a list of things you can and can't do, to try to keep you from feeling ashamed, abandoned, rejected or punished every again.

The first time I encountered my Inner Critic, I was freshly postpartum, trying so hard to love and embrace the body in the mirror. It said to me: "According to Article 14, Section 78:

Your mother loves you more when you're thin. So I'm just trying to help you be more lovable."

Have you ever heard any of these from your Inner Critic?

- "That person seemed annoyed. You should probably replay the conversation 400 times to figure out what you did wrong."
- "You're not tired. You're just being lazy."
- "If you stop making everyone happy, they'll stop liking you."

They aren't facts or truth. They are memories.

The Parts of you that feel hardest to love are the ones that have absorbed the most unkind stories about who you're "supposed" to be or who you must be to be acceptable and lovable. The Parts of you that feel hardest to love are the ones that have endured the sharpest criticism and rejection. The Parts of you that feel hardest to love are the ones you've been told are the greatest threat to your worthiness and belonging.

This isn't random—these are the Parts of you that carry the most shame. And it's deeply connected to how shame sculpts the nervous system over time, creating deeply ingrained patterns that shape how we see and respond to ourselves, others, and the world around us. When we experience shame—especially Relational Shame in childhood—it activates our body's threat response, signaling that connection, safety, or belonging is at risk.

You Struggle to Believe You're Lovable

The idea that you are inherently lovable, that your worth is unshakeable, and that you deserve love no matter what, can feel almost *impossible* to believe when your life experiences have told you otherwise. For many of us, we meet this idea with utter confusion and astonishment, or even anger and outright rejection. We can see and believe that other people are worthy and lovable just for being themselves… but when we try to apply that same truth to ourselves? It feels wrong, it feels impossible. Like, it's a lovely idea but it couldn't possibly be true.

Here's why this is so hard: your worth and inherent lovability *should* have been unconditional. It should have had nothing to do with whether people were happy with you or upset with you. It should have had nothing to do with whether others were proud of you or disappointed in you. But many of us grew up in environments where our parents' love and approval were something that had to be earned—through being "good" and always, always, always behaving. Through making our parents proud with our achievements and successes and never, ever disappointing or letting them down. And through being so mature, so self-reliant, and so put-together that we basically raised ourselves.

We learned that love and approval would be instantly taken away if we messed up, lost control, or if we were "too sensitive" or "too much." We learned that the "most lovable version" of us handled our emotions and needs alone, avoided conflict and was never, ever, ever a "burden" on anyone. We learned that seeming okay on the outside was more important than how we were actually feeling on the inside. We learned that keeping the peace was more important than "ruffling feathers" or asking for help.

From Mikaela

Today, I still struggle to feel good enough. I still struggle to share my struggles with others. Especially if they have shared a struggle with me. I don't want to burden them. I'll even bend over backwards to try and help their struggle go away. I've been working on boundaries and not over exerting myself but it's a battle.

This experience is at the heart of Relational Shame Trauma, which is not about large catastrophic events but about the repeated experiences of being made to feel unworthy, unlovable, or "not enough" in the eyes of the people who were supposed to love us most. When love, approval, and connection felt conditional, our nervous systems adapted to prioritize *those conditions* over our authentic selves. We learned to be a shapeshifting chameleon into whatever version of us would be lovable in that moment. We learned to suppress our emotions, our struggles, and our basic human needs. We learned that it was perfection or bust—that anything other than first may as well be last. We learned to believe that being "good" was the only way to secure love and belonging.

The problem is, over time, these patterns created an inner narrative that love is conditional. Not just from our parents—we unconsciously generalized that to everyone. We also love *ourselves* conditionally.

You didn't ask for this and it's not your fault that it feels so hard to let this go. Relational Trauma happened in relationships and must be healed in relationships. When someone shows up for us in those moments without getting mad and/or going cold, our Inner Critic notices. It starts to rewrite the core beliefs it's got that say we're not worthy of love unless WE earn it. That's where true healing begins: in the safety of connection, where we learn by experience that we're lovable just as we are.

I need you to make it your life's mission to find safe people who can give you that safety, that safe connection, and love you through your messy, human moments. The first person to do this for me was my therapist. I also need you to recognize that the most important relationship to cultivate like that—is the relationship you have with *you*. What if you dared to love yourself through a moment where you feel unlovable? I'm telling you… it would be a significant experience for every version of you.

Taming Your Inner Critic

Your Inner Critic can feel so relentless. It's trying to anticipate anything that could lead to you feeling ashamed, often by holding you to impossibly high standards or pushing you to overperform, over-apologize and hide parts of yourself so nobody *finds out*. While its intention is to protect you from harm, it has the opposite effect: it keeps you in a constant state of unsafety and hypervigilance about looming threats which make it difficult or impossible to relax or trust yourself. Research on Relational Shame Trauma shows that this kind of internalized self-surveillance can keep our nervous system in a perpetual state of dysregulation and stuck in a cycle of shame, self-criticism, and disconnection.

Until we understand all of this, we experience it as bullying, so it makes sense why you feel like telling it to *fuck off*, overpower it, run from it, or distract yourself from it. But when we do that, our Inner Critic has to escalate to get our attention—getting louder and more vicious—to try to protect us. Shame makes everything feel like a matter of life or death and our Inner Critic, tag teaming with our nervous system, will stop at nothing as it tries to keep us safe from the perceived threat.

Your Inner Critic didn't just appear out of nowhere—it rose up to try to keep you safe. But your environment has changed, and you can teach yourself a new way to exist—one that isn't built on fear of failure, disappointing others, or needing to prove your worth. Speak to your Inner Child like you wish a caregiver had spoken to you.

Put your weapons down, sit down next to your Inner Critic, and say to it, "Wow… you've been trying to protect me this whole time. I had no idea, I thought you were the enemy. You've been trying to keep me safe and protect me, all this time? Thank you for trying to take care of me. Tell me more about what you're afraid would happen."

The Part Where You Stop Being Mad at Yourself

Get curious and give it the mic. You will be amazed at the stories it tells you. It likely thinks you're still a child that needs its protection. Gently bring it up to speed that you're an adult now and you don't need its protection anymore because *it's safe now* to not be perfect, to have needs, and to stand up for yourself. From a place of deep gratitude, lovingly ask it to stand down and give you space to live your life in a new way. Let it know you're ready to take the lead now, to show up as your true self without fear of the shame, rejection, and abandonment it's been working so hard to shield you from.

Thank it for everything it's done to keep you safe, and reassure it that you've got this—that you're building a life where you are now safe to be exactly who you are. It's not about silencing that part of you—it's about gently helping it understand that its job is no longer necessary in the same way. You're in charge now, and you're creating space for growth, connection, and healing.

The good news is that you don't have to silence or destroy your Inner Critic to begin healing (you couldn't, even if you tried). Instead, meet it with curiosity and compassion. Look at it with awe, recognizing that its harshness and viciousness comes from a misguided attempt to keep you safe and save your life. Ask it what it's trying to tell you. What has it been carrying for you? What is it afraid will happen if you do that?

Pause when your Inner Critic starts spiraling. Put a hand on your chest and take a deep breath.

Say out loud: "This is not life or death. You are safe."

Remind yourself: "You are still lovable, even when you mess up."

At first, this will feel fake and weird and awful. You might hear these words and immediately reject them, because they go against everything your Inner Critic has been repeating for years. That's okay. You're reshaping your nervous system's response to mistakes, which has never felt safe. It takes time but keep going. This is so incredibly important and you deserve to feel safe to be a human and make mistakes.

This approach, rooted in neuroscience and self-compassion, allows our "hard to love" Parts to soften and integrate. Over time, these once-rejected pieces of you can become sources of strength, creativity, and authenticity.

Just as landscapes can be reshaped, your nervous system is incredibly adaptable, capable of profound healing and rewiring through relational healing, compassion, connection, and feeling seen by yourself and others, and intentionally practicing *pushing through* the shame to offer love and empathy to the Parts of us that feel unlovable and undeserving of love.

Nobody Deserves to Suffer for Messing Up

I've had clients tell me they had to do push-ups or be assigned disgusting chores for making mistakes as kids. In some cases, their parents did the push-ups and disgusting chores too, reinforcing the idea that suffering was the price of messing up. Other clients were spanked or physically punished, sent to their room alone, and had their most cherished comforts taken away. Not just as discipline but as a way to make them feel *bad enough* that they wouldn't do it again. Most of them defend it and believe it made them better.

But here's the fundamental NOPE for me: *People do not need or deserve to suffer for making mistakes.*

They need and deserve accountability, yes. They deserve the opportunity to make things right, yes. But suffering? Nope. Because suffering is not the same thing as accountability. When an attachment figure—the very person a child depends on for safety—intentionally inflicts suffering and pain as punishment, whether it's physical or emotional or both, it leaves behind something far deeper than discipline: Relational Shame Trauma.

Making a child feel like they deserve to suffer, ashamed and alone, doesn't teach accountability the way our parents thought it did. It doesn't teach them that they did something wrong... it teaches them that there is something wrong with *them*. They don't just learn: *I did something bad.* They internalize: *I am bad. I don't deserve comfort. I don't deserve compassion when I mess up. I deserve to suffer. Pain is the price I must pay if I don't do it perfectly, without mistakes.* And when that belief takes root? They seek out relationships that confirm it. They subconsciously gravitate toward people who reinforce their suffering—partners, friends, even workplaces that make them suffer and earn love, belonging, and forgiveness the hard way. Who reinforce and nurture the belief that making a mistake equates being unworthy of kindness.

IFS/Parts Work

Internal Family Systems (IFS), developed by one of my heroes, Dr. Richard Schwartz, is a brilliant and groundbreaking way of making sense of yourself, your thoughts, and your emotions. With IFS, we recognize that we are made up of many different Parts that operate mostly at the unconscious level and sometimes feel confusing and conflicting things. Some Parts of us (Exiled Parts) carry *all* the unprocessed, suppressed emotions, wounds, fear, and shame that we had to pretend weren't there in childhood. Other Parts of us (Protector Parts) rose up and now work tirelessly to protect us and help us navigate life as the most lovable version of ourselves. And beneath all of these Parts, we have Self—our gut, our intuition, our highest Self—who can honor and understand the Parts and their struggles *and* help them work together. We access Self by turning inside to the Parts with curiosity, seeking to understand instead of judging them. Curiosity allows us to do what IFS calls "unblend" from the Part when it's hijacking us, so we can observe it as not who

Good Kids

we are, but a Part of us. From this perspective, we can listen with compassion, honor its intentions, and set loving, firm boundaries with it, which allows our Self to take the lead and help us show up as our real selves.

In healing Good Kid patterns, IFS Parts Work helps us understand how unconscious, hurting Parts of us—often a child Part—desperately try to prove our worth. This Part believes that if it loves enough, gives enough, or keeps everything together, it will finally prove it's lovable and good enough. Often, this Part carries deep shame, believing love must be earned through actions, not inherent value.

Another Part, a Protector Part, might step in to shield you from rejection by pushing you to people please, keep the peace, or take on too much. This Part's goal is to prevent emotional pain by staying in control and ensuring others are happy with you—at any cost. It is trying to protect you, but unknowingly, it keeps you stuck in unhealed patterns of codependency that you're working to break free from.

Healing these deeply ingrained patterns requires us to show up for ourselves with compassion and build a nurturing relationship with our Parts. See their pain, soothe them, and unburden the shame and fear they've carried. Offer the love, care, and validation they've longed for without needing to earn it. Offload the belief that love must be earned by being "good" and that it can be withdrawn because you're unlovable or hard to love.

This healing looks like showing up for yourself with fierce love, no longer needing approval from others. It's about working to believe that you are worthy of love simply because you exist—not because you've earned it. It means going to the Parts of you that feel the hardest to love and approaching them with curiosity and compassion, refusing to be ashamed of them. You reassure them that you won't leave, that they deserve care.

When we do this, it leads to deep, transformational healing—like a plant once thought dead, withered, and cracked, suddenly getting the sunlight and nourishment it's always needed. It transforms into something beautiful and strong, beyond what anyone ever imagined it could be.

Worthiness

Love should not be conditional, despite everything you were told growing up. Use IFS to notice the Parts of you that deeply resist loving all of yourself. Those are the places where you carry the most shame and the belief that you're bad, unlovable, and not enough. Start showing up for yourself without making yourself earn the support first. Stand By Yourself, refuse to leave your own side because you've got you, no matter what.

Notice and get curious about your Inner Critic instead of fighting it. "Thank you for trying to protect me, I see you. What are you so afraid will happen if I say no or stand up for myself?" Offer loving reassurance to the Parts of you that are holding shame and remind them that *it's safe now* to make mistakes. Practice staying non-judgmental and lovingly standing with that Part.

Get curious about the Parts of you that feel unworthy and unlovable without achievements and earning love first, offering them the antidote (the unconditional love, support, and compassion they need). Dare to love them through this moment. Over time, you'll unburden those Parts from the shame they carry and rewrite the rules about how you don't have to earn love anymore and deserve love no matter what.

Listen to all of the Parts with comforting, soothing energy, grounded in profound trust and gratitude. Practice loving yourself through a moment where you made a mistake or didn't do it perfectly, separating your worth from your actions. Approach yourself and your Parts with so much compassion, even when you "fall short" of expectations. You can choose to Stand By Yourself no matter what... and it changes everything.

My Parts need to hear this over and over and over again: "I see you struggling and I'm right here. I will not leave you. I am not going anywhere. I am going to take care of you. I've got you." Practice showing your authentic self in safe spaces with safe people and really notice how it feels inside to be accepted and loved by someone without conditions.

Messy Emotions Are Safe

You were always a feeling being. Long before you learned to be a Good Kid, before you learned to smile when you were sad, nod when you disagreed, and swallow the lump in your throat when you wanted to cry—you felt. Deeply. Freely. Fully. Then your Good Kid conditioning did its thing.

Healing from being a Good Kid requires you to let yourself feel again. Notice and get curious when you dismiss your own emotions to keep the peace so you don't ruffle feathers. Recognize how you abandon yourself and start standing by yourself fiercely and relentlessly, in a way you were never taught to. Instead of criticizing yourself for having emotions, try letting them be there. Don't analyze them, judge them, or rationalize them away. Just let them exist.

- "Of course I feel overwhelmed right now. This is a lot."
- "It makes sense that I'm frustrated—this really matters to me."
- "I don't have to justify my sadness. It's okay to just feel it."

Healing starts with showing up for Today You, Little You and whatever Part of you is hurting right now. Focus on validating your own emotions and needs. IFS Parts Work allows you to reconnect with that hurting Part of you that felt invisible, and offer it the love and attunement you needed but didn't receive. By regulating your nervous system to move out of Fight/Flight and telling your body in a language it understands (regulation) that you are safe now, you can foster and nurture the belief that you matter, your emotions are valid, and you are always deserving of love and care.

Notice when your Inner Critic tries to shut down your emotions, believing they make you a "burden". Then tell Today You and Little You that you are worth being known; you are worth spending time with; and it's a privilege, an honor, and a delight to get to care for you when you're struggling. Acknowledge your feelings and let yourself feel them without judgment. Connect with the Parts of you that learned to hide, reassuring them it's safe to be seen now. You need and deserve to give yourself relentless self-compassion. Turning inside with even a little bit of warmth and softness helps your nervous system regulate out of Fight/Flight and feel safe. Give yourself whatever compassion you've got right now. When your body is suppressing the emotions and won't let them rise, ask your body to help you release them—turn toward that jittery, panicky energy inside and visualize your body helping you release it through movement or lifting heavy things.

Your feelings are not a betrayal of anyone else. They are not an inconvenience, a flaw, or a problem to fix. They are the path back to yourself. You don't have to justify them. You don't have to shrink them. You just have to let them be.

Trust

Forgive yourself for struggling with trust—it makes sense when others have been so inconsistent and unpredictably there for you. Reassure Little You inside that their survival strategies were brilliant but are not needed anymore. Find safe people and be patient with yourself as you gradually rebuild trust in relationships with people who show you they can be trusted. Allow yourself to take small emotional risks while relentlessly having your own back—reminding yourself that you're safe even if someone else has a bad day. Practice co-regulation with safe people and self-regulation through breathwork, Circle Backs with Little You and using movement to Complete the Stress Cycle and calm your nervous system. Look back to the beginning of Chapter 6 for how to do this.

Healing means learning to feel safe in relationships and realizing that other people's emotions and moods are not your responsibility to anticipate, manage or fix. Remind yourself that it's not your job to keep people from yelling at you. You do not need to anticipate and over-explain what might set them off.

Come back into your body when your anxiety flares by speaking to your body in its native language of regulation. Regulate your nervous system through breathwork and/or movement. Through Parts Work, reassure the Part of you that feels hyper-responsible for others and remind it that you are not responsible for anyone else's emotions. Build trust in yourself by taking small steps to express your feelings and needs in safe spaces.

Connect with the Part of you that had to grow up too soon and offer it compassion and validation: "That must have been so hard. You were a kid, but you had to manufacture the maturity to take care of your parent. You needed them to take care of you, but you did not get the support you needed. I'm here now and I'm going to take care of you." Practice asking for help, expressing vulnerability, even in small ways, and receiving help—even when parts of you want to melt into a puddle on the ground out of discomfort. You deserve to be cared for—it does not make you weak, pitiful, or pathetic to need support sometimes. It does not feel like a burden to take care of you—it feels like an honor and privilege and other people feel like the lucky one.

Get Curious

We were raised to be our own harshest critics—we jump right to "Why can't I just get this right?" or "I should be better at this." That Inner Criticism isn't just self-talk—it's the voice of all the ridiculous, unattainable expectations we internalized growing up, where we were expected to somehow be good at everything and never let anyone see us struggle or sweat. Criticism that triggers instant shame in us now just like it did when we were kids. Remember: shame doesn't just feel bad—it feels *threatening*. It sends us head first into survival mode, making us either shut down (*I'm just a failure, why even try?*), lash out at ourselves (*What's wrong with me?!*), or frantically try to prove we are good enough by overcompensating and pushing even harder.

Instead of bracing for self-judgment, shift into curiosity—the way we wish someone had done for us when we were kids. Curiosity softens the Shame Spiral and allows us to access Self—what IFS describes as the calm, steady, compassionate core of who we are that isn't emotionally activated one way or the other. Self is neutral—and neutral is the sweet spot. When we relate to ourselves from Self, we get to show up as the loving parent we needed, the one who doesn't shame us for struggling, who doesn't expect perfection, and doesn't abandon us when we fall short. Self effortlessly stands by us and knows that this is what our best looks like right now—and our best is *good enough*.

So when you find yourself jumping right to "I should know how to handle this" or "Why am I like this?," try shifting into curiosity and asking yourself:

- Why does this feel hard for me right now?
- What if I trust that this makes sense and I make sense instead of assuming something is wrong with me?

- What do I actually need in this moment? More support? Rest? Some freaking compassion?
- Has anyone ever actually taught me how to do this? Or am I just expecting myself to be good at everything, instantly?

Every time you shift from Critical to Curious, you're strengthening your connection to Self—which allows you to be that steady, loving parent to Today You and Little You that says, "I see you. I'm here. I won't abandon you in this." And every time you do this, you're breaking the cycle and teaching yourself what was never taught to you: that you are safe, even when you struggle.

Prioritize Yourself

Healing involves reclaiming your fundamental right to have emotions, needs, and boundaries, and recognizing that you are not responsible for other people's feelings anymore. Reminding yourself that you should never have been responsible for taking care of your parent—it was *their* job to take care *of you*. Use IFS to connect with the Parts of you that feel responsible for others and offer them reassurance that *it is safe now* to say no, stand up for yourself, and set boundaries to take care of yourself. Practice small acts of self-care and notice the *resistance*—the guilt or shame that comes up—reminding yourself that taking care of your needs is not selfish. It is your job to be loyal *to yourself* and what you need.

All Parts of You Deserve Love

I do need you to *expect* there to be resistance to loving that Part of you that feels unlovable—the harder it feels to love it, the more shame that Part is carrying. That resistance can feel overwhelming and make us think we *might* actually be unlovable. It's not that you're incapable of loving yourself or that this Part of you is truly unlovable—it's that another Part of you learned, probably back in childhood, to believe that this Part *doesn't*

The Part Where You Stop Being Mad at Yourself

deserve love. That belief isn't and wasn't a reflection of your worth—it's a reflection of the messages you internalized from a world that didn't know how to see, value, or nurture all of you.

That resistance is a leftover survival strategy. It's a part of your brain and nervous system that's trying to protect you by keeping old wounds buried, believing that revisiting those feelings of rejection, shame, or inadequacy will be too much to bear. But those Parts of you are not the enemy—they are hurting. They desperately need your compassion and care, not your judgment. When you start to approach these Parts of you with loving curiosity instead of criticism and judgment, you will begin to rewrite the story. You can gently remind those Parts that their belief in their unworthiness isn't true—it's just something they learned to survive.

Now let's talk about what you deserve. You deserve to live free from the crushing weight of feeling unworthy and undeserving of love. Your worth isn't something you earn—it's something that should have always been yours, until the world made you feel otherwise. You're able to see that other people are inherently lovable and it's always been true for you, too—every tiny Part of you is lovable and deserving of love. Not because of what you do or who you please, but simply because you exist. That truth is unshakable.

Healing begins when you can sit with the resistance and tell those hurting Parts of you, "I see you, that must have been so hard. I've got you, you're safe now." I carry deep abandonment wounds and these hurting Parts always seem to need to hear some version of, "I will not leave you. I am not going anywhere." Tell these Parts that they don't have to keep carrying the shame they've held for so long. With patience and kindness, those Parts will begin to soften, letting go of the shame that never belonged to them. And as they do, you'll reconnect with the absolute, undeniable truth: every Part of you has always been worthy of love—*no matter what.*

Let Me Tell You A Story

I'm a mom of two now, I've retreated to my bedroom. Rage pulses through my veins, and I have absolutely no idea what I'm even mad about. I stack some pillows and punch the shit out of them. I punch as waves of big, heaving sobs rock my chest, and my body shakes with anger and nausea.

It feels like there's a wrecking ball in my belly. I get curious: it's my Shame Part. I thank Shame for protecting me and ask what it's afraid would happen if it didn't make me feel so worthless.

"Other people will find out," Shame replies.

"Find out what?," I ask.

"That you're pitiful."

I nod in understanding. "Ah, like Poor Little Pitiful Pearl."

That's what my mother called me whenever I was "too sensitive," too needy, making her look bad or couldn't "pull it together" fast enough. Her way of taming me back into being "good" and following the Good Kid Rules.

As as my Shame Part sits back, satisfied that it has warned me and protected me, I say calmly to Today Me and Little Maggie, "I'm not horrified by you. Not even a little bit. I know where that story came from, and I don't believe it anymore. I know who you really are, and I am not going anywhere."

Our Shame Part remembers and holds on tight to the moments we felt most exposed—like someone had ripped the curtain back and seen The Real Us... and didn't like what they saw. For many of us, it was a word or phrase our parents used that landed like a punch to the gut. That word became the name of our deepest, most unbearable shame.

We grow up believing that who we *really* are underneath our Good Kid persona is someone pitiful. Embarrassing. Too much. Unlovable. So we build our lives around hiding it and work our asses off to make sure no one ever sees that version of us again. Because if our parents couldn't love us in that state, how could anyone else?

Your word(s) live in your body, haunting you when you feel like you're "too much" or "not enough." That's why unlearning your Good Kid trauma and reparenting those parts of you are so crucial and utterly transformational.

How to Feel Your Feelings

If I could go back in time to my precious 29-year-old self, when I was first learning how to feel my feelings in therapy, I would tell her, "You are not failing at this, your body is shutting down and suppressing your feelings for a very good reason. You're trying to learn how to feel your feelings by overthinking them, analyzing them, intellectualizing them and burning yourself out trying to make them make sense. That is never going to work, feelings don't make sense. Your job is to help your body feel **safe enough to let you feel**. And then it will know exactly what to do to take care of you."

Good Kids learn to intellectualize their feelings because analyzing emotions is safer than feeling them—thinking them through was a really good way to stay in control, out of trouble, and still worthy of love. But you cannot think your feelings to feel them. You have to actually feel them, as *foreign and forbidden and unthinkable* as feeling feels for you right now.

Let me tell you the most magnificent news that will change everything: you don't need to teach your body how to feel. Feeling is your body's most natural, instinctual ability. It's not that you don't know how to feel. It's that your body *remembers* childhood when you couldn't feel—and it's convinced that feeling is still not safe.

Your Body Still Thinks Feelings Get You in Trouble

When you were a child, there were very real consequences for feeling. Your body learned that messy, inconvenient emotions could get you into trouble, make you "too much," push people away, or overwhelm the very people you depended on.

Your body still believes that feeling will get you in trouble, make you a "burden" and annoying to others and let others down. It shut down your feelings to save you from getting the silent treatment again. So, your brilliant, protective Parts stepped in to save you. They took your big, messy, vulnerable feelings and shut them down before they could make you unsafe. They buried them deep, locked them up, and built walls around them. And now? Those same protective Parts don't realize that you're not that child anymore. That you are safe now to feel. That you don't have to push emotions away to stay lovable. That you don't have to perform, overthink, or self-abandon to be safe. So your job is to start showing your Body that *it's safe now* to feel—so it will actually allow you to feel without shutting it down before it starts.

Get Curious

Instead of forcing yourself to feel, start by listening to the Parts of you that are blocking the feelings in the first place. Sit with that resistance. Get curious and notice the Parts of you that say things like:

- "NOPE. Distracting you from this!"
- "NOPE. We're going to dissociate now."
- "NOPE. This is too much—let's shut it down."

These Parts are not your enemy. They are not broken. They are Protectors—and they have been working their asses off to keep you safe for decades. So, instead of fighting them, get curious about them.

Ask your Protector Parts:

- "What do you want me to know?"
- "What are you trying to protect me from?"
- "How old do you think I am?"
- "What are you afraid would happen if you allowed me to feel?"

The Part Where You Stop Being Mad at Yourself

Don't rush to fix or answer these questions. Just listen. Stay curious. Stay gentle. The goal is to help your body realize that *it's safe now* to feel, not to force your way into feeling. And when your body believes that, it will allow the feelings to surface—but not all at once thankfully. Your body knows exactly how much you can handle, so it will come in waves that you can handle. And for the first time, you won't override yourself. You won't abandon yourself. You won't run. You'll sit with it. You'll let it move through. And you'll finally experience what safe, supported, embodied feeling actually is.

7

You Carry Your Childhood Into Every Relationship

A Rescue Dog Who Didn't Know It Needed Rescuing

2007 was a big year for me. That's the year I met my husband and he just... adored... me? Which felt wonderful and—confusing. I started feeling like a rescue dog that got lucky, like he felt sorry for me and decided to love me for some strange reason I was still trying to uncover. I was endlessly grateful to feel so loved finally, but I also lived in fear, worrying that at any moment, he could realize I was *more trouble than I was worth*. And he would leave.

In the early years, I used to say to him, "Thank you for loving me"—which sounds lovely, I know.

Deep down what I truly meant was: "Thank you for seeing how broken and fucked up I am and still being willing to take on the inconvenient, exhausting challenge of loving me. I'm still not sure why you did and it's amazing to me that you haven't left yet. I'd better enjoy this while it lasts."

I walked around the world, held hostage by the quiet, crushing fear that I was hard to love. It felt both surprising and suspicious when Matt just... loved me—without making me earn it first or prove anything. He was confused but lovingly patient with all of my "You're quiet... Are you mad at me?" moments. Sometimes I would hit the point of exasperation, unable to keep my perfect facade intact, and he would get a glimpse of the parts of me that I felt most ashamed of. Again and again, he was undeterred and... stayed. He seemed to come closer to me in those moments instead of pulling away. It took years for me to stop feeling utterly paralyzed by fear in those situations.

In 2007, I also finally started therapy for the first time. I slowly realized that my "great childhood" was actually full of Relational Trauma and my "personality" was actually a bunch of trauma responses. And at the same time, I experienced stable, safe love for the first time in my life. I realized I had been fending for myself this whole time—feeling emotionally starved and homeless, living in survival mode. It turns out not all love feels like walking on eggshells. Not all love disappears when you mess up. Not all love keeps you on edge, proving, earning, holding your breath. Once I saw the stunning contrast, I couldn't unsee it. In so, so many ways, I felt just like a rescue dog with a gnarly history who had finally found a safe, stable home and person to love them. I had never identified as a rescue because I didn't know I was one.

I would have "overreactions" to things. Shame and fear would hit me out of nowhere, and I would worry that someone was going to hurt me again like before. Sometimes, I asked Matt to stay close to me when I felt insecure. And when I checked to make sure he was still there, he wasn't disgusted by me when I was needy. He was confused but patient. He lovingly reassured me over and over and over again that he was not going anywhere, that he loved getting to love me. That he felt like "the lucky one." He didn't judge me for struggling to trust him or others. He would say, "It makes sense how your life experiences make it feel hard to trust anyone to stay."

My relationship with Matt absolutely changed my life but really changed *me*. Getting to experience safe, stable love changed me. I still feel like a rescue dog sometimes, but I no longer feel like I "got lucky." Most days, I believe in my bones that I deserve this.

You Carry Your Childhood Into Every Relationship

If you've ever felt like a rescue dog too, I need you to hear this: that feeling—like you're too sensitive, too much, too fucked up, a burden—was never the truth. It's just evidence of what you *survived*. It's memories of how you were made to feel. It's the voice of shame talking, painful echoes of a childhood full of love that came with conditions.

This is what Relational Shame Trauma looks like, and it's why it feels so impossible to believe that there was never anything wrong with you. Your brain and nervous system are like, "I mean... that's a lovely idea but I have tons of lived experience that says there is something wrong with me." Because that's how we were made to feel over and over and over again. It's why you go into Fight/Flight trying to stand up for yourself or tell someone no. And it's why you, like me back in the day, live in constant fear that people will decide you're too much trouble and leave.

This isn't actually who you are deep down—it's just the lens you were taught to see yourself through. This is a lens problem, not a *you* problem. You wouldn't get mad at a dirty window for making it hard to see outside, right? When you get your Perspectacles on, you will start to see the truth that was there all along.

When we shift from feeling lucky to be loved to *knowing we deserve it*—we start making different choices. We stop settling for crumbs. We stop abandoning ourselves to keep the peace. We stop believing love is something we have to earn and know that we deserve it because we do. And when we heal this, we also heal future generations.

So if you feel like a rescue dog who got lucky—I see you. And the fact that it feels preposterous to think that you are inherently lovable and worthy is proof of Relational Shame Trauma—and the grip shame still has on you. The rescue dog who finally finds a safe home, a warm bed, and food it doesn't have to fight for, doesn't feel immediately safe... how could it?

Those old, invisible wounds don't just disappear. The first however many times someone reaches out too fast, it will flinch. When the door slams, it will brace for impact. When it makes a mistake, it will expect to be thrown back out into the cold. Not because the dog is broken or unlovable, but because experience taught the dog that love wasn't safe.

That precious dog doesn't need to be punished for struggling to trust or "taking too long" to recover. It doesn't need to "just get over it." That dog needs someone to be endlessly patient, understanding, gentle, and tender with them when they remember the before. That's what you need and deserve, too. You are learning to believe you deserve stable love, a love you can trust and count on. You are learning to believe you deserve to feel safe in your relationships. You are trying to wrap your head around the idea that your worth is actually… inherent? Unshakeable? Just like that dog, you deserve someone who keeps showing up with warmth, again and again, until safety starts to feel real.

Please, try to be that someone for yourself. Instead of criticizing and shaming yourself that this shouldn't be so hard for you, show up for yourself like you would with the rescue dog. Meet yourself where you are with patience, compassion, and hope and hold onto the truth of what you deserved all along. You are not the burden—shame is.

"Good" Kid Relationship Struggles
Your Relationship Set Point

Our **Relationship Set Point** is the relative level of emotional connection or disconnection we *see as safe*—based on what we experienced as a child from our caregivers.

If you grew up in an environment where there was regular emotional disconnection, hostility, unresolved conflict, and instability, your brain and nervous system likely internalized these dynamics as what "love" or "connection" looks like. Your brain and nervous system will prefer familiar, unhealthy, and unsafe dynamics over unfamiliar, healthy, and safe dynamics. You will mistake behaviors and relationships as safe because they are familiar and you'll unconsciously seek to keep hitting your Relationship Set Point—even though it causes emotional pain.

For example, if you got the silent treatment from your parent, you might find yourself pulling away in relationships as an adult, even when you don't consciously want to. Or if you grew up in an environment where you never knew where you stood with your parent and whether they were mad at you, you might unconsciously create chaos in your relationships by picking fights or pushing people away, just to recreate that level of emotional intensity that feels familiar.

We Seek the Familiar

If you were constantly unsure of where you stood with your parent—never knowing if they were upset or pleased with you—your brain might seek out and manufacture emotional chaos as a way to recreate that familiar emotional intensity. This could look like nit picking, baiting a partner into a fight and pushing people away to trigger the familiar "ups and downs" that feel comfortable... even though they're painful. Sometimes our anxiety takes over and starts trying to get a pulse on whether they're mad at you. Other times, parts of us react to the uncertainty by acting out and pushing that person away... hoping they'll fight for the relationship. And us.

When we've always experienced this, we consciously crave love we don't have to earn. And yet we continue to be attracted to people who make us earn their love. If this is you, I need you to remind yourself that this isn't about being irrational or self-sabotaging—it's about *your nervous system's attempts to recreate what it knows*. What was familiar during childhood—emotional inconsistency, unpredictability, hostility, volatility and neglect—is what your nervous system will crave and find "safe."

> ### From Brittney
> My parents divorced when I was three, and I always saw Dad as stable and consistent. He was kind to me, and I considered myself a Daddy's girl. I craved his attention and to be around him because my mom had primary custody.
>
> I didn't realize until very recently that my father was emotionally unavailable. I could scream and cry, or have any emotion really and he would shut that crap down. When I had my first broken heart, I began to cut myself to self-soothe. I begged to be taken to a doctor, but my dad refused until I said that I was having chest pain.
>
> Later, I married a man who didn't show any emotion during arguments. He ignored my requests for emotional connection, choosing to focus on sexual connection only. I discovered that he had cheated on me twice in our relationship, and while I had a full on breakdown, this man fake cried and weakly begged me to stay. We later got divorced.
>
> Years and years later, I realized that being with my ex was just me repeating the pattern of being with a man like my father and begging for attention and emotional connection.

If you learned to associate love with conflict, withdrawal, and earning approval, a relationship with unconditional love can trigger alarm bells and feel terribly suspicious. But your body isn't rejecting love; it's reacting to the absence of chaos, unpredictability, instability, or what it thinks is "love."

The key to healing this is recognizing that these patterns are responses to your past trauma, not an inherent truth about love or your ability to love. By consciously working to show your body that it's safe with steady, unconditional love, you can start to shift your set point for emotional connection and begin to trust that love isn't something you have to work for—it's something you're meant to rest in.

Intense Emotional Arousal Can Be a Red Flag

Relationships that feel familiar in a painful way often trigger a very strong emotional and physiological response in our nervous system because they remind us of childhood patterns where emotional instability, neglect, and/or conditional love were present. Again, we are wired to seek familiarity, even if it's painful, mistaking those dynamics for "safe" based on our early experiences.

The heightened emotional arousal that occurs in these relationships—the anxiety, the fear, the not knowing where we stand with them, the intense push–pull of love and rejection—can feel overwhelming, and our nervous system can react as if we are in a high-stress, high-stakes situation. We experience things like increased heart rate, shallow breathing, and a rush of adrenaline.

Interestingly, we can sometimes mistake this intense emotional arousal for sexual attraction. Polyvagal Theory explains that we can mistake these physiological states because they activate similar areas in the brain and nervous system. So what might feel like "chemistry" or intense attraction in these emotionally charged relationships is often actually our body reacting to unresolved emotional and Relational Trauma (physiological red flags).

How to Spot These Kinds of Relationships

According to Attachment Theory and research on Relational Trauma, when we experienced regular emotional distance and disconnection from our caregivers and attachment figures, our brains are wired to associate emotional distance and emotional unavailability with love, as that was the familiar pattern we learned growing up. In both romantic and friend relationships, we subconsciously try to "fix" the dynamic, believing that if we can just get the person to open up or love us, we'll finally feel worthy. This dynamic feels familiar, even if it's painful, because it's what we've known.

These relationships have that exciting, swirly, whirly butterflies feeling—like having a crush on someone. You are elated when they text you. You feel so incredibly confident and good about yourself when they show you they care. Everything feels like the stakes are high, it feels like the smallest misstep could change everything. One minute you're on top of the world because they picked you... they like you... and then the bottom falls out in an instant if they're quiet or take a long time to text you back. *They're mad. Start preparing yourself now, it's over. You had a good run. And now... you bolt.* It's a freaking rollercoaster.

Be gentle with yourself. Your brain and nervous system are trying to attract partners who will trigger you into healing. Get curious when you notice these relationships in your life. Remind yourself that this makes sense and you make sense. When you get triggered by them because they might have been mad, and your anxiety rockets up—show up to feel the panic, the fear, the longing—and then release them instead of letting them run the show. Circle Back to your Parts and remind them that you don't have to chase love or prove you're worthy of it anymore, that love isn't something you should have to earn with someone and it's a red flag when it feels like you do. And gently remind yourself that real love feels less like a rollercoaster and more like steady ground.

People Pleasing

People pleasing is so exhausting. I know you beat yourself up for it, and I need you to understand that it's way more complicated than just struggling to stand up for yourself. You can't just overpower it by faking confidence. There is nothing wrong with you. People pleasing is a complex survival mechanism deeply rooted in our biology, actually originating in our nervous system and brain. It's a frantic, almost instinctual effort to smooth things over at any cost to try to feel safe. Safe? Yes, safe. For most of us, people pleasing started in childhood as parent pleasing. We have to heal deeper things before our nervous system will *allow us* to not people please. Let me explain.

People pleasing is deeply rooted in the Fawn Response. Kids naturally act out their stress, seeking out a boundary to push against so they can release the stress and regulate their bodies. This resistance shows up in their behavior as pushing back, refusing to cooperate and being disrespectful. Our parents saw these behaviors as "bad" and something they needed to punish out of us.

When we got stressed as kids, our nervous system jumped in to help us handle it. In these moments, it's not that our brain wasn't working—it was dysregulated and disorganized, prioritizing our survival in an environment where love, affection, and care were unpredictable, inconsistent, and conditional. Your brain handed the reins over to your nervous system, which people pleased until the threat went away.

In reality, this was a brilliant survival strategy. Your Fawn Response was a way to manage the threat without fighting or running. It wasn't a conscious choice. This survival mechanism became ingrained over time, which is why you still compulsively abandon your own emotional needs and sense of self to gain love or approval. And why it still feels so impossible to say no or disagree with others. Especially your parents. This makes sense. And you make sense.

But people pleasing doesn't create real safety in relationships—it creates the *illusion* of safety. The love and approval you receive only lasts as long as you are easy, agreeable, and convenient. The second you set a boundary, express a need, or take up too much space, that approval feels like it could vanish. This keeps you trapped in an exhausting cycle of: make people happy to feel safe. Ignore your own needs to keep the peace. Holding your breath, hoping love won't be taken away. And repeat. Deep down, this creates a chronic fear that if you ever stop people pleasing—if you ever let yourself be fully seen, as you are—you'll be left behind. That your worth isn't in who you are, but in how much you do for others.

"Are You Mad at Me?"

It's so crippling and terrifying for someone to be mad at you because nobody has ever been mad at you and still made you feel like they love you... at the same time. In childhood, when your parent was mad at you, they would withdraw *and* withhold love, attention, and affection.

Here's the gentle, steady truth: *their anger was never proof that you weren't worthy of love. It was a reflection of their own struggles, not a measure of your worth.*

As you unlearn these patterns and heal the parts of you that carry this worry and fear, you'll start to feel safer being fully yourself—with your messy emotions, differing opinions, inconvenient needs, and all. You'll begin to trust that your worth doesn't hinge on how others respond to you or whether you can keep everyone happy. It's a profoundly liberating shift when you start to realize that showing up as the Real You doesn't mean risking love—it means building a deeper connection with yourself and those who honor and value your authenticity. Over time, you'll be able to start believing and holding onto the truth that you are *inherently lovable*, even when someone else is struggling to see it or handle it. Because their reaction doesn't define your worth. You do.

People pleasing is a Check Engine Light, signaling that something deeper is happening inside for us, in our brain and nervous system. It's an indicator that we've hit a point where we can no longer tolerate the discomfort of someone being mad at us, disapproving of us, being disappointed in us or disliking us. I need you to notice with curiosity that your body is moving into Fawn Response to try to keep you safe. I often say to myself, out loud: "You are not in danger. I know this feels like a life or death situation, but it's not. You are safe. I've got you." Then do something to help yourself regulate with tools that speak your body's language—my go-to's are the Physiological Sigh with Butterfly Tapping and Completing the Stress Cycle with air squats, wall push-ups or going for a walk. Refer back to Chapter 6 to find out more information on regulation tools.

Healing Relational Trauma in Safe Relationships

Because people pleasing is born from Relational Trauma, it has to be healed *in relationships*. It can't be healed in isolation. You can't outthink it, willpower through it, or "fix" it by yourself (I know how hard you've tried). It's not something you can just journal or therapy your way out of.

Relational Trauma must be healed in a relationship where it feels safe for someone to be upset with you because you can feel they still love you. You have to experience being loved through the very things you've been told make you unlovable. That's how you start to believe it for yourself, that you're enough, that you're lovable, that you deserve relationships that feel safe.

If you didn't grow up with this type of relationship, it makes sense that this might feel impossible. But these relationships exist, and when you find them, your nervous system will finally experience the truth: love does not have to disappear when you disappoint people. And with safe people, it doesn't. You do not have to be agreeable to be safe. And safe people celebrate when you speak up about your feelings and needs. Safe people won't take it personally when you express your opinions and preferences. You get to choose you and be loyal to you. And safe people will cheer you on when you do.

My first safe relationship like this was with a therapist, and it changed my whole life. She was the first person who showed me that I could say how I actually felt, I could fall to pieces and be "pitiful" and express myself fully without losing her warmth or care. This taught Today Me and Little Me that I deserved that. Over time, this changed the way I saw myself and others and the way I believed I deserved to be treated. Alarm bells started to go off when I wasn't being treated the way I deserved.

Build a Tolerance for Being Misunderstood

The way you curb your people pleasing instincts is by building a tolerance for being misunderstood. This starts by dismantling and detaching from the shame you carry. That shame convinces parts of you that their disappointment is a life or death situation, that your survival and livelihood depends on them seeing that you're "good." Their disappointment also feels like proof of something you've always feared deep down: that you really are awful, that there's something fundamentally wrong with you, that you're unlovable. Shame makes it feel like your job is to keep the world from seeing "the truth" about you, to hustle for approval and avoid the pain of being seen as not enough.

> ### From Brittney
> Today, I have learned to set boundaries. I practice the philosophy of "let them," allowing my mother to feel however she needs, while focusing on my family's needs. I refuse to let her treat my children the way she treated me, and I no longer feel obligated to please her. Instead, I prioritize my children's well-being, advocating for their needs and standing up for them, even if it means maintaining distance from my mother.

You Carry Your Childhood Into Every Relationship

Letting people be upset with you, letting them think you're terrible, letting them feel disappointed because you didn't meet their expectations or give them what they wanted—it probably feels unbearable, impossible and... *unsafe* right now. I get it. I remember when the idea of someone being upset with me wasn't just uncomfortable; it felt dangerous. My body would go into full panic mode, my heart racing, my stomach in twisty knots. That fear wasn't about the moment itself. It was stirring up my own shame and the beliefs I had carried for so long: that if someone was upset with me, it must mean I was bad, unworthy, or unlovable. My nervous system had been trained to see other people's disapproval as a threat to my safety, so of course I worked frantically to fix it. Of course it felt impossible to just let them feel their feelings.

But here's the thing, if you do the work—lovingly caring for the parts of you that carry shame, challenging your Inner Critic, and systematically dismantling the lies shame has been whispering to you your whole life—you start to see it for what it is. And the truth is, there is nothing wrong with you. There never was. It's just how you were made to feel by parents who knew no other way to "teach" you how to be "respectful" using shame and fear.

When you notice that it's always your Inner Critic who says you're unlovable—and Self doesn't agree with your Inner Critic on this—you start to know that in your bones, too. You operate from a place of knowing who you are and what you deserve, other people can think whatever the hell they want about you. Their opinions don't hold the same weight because you know they're wrong.

And that's when the game changes. You stop hustling to prove you're good enough. You stop running yourself into the ground trying to manage everyone else's feelings and perceptions. You realize it's not your job to make sure everyone sees you in the "right" light. You already know you're good enough, so it no longer matters what anyone else thinks. It's not just freeing—it's life-changing.

Talk to Your Inner Child

But what if the work isn't about fixing their disappointment? What if the real work is about helping yourself—your body, Today You and Little You—feel safe, loved, and cared for—no matter what anyone else thinks? What if the goal isn't convincing them you're good enough... but convincing *yourself*?

Approach your triggers with as much curiosity and compassion as you can. Seeing your Inner Child's fear, panic, and terror. Recognizing when they are spiraling and gently showing them: "I see you. This is hard. You don't have to go through it alone anymore." This is how we build a sense of safety inside ourselves, by being the stable, solid ground we never had as a child. The soft spot to land. And as we start to notice patterns—the things that always seem to trigger us into people pleasing, shutting down, or spiraling—we make connections about why those moments feel familiar in a scary and painful way.

Let's walk through the experience. Someone is upset with you, and you feel that familiar panic. But instead of rushing to fix it, you pause and take a deep breath. You say to yourself, "You are not in danger. It is safe for them to be upset with you. I've got you and I'm standing with you. You are safe."

You resist the urge to immediately apologize or over-explain. Instead, you let the discomfort exist. You say, "You feel guilty, but that doesn't mean you did anything wrong."

You remind yourself that people are allowed to be upset: "Let them be mad. You haven't done anything wrong. You don't have to fix this for them."

You talk to the part of you that's terrified. "I know this feels scary. I know this reminds you of childhood when being 'difficult' felt scary and dangerous. But it's safe now and you're safe now. I am right here, I will not abandon you."

You know the exact words your Inner Child needs to hear. Say it to them. It might be something like:

- "That must have been so hard—to feel like you had to make sense of something that made no sense, to have to take the blame just to keep the peace and feel loved and lovable."
- "It was so tiring to keep everyone happy to feel safe."
- "You must have felt so frustrated apologizing over and over again even when you didn't do anything wrong."

When you say no without over-explaining, you'll feel like you're doing something wrong. But you're not. When you don't rush to fix someone's disappointment, your stomach will twist with guilt. Let it. When someone gives you a look that says "I don't like that" and you don't immediately bend to please them, your hands might shake. That's okay. This is what growth and healing feels like. Excruciating and liberating, all at the same time.

Take a Step Back

I need you to take a step back and get curious about when people are mad, upset, and disappointed in you. Ask yourself:

- Are they *actually* mad, upset, or disappointed, or am I jumping to conclusions based on my past history?
- Are they being reasonable here? Is it reasonable to be mad at me for what I did?
- Did I actually do something wrong here?
- Is their anger or disappointment a problem I actually need to fix?
- Are they acting like I *owe them* my obedience and my compliance?
- Do I just need to let them have that reaction because I know that I did nothing wrong by doing what I needed to do?

Remind yourself: *Their opinion is actually none of my concern and it's not a problem I need to fix.*

Notice when your body moves into Fight/Flight—your breathing shifts, your neck and shoulders get tight, your heart starts pounding, your stomach twists up. Or you might get what feels like an urgent need to fix, defend, or explain and notice that your body is feeling unsafe. When this happens, speak to your body through regulation. Take a Physiological Sigh or Complete the Stress Cycle with a walk or some air squats to tell your nervous system: *You are safe, there is no danger, you don't have to stay on high alert.*

Approaching these moments in this way will help you build a tolerance for other people being mad, upset, or disappointed in you. With practice, you will notice you have more and more tolerance for people to misunderstand you and disapprove of your choices. At the start, it will feel absolutely freaking intolerable for someone to not like you. Your brain and nervous system might default into Fawn Response, but you will be able to gently reassure yourself that it's not an emergency and it is safe now to take care of yourself, even when it upsets and disappoints others. You deserve to be loyal to yourself and what you need.

Turn your focus from that person to yourself. Let them ignore you for standing up for yourself. Let them be unreasonable and act like you standing up for yourself is a personal attack on them. It's not your job to apologize until they are willing to start talking to you again. It's your job to take care of yourself and let them take care of themselves.

Your Relationship to Your Parents

You cannot heal without getting a little bit of space and stepping back from being so emotionally involved with others—obsessing about how they will react, imagining their angry face, spiraling with fear and anxiety when you don't know where you stand or if they are mad.

Healing is about detaching emotionally a bit from people, especially your parents. It can feel more like betrayal and abandoning them because, for so long, it was your job to take care of *them*. Your emotional well-being was always tied to theirs—so it was your job to fix it if they were upset, withdrawn, or unpredictable. So it makes sense that now, trying to let them be upset feels like abandoning them in their time of need. But, you should have never been put in that position. It's time to learn how to step back from being over involved and let them feel their stuff without rushing to fix. That's breaking cycles for Little You.

Emotional detachment is one of the most powerful tools for surviving difficult family dynamics. As a Trauma Therapist and someone who's had to navigate tough family stuff myself, I want to reassure you that emotional detachment is not about shutting down or denying your feelings. It's more about giving yourself some breathing room—stepping back just enough so you're not constantly yanked around by old triggers. Melody Beattie, author of the iconic book *Codependent No More*, put it perfectly when she said: "Emotional detachment is not about detaching from the person, it's about detaching from the agony of the involvement with the person." It's about noticing when you're too emotionally involved, trying to manage, control, or anticipate someone else's actions and reactions. It's about taking that hook that's stuck in you, dropping it to the floor, and remembering that they are their own person, capable of handling their own stuff—and so are you.

Research on Relational Trauma and nervous system regulation shows that learning how to emotionally detach helps your body stay calmer, which means you're less likely to fall back into old patterns when tension rises in family situations. Emotional detachment might look like pausing and taking a deep breath when your mom's comments hit a nerve, reminding yourself that you don't have to fix anyone's mood and you deserve to take that energy and take care of your own self. It might look like getting curious about your feelings, saying, "Wow, I'm feeling really frustrated" or "I'm sad," without acting on those feelings right away.

It's not about being cold or unfeeling. It's about holding onto yourself, no matter how messy things get. Over time, this skill gives you space to engage with your family without falling into codependency. It helps you feel more in control, more compassionate toward yourself, and ultimately gives you a better chance of leaving family gatherings feeling like you stayed true to who you are, not who you had to be when you were a kid.

8

Giving Yourself What They Couldn't

A few years ago, I had a full-on come-apart with one of my best girlfriends, Logan, a fellow Trauma Therapist and cycle breaking mom. My impulse control was down, and I said some things out loud to her that I'd sworn I'd never tell another soul—because shame told me nobody could love me if they knew. The second the words left my mouth, I had an immediate vulnerability hangover. I braced myself and joked, "Wow, I swore I would never say those words to another human being."

Logan just smiled warmly and said words I will never, ever forget: "Tell me the other things you don't believe anyone can love you through... so I can show you that I will."

Full-body goosebumps just remembering that moment. That's the energy I try to bring to parenting my kids *and* reparenting Little Me. Being that unwavering presence I've searched my whole life for that says, *I see you struggling and I still love you. I will not leave you. I will not turn away from you. I will love you through everything you believe makes you unlovable.*

Reparenting ourselves is about stepping into the role of fierce protector—not just for others, but this time, it's *for yourself*. It's about awakening your Inner Mama Bear/Papa Bear—that raw, primal energy that fiercely guards their young, no matter the cost. Unapologetically ferocious when necessary. It's the energy of: *Get the hell away from my little one or I'll have to handle you myself.*

This Part of you has been dormant for most of your life, for your survival. Awakening it and allowing it to rise up on behalf of Today You *and* Little You is one of the most powerful things you can do to heal.

Awakening Fight Response

This is a crucial part of healing childhood trauma—going from a helpless and powerless place of "Why did this happen to me?" to a place of: "What the hell?! How could they have done that? How could they have allowed that to happen? I deserved to be protected, loved, and cared for."

Allowing your anger also signals a fundamental shift in the way you're relating to your trauma *and* triggers. Consistently talking to your body in its native language of regulation will help your body stop shutting down Fight Response and allow you to have access to it through an anger response. Fight Response doesn't have to mean "fighting"—it's about having the ability to rise up to the perceived threat and protect yourself, and stand up for yourself or call bullshit, instead of appeasing and people pleasing to avoid conflict.

What does it feel like when we awaken this protective energy? It feels like a surge of strength, something deep within us that has been waiting to be tapped into. Suddenly, we feel a rush of clarity and confidence, knowing that we are worthy of protection—both from others and ourselves. When we allow our inner Mama Bear to rise, it feels like an electrifying activation of our own power. It's not just an emotional charge; it's a bodily sensation. You might feel your posture shift, shoulders square, as your breath deepens and your body feels more solid, like you're ready to stand your ground. It's a visceral experience of stepping into your own space, unapologetically, and refusing to let anyone—whether it's a partner, parent, or friend—disrespect or diminish you. It's like a switch is flipped, and suddenly, you know without question that you are worthy of fierce protection by you, for you. It's not just a feeling. It's an embodied experience of power you've never known.

When we rise up to protect ourselves, something profound happens in our brain, too. The prefrontal cortex, responsible for reasoning and decision-making, starts to take charge, moving us away from automatic people pleasing or submissive patterns. At the same time, the amygdala—which is responsible for processing fear and threats—becomes less active.

We stop reacting from a place of fear, and instead we shift into a more grounded and empowered state. This shift helps us break free from the cycle of hypervigilance and emotional overwhelm that comes from living in a constant state of emotional neglect or fear. As we step into this protective role for ourselves, dopamine and oxytocin levels rise, helping us feel calm, centered, and more connected to ourselves. These "feel-good" chemicals flood our system, reinforcing the idea that we are safe, worthy, and in control.

On a biological level, this process rewires the nervous system. When we protect ourselves—when we rise up in defense of ourselves and our inner child—our body begins to recalibrate. Cortisol, the stress hormone, starts to drop as we feel more empowered and less reactive. We begin to create new neural pathways that reinforce self-protection, self-worth, and self-love. This neuroplasticity is key to healing trauma, especially Relational Trauma and Shame. The more we practice remothering ourselves and stepping into the role of our own fierce protector, the more we rewire our brains to feel confident and secure, rather than small and afraid. We learn that our needs matter, that we are allowed to take up space, and that we deserve to be treated with respect—both by others and by ourselves.

In practice, reparenting ourselves looks like setting boundaries with others, even when it's uncomfortable. It means saying "no" when we need to, even if we're afraid it will upset someone. It's recognizing that Little You, the Part of you that carries the old wounds, needs to be cared for, just as much as your adult self. It's about showing up for yourself when you feel small or scared, and actively nurturing and protecting that vulnerable Inner Child. If someone violates your boundaries, instead of shrinking or apologizing, you stand firm—knowing that you are worthy of respect. When you face situations that bring up fear or anxiety, you can call on that Mama Bear or Papa Bear energy to protect your peace and your emotional well-being, refusing to let external stressors disrupt your inner safety.

This protective energy also means tending to your own emotional needs. Just like a Mama Bear would comfort her cubs, you become your own source of comfort. You soothe yourself when you're hurt, acknowledge your emotions without judgment, and create space for healing. This could look like:

- taking time for rest;
- enjoying hobbies that nourish your soul;
- speaking kindly to yourself when you're feeling overwhelmed.

It also means reparenting yourself—giving your Inner Child the nurturing love and protection they didn't get in the past. This may involve confronting the stories of unlovability (is this a word?) or unworthiness that have been passed down through generations and re-writing those narratives. By doing this, you create a solid foundation for both the adult and the child within to feel safe, supported, and empowered.

Ultimately, learning to protect both Today You and Little You is a transformative process that fundamentally alters our relationship with ourselves. It shifts the way we show up in the world, in our relationships, and in our own bodies. We stop living in fear of rejection or abandonment, and start living from a place of strength, compassion, and deep self-respect. Through this process, we not only heal past wounds, but we also reclaim our personal power, one fierce, loving step at a time.

For me, awakening this primal energy felt like a tidal wave of sparkling confidence rushing through my whole body. It felt like every cell in my body stood up, knowing it was time to rise up and defend everything I've ever been. My body felt tense but not in a bad way—like the tension was a taut string about to snap with the stunning clarity that just hit me that *I did not f%@ing deserve that*. It's this energy of no longer feeling the need to ask for permission to take up space… you just freaking *claim it*. Asking permission suddenly feels… unnecessary.

The surge is not just emotional, it's visceral. It's primal, and it's yours.

You and Anger: It's Complicated

If you're a recovering Good Kid, chances are your relationship with anger is complicated. Maybe you bottle it up so tightly that when it finally breaks through, it feels explosive and out of control. Maybe you find yourself getting mad at little things—like snapping at your partner or kid over something small, while staying silent and internally fuming in situations where you're actually being mistreated. Maybe you feel like you "should" know how to handle it by now, that it's embarrassing to still be struggling with something so basic.

But here's the truth: most of us were never taught how to handle anger. We were taught to suppress it, to swallow it down and pretend it wasn't there, to "control" it—when really, that just meant avoiding it until it inevitably leaked out sideways. And when anger broke through? Goodness, we were made to feel so ashamed of ourselves. But shame fuels anger into aggression. It makes us lash out, shut down, or turn the anger back onto ourselves, reinforcing the belief that we're just *bad* at this, that we *should* be able to do better. And that shame keeps the cycle going. You deserve to move out of this shame-driven cycle.

So let's pause.

Take a breath and get curious.

What if anger wasn't the enemy? What if anger was actually that epic, badass best friend who refuses to stand idly by when you're being mistreated? The one who pipes up to say, "Hey, this isn't okay" or "Ummm... I call bullshit." The problem was never having anger. The problem was that no one taught us what to do with it... except push it down and pretend not to be angry. So now, it's your job to be your own Confident Loving Leader—to Today You and to Little You, to show yourself the patience you would show your own kid if they were just learning this for the first time—because *you are*. Decades into life, you are learning something that was never modeled for you, and that carries deep, layered shame.

From Michelle

I grew up with an older brother who is likely on the spectrum. My parents constantly fawned over his demands (they even nicknamed him King Tut), terrified of upsetting him, while desperately trying to mold him into a "normal" kid—a role he was never going to fit.

When I was nine months pregnant, I attended my brother's (at the time) fiancée's bridal shower. Shortly after arriving at the end of the event, my brother came to my table and demanded that I give his fiancée a bible that our deceased grandmother gave to me. The bible had her signature inside but otherwise had no material value.

After I refused and rolled my eyes, he raised his voice, pointed his finger at me, and threatened, "I don't care that you're nine months pregnant; I'll punch you in the stomach."

My Mama Bear instinct kicked in. I stood up, ready to fight, but thankfully, we were separated before things escalated further.

Afterward, as always, the blame somehow shifted to me. "You instigated him, you egged him on," my mother said. Even now, she genuinely still believes it is my responsibility to somehow manage my father's and brother's toddler-like temper tantrums. Unfortunately, she won't educate herself and see that this was not and NEVER should have been my job...

Anger isn't something to fear. It's something to release. It's something to move through your body in a way that doesn't hurt you or anyone else. Stomp your feet. Tear up paper. Throw a pillow. Scream into it if you need to. And when it comes, talk yourself through it:

- To your body: "Body, it's safe to let that anger rise, let it come."
- To yourself: "It's okay for you to be angry, your anger is trying to show you that something is not okay. Let yourself lean into the anger and move it out."

You don't have to keep bottling and exploding. You don't have to stay stuck in shame. You get to learn a different way. It's safe now.

You may have heard mental health professionals or even research studies claim that allowing yourself to feel anger will make you more aggressive, but let's break that down. Studies that make this claim often fail to account for shame as a key variable. Research consistently shows that it's not anger itself that fuels aggression—it's shame about anger that does. When people feel ashamed of their anger, when they've been taught that it makes them bad, unlovable, or unworthy, that's when it festers and turns into something explosive. Shame makes anger feel unbearable—like something that must be pushed onto someone else to escape it. But when anger is processed in a safe, shame-free way? When people are given space to feel it, move through it, and release it without being punished or judged? They don't become more aggressive. In fact, research shows that people who develop healthy emotional regulation—including safe anger expression are less likely to exhibit aggression or chronic stress responses later in life.

So if you're worried that letting yourself feel anger will make you an angry, out-of-control person—take a breath. The science says it's *shame* that warps our relationship with anger.

Learning to release it rather than fear it sets us free to have a healthy relationship with anger that helps you take care of yourself, which is what you always deserved.

There's a good chance you've been feeling a great deal of anger as you've been processing your Relational Trauma. As a child, you were not asking for too much. And you were not "too much." You were never a failure. The love and care you needed weren't things you should have had to earn. And while the past can't be rewritten, the story you tell yourself about your inherent worth and lovability can. The shame you've carried all these years was not yours to hold, and it's time to start putting it down. You've always been deserving of the care, compassion, and safety that you fought so hard to create for others. It's time to start creating it for yourself—please make it your most important job to love the shit out of Today You and Little You. To be that stable anchor, that soft spot to land, that relentlessly encouraging and supportive—not critical—parent you needed.

When the anger comes up because you start to realize that it is *some bullshit* that you were a child who had to be the parent to your parent... and now you're still having to be the parent—maybe with your parent, maybe with your kids—and *when is it your turn to be taken care of?* Please know it is totally normal to feel that way, of course you feel that way. I see you. Let yourself say all the things that are swirling around. Shout it into a pillow, say it under your breath or say it loudly while you're driving down the road. Stop pushing that down and pretending it didn't bother you. Little You carried enough in childhood—honor what they went through and help them release that sacred anger, frustration, resentment and rage.

It's okay to be mad, frustrated, resentful, and full of rage about it. Of course you feel that way. Cheer Little You on as you help them feel safe to *stop* pretending and suppressing it. Cheer Little You on as you help them unload it. Rub your

Younger Self's back while they scream about it, cry about, fall to pieces in grief about it. Stand By Your Younger Self. Refuse to let them do it alone. Refuse to abandon them. Validate their feelings. Soothe them, comfort them. Love them through *all of it*. Say things like:

- "That must have been so hard, having to do it all by yourself."
- "You deserved to be cared for. It's okay to be mad and sad and grieve the love and care you deserved but didn't get."
- "I'm going to take care of you now—I've got you, and I'm learning how to show up for you and help you feel safe."

Good Kid Recovery

Reparenting is taking on the privilege—not burden—of getting to love and care for yourself. For Today You, Little You, your Parts and your body. It's the daily practice of reclaiming yourself—your needs, your emotions, your worth. It's choosing, every day, to Stand By Yourself—to belong to yourself first, before seeking belonging anywhere else.

Reparenting is the practice of showing ourselves, over and over, that love stays, even when we're messy, struggling, or falling apart. We don't have to earn our belonging. Even at our most unfiltered, our most exposed, we are still worthy of being held.

Unconditional Positive Regard

Close your eyes and imagine the parent you always needed, the one you've always wished you'd had. You make a mistake, and you run to them for support, knowing they'll be a soft spot to land—warm, comforting, and unwavering. This is a parent who sees your struggles, your mistakes, your messiest moments and never pulls away, who leans in and reaches for you when you need to cry, who doesn't withdraw or withhold warmth, support, or love when you disappoint them. That's what Unconditional Positive Regard (UPR) is and what I want you to start giving yourself now.

UPR is about showing up for yourself with the same compassion you would offer a struggling child. It is the opposite of our Inner Critic with its harsh, critical voice—the one that says we have to be better, do better, and never mess up to be worthy. In Internal Family Systems (IFS) and Parts Work, we learn that every single Part of us has a positive intent, even the ones we struggle with. When we stop attacking ourselves and instead get lovingly curious—when we assume that we are doing our best with the tools we have right now—something incredible happens: we soften. We are able to stay warm, connected and loving instead of going cold and moving into disappointment. And we feel safe enough to actually heal.

This isn't about making excuses for ourselves or avoiding accountability—that parent would absolutely hold us accountable for our impact, but they would do it from a place of unwavering belief in our inherent goodness. UPR is love that stays, love that doesn't get taken away when we mess up. When we practice UPR, we stop using shame as a tool for "growth." We operate from a place of belief in our own inherent goodness, even when we struggle.

You deserved a parent who would sit beside you when you were hurting and remind you that you are loved no matter what. And now? You get to be that parent for yourself. Because this is what your best looks like right now—and it is enough.

Set Boundaries with Yourself

Set boundaries with yourself from a place of relentless self-compassion, ruthless boundaries and what you deserve. This could look like:

- "You deserve to feel good about yourself so we're going to turn off TikTok and put your phone down. I've got you, I'm

here to help you when you struggle to take care of yourself. Because you deserve to feel good."
- "You deserve to feel good in your body so we're going to stop after one glass of wine tonight. I've got you, I'm here to help you when you struggle to take care of yourself. Because you deserve to feel good."
- "You deserve to feel good mentally so we're going to keep it surface level with (that family member who's very intrusive). Simple answers and 'I don't want to go there' when they ask to go more in-depth. I've got you, I'm here to help you when you struggle to take care of yourself. Because you deserve to feel good."

Stop Blaming Yourself for Needing Help

I now ask you: how long have you been telling yourself that you "should" be able to handle this on your own; that you should have it all figured out by now; that if you were stronger, smarter, better—you wouldn't be struggling?

If you're a recovering Good Kid, chances are you don't even consciously think of yourself as someone who needs support. You just push through, suppress your exhaustion, tell yourself you're fine when you're not, and carry the weight of the world like it's your job. Because when you needed help as a kid, how was it received? Were you met with a sigh? Did you get an eye roll? Did your parent give you a dismissive, "You should know this by now," or "I can't do everything for you," or "Figure it out on your own?" Maybe your needs were ignored entirely. Maybe you learned that asking for help only led to more disappointment, more proof that you were on your own.

So you adapted. You learned *to not need*. You became the strong, self-sufficient, never-a-burden Good Kid who took care of things yourself, who never made waves, who got things done without needing extra guidance. But you didn't stop needing help—you just stopped allowing yourself to ask for it.

You learned to shame yourself for struggling, to believe that your exhaustion meant you weren't trying hard enough. To push through, bottle it up, and keep going, even when you were completely depleted. And now, that pattern is running in the background of your life—making it nearly impossible to recognize when you're drowning, let alone reach out for a lifeline.

This is the cycle we deserve to break for ourselves: we shame ourselves for needing help, then withhold help from ourselves... *just like our parents did*. But what if needing help isn't a weakness? What if struggling doesn't mean you're failing? What if getting support isn't a sign that you're broken—but a radical act of self-love and trust? Because the truth is, you're not weak for struggling. You're human. And that means *you deserve care and support*, just like anyone else.

So what does actually helping yourself look like? It looks like therapy, if that's accessible to you. It looks like admitting you're struggling instead of pretending you have it all together. It looks like finding one person you trust and telling them the truth when they ask how you're doing. It looks like pausing before you push yourself past your breaking point, and asking yourself, "What would I tell a friend in this situation?"—then actually taking your own advice. It looks like allowing yourself to rest without guilt. It looks like finding compassion for the Parts of you that are still learning how to receive care, that still flinch at the idea of being seen in your struggle.

Because here's what I need you to hear: needing help was never the problem. Being made to feel ashamed for needing help was. That shame is not yours to carry anymore.

You Are More Than Your Achievements

The way you were made to feel as a kid was that the "Most Lovable Version" of you was perfect, always accommodating, selfless, and a shape shifting chameleon. It felt like your worth

Giving Yourself What They Couldn't

had to be earned by accomplishing and pleasing and achieving and doing things perfectly and never making anyone mad. So yes, that was your experience of things as a kid and all along, but that's not truth—it's memory. That was a made-up idea and it was incorrect. And I'm absolutely thrilled to inform you that you get to decide now if you're good with that.

Are you good with your worth, your value, your innate lovability being something that you have to work for and prove every day? Are you good with feeling like you must be a certain level of productive every day to be lovable—even when your body is screaming at you because it needs a break? Are you good with that?

You're comparing yourself to some perfect version of yourself who doesn't actually exist. You learned this from your parents—they were also comparing you to some perfect version of you that didn't exist, saying you "weren't measuring up to your potential." It's a trap, friend. You will *always* fall short, you will *always* feel like a failure, you will never, ever feel good enough.

So ask yourself: "Am I good with that? Or am I *done* living like that?"

You can choose to call bullshit. You can choose to see that this is old wiring, old conditioning that is *not* serving you. You can dare to believe that you're still lovable even when you don't get shit done. Even when the to-do list is still there. Even when the day gets away from you. You can dare to believe you're still lovable *no matter what*. You can dare to love yourself anyways. You can dare to be proud of yourself for taking the break you needed or doing something to care for yourself. Think about a child you know—do you believe deep down that they need to accomplish a certain amount to be lovable? Why would you be any different? You're not different and you can show up and say NOPE. *I'm not doing that anymore. I deserve better than that.*

Empathy

You deserve to give your younger self something they desperately needed but never got—empathy. Compassion. Understanding. Seeing and acknowledging the hurt and shame they've carried for so long.

It's about saying to your younger self:

- "That must have been so hard that you had to hide your emotions and the parts of you that were hurting, to feel loved."
- "You never should have had to carry that pain alone."
- "You felt like something was wrong with you for having big emotions—but there was never anything wrong with you."

It's not about blaming your parents—it's about breaking the cycles and recognizing those inherited patterns that have shaped you and choosing to heal so that pain doesn't get passed down. Healing Relational Shame means learning to separate what's happening now from the wounds of the past to consciously choose to respond differently. When we do this work, we create new patterns built on softness, warmth, and steady connection instead of harshness, fear, shame, and control.

> ### Client Story
>
> Becca* was about a year into counseling with me when she noticed an inner resistance to looking at pictures of her from childhood.
>
> She said it now felt "like a gut punch." She asked if she could bring some pictures in and look at them together so I could support her through it.
>
> She took a deep breath and looked at the first picture of her as a baby. Her eyes welled up with tears. "Look at those chubby cheeks. God, my daughter is just the same." She rubbed the picture lovingly with her finger. When she pulled out the second picture, her energy shifted. She let out a long breath, her back stiffening, her watery eyes hardening. She held it up to show

me—her at about seven or eight in a big, poofy dress and a smile that lit up her whole face. After a few minutes, she said, "I hate her. I can't even look at her."

It was Shame. Becca's Shame Part had hijacked her.

I took a deep breath and said, "Okay. Can you notice that Part that's feeling so disgusted by her? Find that disgusted energy in your body—where do you feel it?"

She waited a beat, thinking. "My stomach," she said.

"Try to notice it as a Part of you," I said gently. "Notice it with warm, loving curiosity. Thank it for trying to protect you. Then when you're ready, ask it to step back and give you some space."

Becca let out a few long breaths. Her energy started shifting into something softer. "Were you able to get it to step back and stand down?" I asked. As she nodded, I asked, "How does it feel to look at that picture of little you now?"

"So different," she said, tears streaming down now. "She's so little. She's so cute. I loved that dress so much," she sobbed. "I knew I was eight when all of that stuff happened, but looking at her now... I was so little."

"She deserved protection and safety and care," I said.

"She did. 'I'm sorry it's taken me so long to come back for you,' she said to Little Her. 'I'm sorry all of that happened to you. You didn't deserve that. I'm sorry I wasn't able to protect you. I'm here now. I'm going to take care of you now and help you heal.'"

(*not her real name. Shared with her permission and encouragement.)

This moment perfectly captures why loving ourselves, being kind to ourselves, and believing we deserve care feels so hard. It's not because we're broken. It's not evidence that we are actually unlovable. It's because we're carrying shame that's contaminating how we see ourselves.

Little You is waiting for you to find your way back—to see how shame has you hijacked and ask it to stand down. So you can notice Little You, to hold them, to finally give them the love and safety they've been searching for all along. To finally be that person who believes they are deeply, completely lovable.

3
PARENTING

9

Facing Your Stuff So Your Kids Don't Have To

When we become parents, just like our parents and grandparents before us, we see it as our job to roll up our sleeves and basically... break our kid's spirit with punishments until they become good and respectful. We tell ourselves, "I don't enjoy this either, but it's my job to raise you to be respectful. And if it takes punishment after punishment to make you be obedient—then so be it." At the core of this belief is the idea that a Good Kid doesn't fight back.

At some point, after enough punishments, they learn to stop pushing, mostly obey, mostly stay quiet. We pat ourselves on the back. We did it. We raised a Good Kid.

Maybe we have another child—one whose spirit is harder to break. This child still has *the audacity* to say no and stand their ground. This child doesn't seem to "learn" from punishments. Ultimately, this child makes us feel like we've failed. Deep down, we also believe they are failing at being a Good Kid. Because if success means raising an obedient child, then a defiant child must mean we've done something wrong.

Our parents and all parents before them got this part so wrong.

Children *should* have access to their Fight Response. The child who never misbehaves or challenges us has shut down their natural, physiological response to stress and is instead just bottling up their feelings and emotions to please us.

The real problem here is the misguided belief that discipline should involve suffering and making kids feel ashamed to come to us for support. It's the belief that kids deserve to be punished for challenging our authority and that kids deserve to languish, alone, when they mess up because it somehow helps them "learn". The research continues to show that it not only doesn't help kids learn... it blocks their ability to learn.

Parenting triggers us into healing, and I believe the most important work we will ever do as parents is in learning how to nurture and show up for our kid's emotional well-being with empathy and love without conditions, allowing them to be Feeling Beings, and pivoting the hell away from punishments and making kids feel scared and ashamed for messing up. Instead, we should learn how to hold them accountable, teach them to show up for their impact and Stand By Them through the whole thing.

We have a choice. We can repeat the cycle, raising another generation of Good Kids who spend their adulthood trying to recover the parts of themselves they had to shut down just to survive, or we can raise kids who:

- are allowed to resist to release to regulate;
- are held accountable for their impact with consequences, not shame and punishments;
- feel loved and supported while also learning responsibility;
- know, deep down, that they are inherently worthy and lovable, no matter what.

When we do this, we don't raise kids who are fragile, rebellious, or out of control. We raise kids who can handle big emotions, navigate hard times, and move through life with confidence without being crushed by shame. We can parent kids who don't have to recover from their childhoods like we have. And we raise kids who feel safe needing us and needing support. Who, when life deals them a hard blow, run to us for support—instead of hiding their struggles and pretending they're fine when they're not. Because we've made it feel safe to not be okay, to show their imperfect self and they can trust we will make them feel safe and better... not worse. That's what we want.

You're Going to Mess Up... A Lot

Hi, I'm a Trauma Therapist, parenting expert, and mom myself and I'm here to say... you are going to mess up as a parent. All the damn time. I am so sick of the toxic, perfectionist narrative that being a Cycle Breaker means you never lose your patience, never raise your voice, never react instead of respond. Expecting yourself to be able to always have endless patience for the bullshit of parenting. That's not breaking cycles—that's breaking yourself.

I live and breathe generational trauma. My brain never stops thinking about it. I see counseling and coaching clients around the world to help them with this—and *I still mess up all the time.*

The goal is not to never mess up. The goal is to break the damaging cycles *when* we do. When we raise our voice, we don't gaslight our kid or make excuses; we Circle Back and own it. When we lose our patience, we apologize. When we react instead of respond, we don't put that on them—we say, "I'm sorry for scaring you. That wasn't okay." This is how we stop passing down the shame, fear, and emotional disconnection we grew up with. Not by being perfect, but by showing our kids what it looks like to try something and not do it perfectly, and what to do next. We show them how to Circle Back to start that awkward conversation, how to take accountability for how we made someone feel, how to apologize without the word "but," and how to love someone through the tense moments of conflict. Boom. Our kids learn how to do that *and* they go into the rest of their lives believing they deserve that when someone hurts them.

The perfection you're chasing is a set-up. You are set up to fail. It's impossible. We all get upset and lose our cool, but our ability to be the parent we want to be is profoundly impacted by our stress level. We were all raised to bottle our feelings, so we are walking around like a balloon about to pop, beating ourselves up for not having enough patience. But how? How can you be patient and warm when you feel like you're about to burst? You can't. That's not a moral failing—it's biology. You have to release what's bottled up first. You have to give yourself what you're trying to give them.

So let's stop aiming for perfection and start aiming for repair when we don't get it quite right. Let's commit to doing our best—whatever that looks like in the moment. We can raise kids who don't have to spend their adulthood in therapy untangling their worth from their mistakes because they grew up knowing that love isn't something you have to earn, and repair is always possible.

Parenting and Reparenting, Together

The only way I know how to teach parenting is by talking through the stuff we, as the parent now, struggle with now. These are the things that feel the most triggering for us because those triggers are all wrapped up in how *we* were parented. That's why I teach parenting and reparenting together. You can't separate the two.

We can want to parent differently. We can listen to the podcasts, read all the books, and be in all of the social media groups for parents who are doing it differently. We can know in our minds that something we're doing isn't good for our kids—maybe even hurting or traumatizing them. But knowing and understanding it intellectually are not enough. We have to be brave enough to sit with and face the reality of the impact our parents had on us… and the reality of the impact we are having on our children now.

Our reactions as parents are shaped by wounds we haven't fully healed. When our kids remind us of our younger selves we instinctively try to protect them from what would have happened to us as kids. But that instinct often backfires, and we end up shutting them down in the same ways we were shut down.

I've been there. When my oldest was a toddler and got clingy or needy, I was so damn determined not to make her feel pitiful or pathetic for needing me. But when she got needy, I'd shut her down anyway, making her feel bad about herself. It was gut-wrenching. It took multiple incidents, a lot of therapy, and so much pillow punching to process the sadness and anger I felt about how my mom had responded to *me* as a child. Only then could I start being the soft place to land for my daughter—most of the time.

Here's what's happening: our nervous system isn't thinking about happiness or joy when we're triggered. It's focused entirely on survival, constantly scanning for threats. The kicker? It processes a crappy text from someone or a screaming toddler the same way it processes a bear attack—like your life is in danger. Your body floods with thousands of biochemical reactions, shifting into Fight/Flight.

If you were made to feel pitiful or pathetic as a kid for being needy or having Big Feelings, then your nervous system sees your needy, emotional child as a threat—as if that same "bear" from your childhood is back, ready to maul you all over again. And if your parents made you feel like you were never good enough, then when your child refuses the meal you just made, this might hit you in the exact same place, sparking that old, familiar ache of inadequacy and failure.

These moments aren't just triggering—they're laced with a familiar shame. They stir up the belief that maybe, just maybe, your parent was right: you're not enough and there *is* something wrong with you. And without even realizing it, that shame becomes the filter through which we see our child's behavior, twisting it into something personal, when in reality, it's not about us at all. It's about a child who is dysregulated and needs help from their parents. Just like Little You back then.

Sometimes, parts of you will come out of nowhere to try to protect your child from what would have happened to you as a kid by responding that same way. It seems counterintuitive but it happens to every last one of us.

I'm going to keep reminding you that we are doing our best, parenting the only way we know how, loving our kids the only way we've been taught. Knowing deep down that we needed something different and trying to get there without a roadmap is incredibly difficult. I see you trying every damn day to be the parent your kids need, to give them what you know kids need but didn't get yourself. I see you feeling frustrated and kind of devastated when the reality of your parenting looks nothing like what you had hoped it would be. Please hear me when I say this: that distance between what you want and where things are now *does not* make you a bad parent. It's not a reflection of your worth or love or how hard you're working. It's a reflection of the insidious, sneaky nature of shame-laced parenting and discipline. Shame is like freaking glitter—it gets everywhere, it sticks to everything, and it's nearly impossible to fully clean up without deep, intentional effort.

The good news is that we can absolutely do this. Yes, it takes work, but it's the kind of work that transforms everything. Showing up and being brave enough to do this work will not only liberate your child from the devastating long-term impact of shame-laced discipline, but it will liberate *you* from the shame that's been running the show for years, keeping you stuck in patterns you don't even want to repeat and hijacking you when you get overwhelmed. This work will also liberate the child you used to be from the idea that you ever had to earn love or be perfect to deserve it.

That means showing up for the hard, messy process of getting honest with ourselves. Brutally honest sometimes. Sitting with how it feels in our body when we notice those patterns, and being curious about the sadness, the anger, the fear, the shame, and the pain that surface. It means facing the guilt of realizing we've hurt our child, even though we tried so damn hard not to. It means letting ourselves remember what it really felt like to be on the receiving end of things as a child. Acknowledging that we didn't deserve that then—and our child doesn't deserve it now.

Healing ourselves is the only way through. It's the only way to become the parent you want to be: the one who breaks the cycles of generational trauma, the one who raises children who don't have to recover from their childhoods. In the moments where you're hanging on by your fingertips, remind yourself what it felt like to be the kid. Feel those feelings so you don't explode on your kid. Circling Back to start the awkward conversation and apologizing to your kid. Show up to therapy in the middle of a busy day. In these moments, you are profoundly transforming the lived experience of not just yourself, but your children, and generations to come.

How Kids Actually Develop

Kids are always in motion, constantly developing in ways we can and can't see. Their brains and bodies are working around the clock, taking in every little thing, forming new neural connections, refining skills, and reorganizing what they already know. Unfortunately for all of us, development isn't linear, smooth, or predictable—it happens in waves, through cycles of balance and imbalance—what scientists call equilibrium and disequilibrium.

The Cycle: Equilibrium and Disequilibrium

Development isn't a steady climb—it's a back-and-forth dance between moments of stability (equilibrium) and moments of chaos and struggle (disequilibrium).

Equilibrium refers to the "golden phases" when things tend to run more smoothly and our kids seem more regulated, adaptable, and able to control themselves more consistently. Emotions seem relatively manageable, everything is not a fight, and they tend to be able to be more independent.

Disequilibrium is when, seemingly suddenly, everything changes and things feel unstable and unpredictable. Our kids become clingier, more emotional, more impatient, and struggle with things they had previously mastered. You may see a regression in sleep or consistent struggles to separate from you at bedtime. Kids become extra sensitive to everything, or seem off in ways that don't make sense. This isn't them "going backward"—it's their brain reallocating resources to build something new elsewhere in their body.

A developmental leap pulls kids out of equilibrium and into disequilibrium. A developmental leap is one of those big, intense shifts where their brain is rapidly upgrading itself all at once. This means less capacity for emotional regulation, motor coordination, and everyday skills. This is why leaps often look like regressions first—our child is adjusting to a new, more advanced way of thinking or moving, and things get bumpy before they get better. Think of it like a software update: while the system is installing new, upgraded features, other functions slow down or glitch. Your child isn't "losing progress"—they're getting ready to uplevel to a whole new level of ability.

Kids don't just have occasional developmental leaps—they are constantly growing, refining, and adapting. Leaps are just the moments where the shift is so big that we can't miss it. But the brain and body are always in motion, moving through these cycles of equilibrium and disequilibrium over and over again. So if your child suddenly seems out of sync, struggling with things they used to handle, or acting like a completely different kid overnight—please remind your worried, confused self that they're not broken, falling behind, or backsliding. You're not failing as a parent. They're deep in the process of becoming someone new.

The 6 Core Needs: What We Need Most

Kids have core needs inside their relationship with their caregivers—relational needs. A child's sense of self is shaped by how their caregivers respond to their relational needs—when they are scared, sad, mad, joyful, or simply being themselves. The painful truth here is that our parents didn't know we had relational needs—their parents didn't know it either. Kids having emotional needs that parents needed to meet wasn't modeled, taught or named. So they didn't know they were supposed to meet them for us... or how one would even do that.

Which means our core needs went unmet. And there is an impact when these core needs go unmet—one that doesn't disappear when we grow up. We carry those unmet needs with us into adulthood—playing out in our relationships, our self-worth, our ability to regulate, and our struggles with shame.

The first four core needs come from the 4 S's of Secure Attachment (Dr. Daniel Siegel & Dr. Tina Payne Bryson's work) which are fundamental to building a secure, resilient child. But I believe there are two additional core needs that are essential to breaking the cycle of "good" kid trauma—needs that aren't widely discussed, but are absolutely crucial for kids to thrive: the need to feel inherently lovable and the need to release stress and Big Feelings without shame.

And since we're talking about all of this, it feels like a good time to remind you: you are not going to do this perfectly.

Sometimes, you will try to stay calm, and then—*bam*—you'll get triggered out of nowhere and suddenly you're yelling. Same. Remember, our job as cycle breaking parents isn't to never mess up or do everything flawlessly. We are all still learning that feelings and vulnerability are safe, as we try to raise kids who know that, too. We're going to make mistakes, *all the damn time*. Same! The work isn't about getting it right every time—it's about recognizing when we're slipping into the old ways of doing things and showing up to course correct. To see when we've scared, hurt, dismissed, or shamed our kid—and to own our impact and repair. That's what actually breaks cycles: showing our kids what it looks like to try, to struggle, to not get it right, and then how to make it right.

Let's break the 6 Core Needs down:

1. SAFE

Kids need to feel physically and emotionally safe in their home and in their relationship with their parents. They need a safe environment to express all their needs and emotions without being made to feel ashamed or punished. Safe also means safety to make mistakes without fear of physical harm or emotional withdrawal and withholding of love, attention, affection, and a willingness to care.

- Emotional safety—kids need to express their emotions without being shut down or shamed.
- Physical safety—kids need to know our stress or anger won't become their problem or hurt *them*.
- Relational safety—kids need to trust that love won't be taken away when they struggle.

This Breaks Down When:

- A parent makes their child feel ashamed or scared for having big emotions. When parents rage, yell unpredictably, or use intimidation and aggression, kids don't just experience momentary fear—they internalize the message that the world (and the people they depend on most) are unsafe.

When This Need Isn't Being Met
Kids learn to stay small, stay quiet, stay safe. They monitor moods, walk on eggshells, and learn to anticipate your disappointment before it happens. This is why relaxing feels impossible—because their nervous system is bracing for the next emotional blow.

Reparenting Yourself Now
Relaxing feels impossible because a part of you is always bracing for impact. Reparenting means teaching yourself that safety isn't something you have to earn. Your emotions aren't a problem, your worth isn't tied to how easy you are, and love isn't something that is taken away when you struggle. Every time you take up space, honor your body's call for rest without shame or guilt, or feel your feelings without shutting them down, you're showing Little You what safety really feels like. And that is how we break these cycles.

2. SOOTHED

Kids deserve comfort and care, not criticism. They deserve co-regulation, not isolation. They need a parent who can hold space for their emotional release without shutting them down or making them feel ashamed for needing to fall apart.

As parents, we must be able to manage and regulate our *own* stress to have the capability to stay calm while our kid falls apart and flails on the other end of the rope. The more we practice staying steady, the more our kids learn how to steady themselves. This is how we show them that Big Feelings aren't too much, aren't a problem, and won't make them unlovable. This is also how we teach them to regulate through painful and uncomfortable emotions without bottling them up, without shutting them down, and without rushing them to "calm down." We lovingly hold space and *stay with them* (instead of abandoning them) when things get messy and rocky.

And here's the big one: kids also need a soft place to land even when they screw up. When they make a dumb mistake, when they ignore our warnings, fall flat on their face, and come crawling back after we told them this would happen, we need to be there for them. Most of us didn't get that, so we need to do better for our kids. They need to know that messing up doesn't make them unworthy of love.

This Breaks Down When:
- A parent refuses to comfort a child who is struggling. When a child is told they "shouldn't" be so upset or when a parent punishes a child for expressing their emotions. Emotional regulation is a learned skill—and it's learned through co-regulation with a parent who can show them how to navigate hard feelings safely.

When This Need Isn't Being Met
Kids become an expert at self-soothing in secret (see "Good" Kid Check Engine Light #10, Hidden Self-Soothing Behaviors, in the next chapter). They learn to push through, hold it together, cry alone. Asking for help feels shameful and forbidden and admitting you need comfort feels wrong.

Reparenting Yourself Now
When you're overwhelmed, your instinct is to shut down, isolate and pretend you're fine. I call this "Turtling"—I pull into my shell and it takes an *incredible* amount of strength to push through the shame and say or type out the words, "I am not okay. I need support." But you deserve comfort—you did then and you do now.

If you don't consciously and intentionally soothe yourself, your body will find another way. This is how we end up with Hidden Self-Soothing Behaviors (emotional eating, skin picking, online shopping, scrolling for way too long on social media, etc.) that can bring short-term relief but create bigger problems in the long run. The key is to notice we need soothing and meet that need on purpose, in a healthy way that actually serves us. Call that friend who feels like a soft spot to land. Ask a safe person for a 30-second hug to help you regulate. Take a soothing bath. Put on those soft, cozy pants that make your whole body unclench and snuggle up in that soothing blanket. Take a walk to release the pressure and stress that has built up inside. Say, "Body, I see you trying to soothe and regulate. I'm listening, how can I care for you right now?" And do your best to give your body whatever it asks for.

Reparenting means dismantling the messed-up belief (really, it's a lie) that needing support makes you weak, and offering yourself kindness instead of criticism, softness, and warmth instead of shame. Reparenting means finding safe people who don't just tolerate you when you're struggling but who actually *delight* in caring for you and showing up for you. Show Little You that you don't have to hold it all alone anymore. Reparenting also means sitting with the parts of us that feel unworthy and carry all that old shame and say:

- "I will not leave you. I will stay with you."
- "You are not bad. You are hurting. And I will take care of you."

Because healing from Relational Shame Trauma isn't about never feeling shame again. It's about learning how to hold ourselves through it—without abandoning, shaming, or rejecting the younger versions of us that still desperately need love.

3. SEEN

Kids deserve to feel truly known and understood, not just managed, tolerated, or praised only when they get it "right."

Kids need their parents to see beyond the behavior—to recognize that meltdowns, outbursts, and acting out aren't about manipulation or defiance... they're a release, a sign that their nervous system is overloaded, overwhelmed, and out of options. Their real self is still there, underneath the dysregulation. They need parents who are adjusting their expectations in real-time, not frustration for failing to meet impossible standards. Kids also need to be noticed for who they are, not just how well they behave and what they do right.

This Breaks Down When:
- We assume kids are choosing to act out instead of recognizing that they're overwhelmed. When we take their struggles personally, expect them to "know better," or make them feel like they've let us down for not handling things perfectly, they internalize the belief that struggling makes them unlovable.

When This Need Isn't Being Met

Kids learn that being "good" means not needing anything from anyone, figuring everything out on their own, and attention must be earned through excelling, behaving, or making life easier for everyone else. Shame makes kids feel *seen in the worst way*—like their "real self" is bad and if people really knew them and *found out* the "truth" about them, they wouldn't love them and they'd leave.

Reparenting Yourself Now

Reparenting is finally letting yourself be seen, not just for what you do, but for who you are inside without the perfection-based performance, without the hustle, and without the shame. See yourself the way you have always needed to be seen, and see the ways you are *trying so hard*. This means noticing when you're holding yourself to an impossible standard and Checking Your Expectations in real time. Noticing when you're hustling to be seen by someone else as "good enough." And noticing when you're pouring into others from a place of secretly wishing someone would hold space for you like that.

Reparenting means looking at Little You and saying, "I know who you really are. You don't have to do more to be worthy anymore." And looking at Today You and saying, "I see you trying" and "This is what your best looks like right now, and it is *good enough.*"

4. SECURE

Kids don't need a "perfect" parent; they need a *steady* one. They need a Confident, Loving Leader who can set and hold consistent, sturdy boundaries with warmth and reliability, not control, fear, and shame.

Some key cycles from our childhoods that we need to break to help our kids feel secure are:

- Kids need someone who can handle their big emotions without making them feel like they're bad, broken, or too powerful.
- Kids need boundaries that *hold steady* instead of collapsing under pressure and turning into a power struggle.
- Kids need parents who learn how to stop taking their outbursts and resistance as personal attacks, shifting from Critical to Curious and finding neutral ground (instead of going cold).
- Kids need to feel that their emotions don't threaten the relationship.
- Kids need us to recognize when we're expecting them to hold boundaries for themselves way before they're capable—and not make them feel ashamed and punished when they can't.

This Breaks Down When:

- When we're afraid to say no because we don't want to deal with our kid's meltdown, or when their big emotions trigger something in us and we react out of frustration, fear, or guilt, they start to feel like *they* are the ones in charge. Instead of feeling safe, they feel powerful in a way that actually makes them more anxious and unsettled. If boundaries are only sporadically enforced—they'll keep testing. Not because they're bad or "manipulative," but because they're prompting us to give them stability they need *and* want.

Without a parent who feels steady and confident in their leadership, kids either try to take on that role themselves, or they shrink, becoming hyper-aware of how to avoid upsetting others. Either way, they don't get to just *be* a kid. They learn that boundaries mean conflict, rejection, or unpredictability, instead of something that actually helps them feel safe and loved. Kids also need a parent who will actually parent—not tell them something once and then expect them to hold the boundary for themselves, and then be ashamed if they can't.

As quoted in Janet Lansbury's book *No Bad Kids: Toddler discipline without shame*, educator Janet Gonzalez-Mena describes the "Boundaries Bridge" as having railings that provide security for kids as they navigate their world. The way I think about this is that we, as parents, are the planks of that bridge. Our kids need to feel like they are walking on solid, sturdy planks—not wobbly, unpredictable ones. When we avoid saying no to prevent a meltdown, or react out of frustration, fear, or guilt, they don't feel reassured—they feel like they're in charge, which is overwhelming.

When boundaries are inconsistent, our kids' nervous system compels them to check: can I trust this rule? Can I trust you to hold it even if I push back? Just like someone crossing an unstable bridge who instinctively pushes against the planks, trying to find solid ground. If whining, begging, or escalating has worked before to get you to change your mind, they'll try harder before giving up—this is called an "extinction burst." But if we stay firm—not cold, not cruel, just steady—they stop testing. Not immediately, but eventually, because their brain registers: *This plank is solid. I can trust it. We can move on.*

The reality is, we will be wobbly planks sometimes—parenting is unrelenting, we weren't raised to regulate our emotions and we weren't given a sturdy Boundaries Bridge to walk on ourselves. We were expected to hold ourselves to impossible standards, without guidance or repair when we fell short. And that's what we're breaking here: we're showing our kids that boundaries don't have to come with shame and rejection. We don't have to get it right every time—we just have to be steady enough, often enough.

So when you find yourself in a power struggle, when you feel triggered and frustrated, ask yourself: *Am I being a wobbly plank on the Boundaries Bridge?* And if the answer is yes, don't shame yourself—just start there. Regulate. Steady yourself. When we can hold ourselves steady, our kids can finally stop testing. What matters most isn't never wobbling, which is impossible anyway; it's coming back to steady ourselves again and again so our kids feel the stability and security they need. By knowing we've got them, so they can be free to be a kid.

When This Need Isn't Being Met

When a child doesn't feel secure in their parent's leadership, they can end up walking on eggshells, constantly trying to predict how their parent will react. This can create a deep fear of disappointing others or a sense that their emotions are "too much" for the people around them. When a parent struggles to be consistent, kids don't know what to expect—will today's no stay a no, or will they give in if I plead for it? This uncertainty fuels more testing, not because kids enjoy it—they don't, it feels scary—but because they need to know where the boundary actually is.

Reparenting Yourself Now

Give yourself the stability and security you've never had by showing up to set and hold boundaries for *yourself*. Most of us set boundaries from a place of, "Oh gosh, here you go again. You're pathetic!" That's the approach our parents took with us. It's paralyzing and crippling, not motivating. You deserve to show up as the parent you needed:

- "You have to wake up early tomorrow and you deserve to feel good and have enough energy, so we need to turn this off, and go to bed now."
- "Those cookies were so delicious. Let's stop after this one because too much sugar tends to give you a headache and you deserve to be able to enjoy this today instead of feeling awful."
- "It makes sense that you're upset and I'm right here with you. But let's pause before reacting—I know it's tempting but you don't actually want to lash out from this place. You'll say things you can't take back that could cause hurt and damage. Let's honor that anger and we'll respond once we've settled."

Learning how to Stand By You, no matter what. Ready to help yourself regulate through the shame that flares because, when you were a kid, trying to set or hold a boundary often led to punishment, rejection, or being called *selfish*. Of course it can feel unbearable now to let someone be upset with you, when you spent your childhood keeping the peace.

But you deserve to be loyal to *yourself* and what *you* need. The people who truly love and respect you will adjust. The ones who don't have been relying on your lack of boundaries all along. Start noticing when you're walking on eggshells, second-guessing yourself, or bracing for someone's reaction.

- Ask yourself: "Are you making this decision because it's what you want, or because you're afraid they'll be mad?"

- Remind yourself: "You don't have to manage anyone else's emotions. You are safe now. You get to take up space."

Reparenting isn't about suddenly feeling fearless. It's about learning to *hold yourself steady*, even when the fear, anxiety, and shame is there. Trusting that you no longer have to earn your stability and security. Because you can create it for yourself.

5. LOVABLE

Kids need to feel loved for who they are, not for what they do. Love should never be dangled as a reward or withdrawn as punishment. This is such an easy trap to fall into, just like our parents did, when we're frustrated, mad or disappointed. Kids need to feel like they are loved (and thus lovable) even when they're not easy to be around, achieving something impressive, or making other people happy. Kids need to believe that their authentic presence alone is enough to be accepted, loved, and belong.

This Breaks Down When:
- A parent pulls away—goes cold, gives the silent treatment, acts like their kid doesn't exist or they don't care about them anymore. This tames the child back into submission and "good behavior" by making them feel completely alone and undeserving of love right now. Our parents did this to "teach us a lesson" but the only lessons it teaches the child are that love is not guaranteed, it's conditional and dependent on their good behavior. And that love goes away when they mess up. They don't learn that mistakes are a fundamental part of being human—they learn that mistakes make them unlovable. Instead of feeling safe in their relationships, they become focused on earning approval and avoiding disappointing others at all costs.

- The other way shame undermines this core need to feel lovable is that it makes kids feel like: "My parents love me when I behave. But when I misbehave, they don't love me like that." As Cycle Breakers, we're learning how to hold them accountable with boundaries and consequences when they misbehave—but make them feel like our love is steady and there to support them through the entire thing.

When This Need Isn't Being Met

They learn that their worth as a person comes from being "good" and useful to others, so when they're not being "good," achieving, or proving their value, they feel like they're falling short. Deep down, they believe love is something they earn, not something they deserve.

They believe they are *hard to love*—that loving them is a burden on others. They believe their worth is something other people get to decide instead of it being something that is inherent and unshakably theirs.

Reparenting Yourself Now

As an adult, this belief doesn't just disappear. It follows you into your relationships, your work, your daily life. The idea that you are inherently lovable feels like a nice thought, one that makes sense for other people, but somehow not for you. Instead, you carry around the quiet fear that loving you is a burden and an inconvenience. You might even find yourself feeling surprised—or suspicious—when someone chooses to love you without conditions.

This is why slowing down feels so uncomfortable and why rest feels wrong, like laziness. It's why disappointing someone—even in small ways—can trigger an instant, crushing Shame Spiral. Because if your worth has always been tied to *what you do* instead of *who you are*, then stopping the performance feels too risky because what if they "find out?"

But the truth is, love shouldn't be something you ever have to perform for. It shouldn't have been something that disappeared when you were struggling. Love should have never been something you had to convince people to give you by being likeable, impressive, and never annoying or "too much." That is how many of us felt in childhood—but that wasn't a reflection of *us* and our worth. All of that was never truth—that was evidence of what we survived.

Reparenting yourself now means reminding Today You, Little You and the Parts of you that still believe love is conditional: "You are not hard to love. You are not a burden. You don't have to earn your worth—you already have it. And I'm not going anywhere—I will stay with you, no matter what."

6. FEELING BEING

For generations, we've been taught that thinking is superior to feeling. Western culture has long valued logic and reason above all else, reinforcing the idea that emotions are inconvenient at best and a sign of weakness at worst. We were told to "think things through," to "not be so sensitive." The unspoken message was clear: don't feel. Think. Stay calm, composed, and in control at all times.

We stuffed our emotions down. We numbed them. We ignored them. But neuroscience, psychology, and behavioral research all confirm that we are, and always have been, Feeling Beings who occasionally think—not Thinking Beings who occasionally feel. Emotions don't just happen in the background of our lives; they drive everything. They shape our relationships, guide our decisions, and influence every action we take. In fact, logic and reason usually show up after an emotional decision has already been made, working to justify what we've already felt.

This Breaks Down When...

- Children are expected to suppress emotions instead of express them. When Big Feelings like sadness, frustration, and anger are punished, ignored, or shamed, kids don't learn how to regulate—they learn how to hide.

A child's resistance isn't defiance; it's their body's attempt to regulate those Big Feelings. Kids resist to release to regulate. So the pushback, the tears, the outbursts? Those aren't bad behavior—they are the release that allows their nervous system to regulate and come back to balance. This is so tricky and triggering because when we were kids, our parents treated us with rejection, punishment, or coldness in those types of moments.

When This Need Isn't Being Met

Kids will bottle and suppress their feelings to avoid getting in trouble and then have to find *some way* to soothe and regulate. Suppressed emotions build up and cause other problems like headaches, digestive distress, and tension in the body. This is where we see kids turn to Hidden Self-Soothing like emotional eating, picking their scabs or skin—just trying to find a way to stop hurting and feel better. Kids feel shame about this already, like, "What is wrong with me? Why do I do this to myself?" That shame is so overwhelming that they have to soothe through that, too, and it keeps the cycle going. This is why we *must* see this as our kid just trying to stop hurting and feel better—and approach with that loving, understanding energy. More on this in Hidden Self-Soothing Behaviors, coming up next.

Reparenting Yourself Now

You spent your whole life trying to be a Good Kid, believing that your natural emotional self was wrong, bad, and a burden. You forced yourself into the role of a Thinking Being, suppressing everything that wasn't logical, digestible, or easy for others. Maybe you battled anxiety, depression, an eating disorder, addiction—all the ways your body tried to cope with the unbearable pressure of pretending emotions didn't exist.

Emotions aren't dangerous. You were never meant to earn permission to feel. Reparenting yourself now means creating space to be a Feeling Being again. It means reminding yourself, "You don't have to suppress who you are to be worthy of love. Your emotions are not too much. You are safe to feel. I've got you and I am not going anywhere."

Anger is like that friend who has your back and is incapable of just standing there quietly when someone is mistreating you. But this sacred emotion has had to just stand there quietly for decades, incapable of helping you move that charged, loaded energy out of your body. Practice letting your anger rise up to protect and take care of you—because you deserve to be loyal *to yourself* and how you feel inside.

I've helped so many clients learn how to actually *feel* their feelings by starting with frustration because it's the outlet our nervous system has been searching for all along. Shame hijacks our nervous system, shutting down anger and sadness before we even realize they're there. But frustration seems to fly under the radar, sneaking past those internal defenses, and this makes it a powerful way to tap into and release deeper emotions through a Fight Response instead of shutting it down or bottling it all up.

Immediate and profound relief from tension headaches, stomachaches, nausea, and insomnia is often right on the other side of allowing that frustration, that anger, that sadness to rise and releasing it. When you stop suppressing and start releasing, your nervous system can finally shift out of a chronic stress state (Fight/Flight) and regulate back into parasympathetic—the state where your body can rest, heal, and restore balance.

You may have to coach your body through it: "Body, let that anger/frustration/sadness come. It's safe now. I've got you, I'm going to take care of you and help you release this, so you can feel better."

Practice Standing By Yourself, fiercely defending your sacred emotions and loving yourself as hard as you can through the whole thing. Use Butterfly Tapping, Physiological Sigh and Completing the Stress Cycle (Chapter 6) to regulate your body through it.

When You or Your Kid Are Struggling... Come Back to The 6 Core Needs

When your child is melting down, acting out, or struggling, come back to these core needs.

When you are in a funk, getting snappy or shutting down from your people, come back to these core needs.

Instead of jumping to correction or control—shift from Critical to Curious:

- Is your child or Inner Child feeling unsafe?
- Are they feeling unseen?
- Do they need co-regulation and soothing?
- Do they need reassurance that they matter and are lovable?
- Are they struggling to release stress in a safe way?
- Am I avoiding a hard no because I'm afraid of my child's reaction?

The breakdown is always somewhere in there. And when we can meet them in their needs, we don't just correct their behavior—we build the foundation of resilience, emotional intelligence, and secure attachment. That's the work.

10
Seeing the Signs and Showing Up Differently

Check Engine Lights for Good Kids

As you know from experience, Good Kids hide their struggles and suffer in silence, but they have their own indicators that something deeper is happening beneath the surface and they need our support. These signs often reflect Relational Shame, emotional suppression and an internalized pressure to perform, please, and avoid conflict. Recognizing these indicators allows you to offer connection, support, and boundaries instead of assuming that if you're not seeing any struggles on the outside… they're fine.

By approaching these "Check Engine Lights" within ourselves and our children with curiosity and compassion, you can uncover the unmet needs beneath the behavior, offering our kids and ourselves the safety, support and connection we all truly need and deserve.

1. Perfectionism and Debilitating Fear of Failure

What It Looks Like
Over-apologizing for minor mistakes, avoiding tasks they struggle with, paralyzed by a fear of getting it wrong and excessively seeking reassurance about their performance.

The Deeper Struggles
They've internalized the belief that their worth and value isn't in who they are, but in what they do. Failure doesn't just feel

like a mistake; it feels like a betrayal of the unspoken contract between them and the people they seek approval from—usually parents, teachers, or other authority figures. Messing up feels like letting people down in a way that threatens the relationship and connection they need. Deep down, they fear that if they fall short, then approval, affection, and even love might be taken away.

Where to Start (Parenting a Good Kid)

Instead of reinforcing achievement-based validation and perfect outcomes, focus on their effort, growth, pushing through frustration, creativity, problem-solving, self-compassion and resilience. One of the most impactful things we can start doing is to normalize and humanize struggling and making mistakes, modeling self-compassion when we struggle with something or mess up. Let them overhear you lovingly talk yourself through it without reproach and Stand By Yourself without beating yourself up—"I see you trying. This is hard. I've got you and I believe in you, keep going."

What They Need to Hear

- "This is what your best looks like right now and your best is good enough."
- "I still love you—and you are still lovable—when you mess up."
- "You don't have to prove anything to me. I already think you're incredible."

Where to Start (Reparenting Yourself)

Healing starts with giving yourself permission to be human—to mess up, to struggle, to not have all the answers and Stand By Yourself.

What Your Inner Child Needs to Hear
- "This is what your best looks like right now and your best is good enough."
- "Failure and mistakes are proof you're trying and being brave, not proof that you're bad or unlovable."
- "I love how hard you tried. I'm proud of you for sticking with it."

2. Chronic People Pleasing

What It Looks Like
Saying "yes" automatically, to everything. Asking, "Are you mad at me?" after a conversation, text, or even just a slight change in tone. Feeling intensely uncomfortable when someone is upset with them—racing to fix it, over-apologizing, or smoothing things over to "get back in good favor." Monitoring people's mood constantly, looking for any evidence that they're in trouble.

The Deeper Struggles
Good Kid people pleasing isn't just about being "nice"—it's a desperate attempt by their brain and nervous system to stay emotionally safe because being easy, agreeable, and pleasant keeps them in good standing with others. Over time, this pattern becomes automatic—agree first, suppress everything, pretend you're fine.

One of the most invisible forms of people pleasing is the desperate need to make sure everything is okay in a relationship because of a core fear that love and conflict can't exist at the same time. It feels like someone can't be mad at them and still love them. They don't just fear the conflict itself—they fear what it means about them:

- "If they're mad, does that mean I messed up too badly this time?"
- "If they're annoyed with me, does that mean they don't like me anymore?"
- "If they're disappointed, that means I am a disappointment."

So they scramble to fix it. Over-apologizing, smoothing things over and doubling down on the people pleasing because they have learned that keeping the peace means keeping the relationship.

Where to Start (Parenting a Good Kid)

We don't mean to teach our kids to people please, but it can happen in the tiniest, most unintentional ways—like when we sigh or tense up when they ask for something, when we get irritated when they say no or push back, and when we withdraw when we're upset. Over time, this makes them feel like they have to people please to stay safe and connected.

Your child may feel like speaking up and telling you what they actually feel and need are a burden. I need you to help those things feel safe. But before you run to tell your child, "You're not a burden"—I'm going to stop you right there. We will *all* make kids feel like a burden sometimes. Myself included. Parenting is so damn unrelenting; we are trying to parent in ways we have never seen or been taught all while facing our own stuff and showing up for the agony of learning how to be brave with our boundaries and say no without going into Fight/Flight.

We need to get curious and notice our impact in these moments. And we need to show up to have these uncomfortable, "brutiful" (brutal + beautiful, thank you Glennon Doyle) conversations with our kids about this generational struggle of feeling like a burden. Because being told "You're not a burden" by your parents while very much *feeling like a burden* creates another painful internal conflict for kids—because which one is true? For Good Kids, this disparity creates Relational Shame—the deep, gut-level belief that their presence, needs, and emotions are inherently too much.

Kids are wired to pick up on our tone, body language, and energy more than the words we say. If they feel like their emotions, needs, or struggles make us overwhelmed or annoyed, they think, "I'm too much," "I need to handle this on my own," and "I have to need less to keep from burdening my parents." Kids are not capable of the critical thinking required to get to, "Their response wasn't about me—they're just having a hard day." Instead, they absorb the experience as truth about themselves, not about us. And that truth, if reinforced enough times, doesn't stay in childhood—it follows them into adulthood.

Pay attention to how your kid reacts when you're frustrated or upset. Do they scramble to please you? Do they apologize even when they haven't done anything wrong? Do they shrink or jump to help you? These are signs they're feeling like they need to manage your emotions instead of feeling safe to have their own.

After a tense moment or conflict with them, don't just move on—show up to talk about what happened, take responsibility, and apologize for your actions and impact on them. The way we respond to their emotions and needs teaches them whether it's safe to express themselves freely in their relationships. We don't have to do this perfectly, but over time, this reinforces what it feels like for someone to be upset with them but still loved. We must commit to noticing our impact and showing up for it by saying something like, "You asked me for help, and I sighed really loudly. I'm sorry if that made you feel like you were a burden. You're not—I'm just running on fumes today. But I love helping you, and thank you for telling me what you need."

Show your child that it's okay for people to be upset, and that it's not their responsibility to make everything okay. Work on healing your own people pleasing and let them see *you* letting others have their feelings without scrambling to fix, apologize, or smooth things over. Let them see you hold your ground, let someone be mad, and not shrink or over-explain to make it better. Your kid will learn they can do the same, *and* they'll start to believe they deserve to do that, too. When they push back or say no, *cheer them on* for disappointing you instead of disappointing themselves.

The goal isn't just to tell them that their needs matter—it's to show them, over and over again, that love isn't something they have to earn by being easy, agreeable, or small. Standing By Them and loving them through the messy moments.

What They Need to Hear

- "Loving people doesn't mean saying yes when you mean no."
- "It's not your job to manage my feelings. I'm working on managing my feelings better in the future."
- "It's safe for us to love each other and feel frustrated with each other sometimes."

Where to Start (Reparenting Yourself)

Most advice about overcoming people pleasing stops at, "Just say no and set boundaries!" But come on, it is not that damn simple, and it pisses me off. The real work isn't in what we say—it's in how we regulate and calm our nervous system and Inner Critic so they will *allow us* to say it in the first place. Healing people pleasing means slowly teaching our nervous system that it is actually safe to disappoint people and be misunderstood. The same way we reassure our kids when they're overwhelmed, we have to be that steady, loving presence for our Inner Child. Approach our triggers with curiosity, see our Inner Child's fear, panic, and terror, and recognize when they are spiraling and gently tell them: "I see you. I've got you. I love you."

Because people pleasing is born from Relational Trauma, it also has to be healed in relationships. Healing happens when someone shows up for you—not when you're at your best, but when you're at your messiest: when you've made mistakes, when you're feeling unlovable. That's how you start to believe you deserve it so you can start doing that for yourself.

What Your Inner Child Needs to Hear
- "That must have been so hard to keep everyone happy just to feel safe."
- "You are not a burden. It's a privilege and an honor to take care of you."
- "Let them be mad. You haven't done anything wrong. I've got you."

3. Bottling Their Emotions

What It Looks Like
This looks like brushing off sadness, frustration, or disappointment with a laugh or a joke, saying "I'm fine" when they're clearly not, and exploding over the slightest thing after holding everything in for too long. They might be numbing out with screens, food, or distractions instead of acknowledging feelings or having an hour-long meltdown over something seemingly insignificant, like stubbing their toe.

The Deeper Struggles
For Good Kids, emotions feel dangerous. When expressing frustration leads to being labeled "disrespectful" and sadness is met with "You're fine. Get over it," their nervous system learned to shut it down before it even reaches the surface to avoid rejection, disapproval, abandonment, and the possibility of punishment.

After years of ignoring their emotions and *focusing out* to monitor and manage other people's emotions, Good Kids lose touch with what *they* even feel. Ask them what's wrong, and they might say "I don't know." Not because they're hiding it, but because they've been so conditioned to ignore their feelings that they genuinely can't name them anymore. This makes emotional regulation even harder. How can they process what they don't recognize? Instead of addressing emotions as they come, they build up until they overflow in ways they can't control—like random outbursts, panic attacks, or complete shutdown.

Where to Start (Parenting a Good Kid)

When your child is releasing feelings, your job is to *allow* it to happen—not to rush them to the part where they see it'll be okay, not to get them to understand the bigger picture, not to minimize it because it won't matter in the grand scheme of things. When all of *your* feelings were shamed or punished, it can be *hella* triggering to sit with your child while they fall apart. You might feel an overwhelming urge to jump in and rescue them. You might feel like letting them sit with overwhelming emotions is abandoning them. But that's not the truth—that's your *own* Relational Trauma talking.

This is where you break the cycle. *Hold steady,* and that's it. Give your child what you never got to experience—someone staying close, staying warm, staying present, while the storm passes. You show them that emotions aren't dangerous, that their feelings won't make them unlovable, that they don't have to hold this alone.

Good Kids will stub their toe and fall apart, or spiral down over something their teacher said. On the surface, it doesn't make sense. But these "over" reactions happen because they've been bottling up emotions for so long their body can't contain it anymore. The Thing is *not* The Thing. It's not really about the toe, or the teacher—this is their body masterfully facilitating a release, regulating the only way it knows how. *Trust, trust, trust.* Do not shut it down or talk them out of it. Get out of the way and stand by, staying warm and curious.

Trust that it does feel this big, this overwhelming, this scary, this hopeless *to them right now.* Stand By Them. Once their nervous system has completed its process, they'll see that this isn't actually the end of the world. If you don't know what to say, use The Magic 9—the nine words all humans need to hear when they're struggling: "I see you. I've got you. I love you." That's it. Your trust in their ability to release and recover teaches them that emotions *aren't* dangerous—and that they don't have to carry them alone.

And then comes the Shame Spiral. Good Kids, especially, start to panic mid-release, fearing they've "overstayed their welcome" in their pain. They believe they're only allowed so much time to struggle before they become *too much*—before they risk rejection, before they push people away. But their body isn't fully regulated yet, so the tears won't stop, the frustration lingers, they stay stuck in resistance. This is when they need you to keep holding steady, to show them their feelings are not a problem, that they don't have to shove everything down just to keep your love.

What They Need to Hear

- "I think I've made it feel scary to upset me, is that how it feels? I'm learning how to be okay with you needing to be mad at me sometimes."
- "Sometimes, I wonder if you're pushing your feelings down to avoid making me mad or letting me down. I want to help you feel safe getting those feelings out with me."
- "You don't have to pretend you're fine when you're not."
- "I see you trying to hold it in. But you don't have to—it's safe to let your body release. I've got you."

Where to Start (Reparenting Yourself)
You learned that showing big emotions made you "difficult" or "too much," so you pushed them down. But bottling them up only hurts you. Practice letting your emotions come up without judging them.

What Your Inner Child Needs to Hear
- "I'm sorry for the ways I've made you feel like you and your Big Feelings were too much for me."
- "It's okay to feel angry, sad, frustrated, scared, etc. I'm right here and I've got you."
- "You don't need to push your feelings down to avoid making them mad or letting them down. We're going to let them be mad or disappointed—and it's safe to get those feelings out with me."
- "We're not pretending we're fine when we're not anymore. We deserve better."

4. Anxiety and Hypervigilance (Being on Edge/on High Alert)

What It Looks Like
Constantly worrying about making mistakes or upsetting others, vigilantly watching the environment and other people's moods, overthinking interactions and replaying conversations, being overly focused on rules and routines—not out of preference, but out of fear of what will happen if they don't.

The Deeper Struggles
Good Kids feel that love and approval are *fragile*, so their nervous system adapts by constantly scanning for signs that something is "off." A sigh, a change in tone, a look—anything that might mean someone is disappointed or upset with them can feel like a threat to their belonging. They're not just

overthinking—they're on high alert, bracing for the moment they might be in trouble, might let someone down, or might be seen as "too much" or "not good enough."

They don't just fear making mistakes—they fear what those mistakes mean about their inherent value and worth. Every interaction feels like a test: *Am I still okay with them? Do they still like me? Did I do something wrong?*

When the world feels unpredictable and other people's emotions feel like potential danger, control becomes the antidote. If they can follow every rule, plan every detail, anticipate every possible outcome, maybe—just maybe—they can prevent the feelings of shame and panic that come with getting it "wrong." Being overly controlling isn't about wanting power—it's about managing fear and trying to find safety.

Where to Start (Parenting a Good Kid)

I need you to notice how you react when your kid is anxious and on edge. Notice if you dismiss it as ridiculous or dramatic. Notice if you make them feel like they *shouldn't* feel that way. Notice if you expect them to shut it off like a light switch. They're not choosing to be this way. Their nervous system is stuck in survival mode, and they need us to help them and be their safe place.

First, you need to be calm, rational, and regulated. Breathe into your belly. Do it again. Steady yourself. If we come in tense, dismissive, or impatient, we'll only add to their overwhelm and make them feel ashamed for feeling and struggling like this. Remember that we set the emotional tone of the interaction.

Then meet their fear with curiosity. Saying, "That's ridiculous. Nobody is mad at you" may be true, but it doesn't make them feel safe. When their anxiety is high, their thinking brain is offline. This isn't the time for logic or pep talks; it's time for validation and co-regulation by sitting with them and helping them work through their emotions. Try,

"It sounds like you're really worried about how that went." Help them feel safe first, problem-solve second.

We worry that validating anxiety will make it worse, that if we acknowledge their fears, we're somehow reinforcing them as *real and true and correct*. So we rush to talk them out of it, to reassure them, to explain all the reasons why they don't need to feel this way. But this just makes them feel even more alone and ashamed for "being dramatic" and "overreacting."

When a child is stuck in an anxious spiral, they don't need logic—they need to feel seen and understood. They need us to stop focusing on whether their fears are rational and instead see that *this is how it feels inside for them right now*. And when we meet them with curiosity and validation, we help their nervous system feel safe enough to settle. And once that happens, they can regulate down. But they can't get there on their own. They need us to walk them back to safety first.

Hold space for their fear and trust that it feels very real and very scary for them. Instead of pushing them to "calm down," become their solid ground. Trust that their nervous system knows how to settle—once it feels safe enough to do so.

What They Need to Hear

- "Tell me more about how it feels inside."
- "You're not in trouble. You are safe with me, no matter how big this feels."
- "Your brain is working really hard to keep you safe right now. But you don't have to figure this out alone. I'm here."
- "It's okay if this doesn't make sense to me. It makes sense to you—so let's sit with it together."

Where to Start (Reparenting Yourself)

Just like we wouldn't expect a dysregulated child to *think* their way out of panic, we can't expect ourselves to simply convince our Inner Child that they are safe. We have to *show* them. When our brain starts spiraling, it's a sign that our nervous system is on high alert, scanning for danger. Instead of shaming ourselves for overreacting, we can pause and recognize: "Oh, this is my hypervigilant Part trying to keep me safe."

You need to speak to your Inner Child with compassion: *You're scared, but you're safe. We're going through this together.* If we don't feel safe inside our body, we will always look for safety outside of ourselves—through people pleasing, hypervigilance, or trying to control everything.

This work feels uncomfortable and excruciating because it's activating our Relational Shame Trauma, and it goes against everything we were wired to believe. But, every time we sit with the discomfort and tolerate the struggle, we are reteaching our nervous system that love doesn't get taken away when we stop people pleasing, that our worth isn't tied to keeping everyone happy, and that safety isn't found in hypervigilance—it's found inside of *us*.

What Your Inner Child Needs to Hear
- "I know everything feels scary and overwhelming right now. But I promise, you are safe."
- "It makes sense that you're scared—this feels familiar. But I've got you, I am right here and I will not leave you. We're going to get through this together."
- "You don't have to chase love from people by shapeshifting into a 'more likable or lovable' version of yourself—You deserve it by just being you."

5. Only Having Two Speeds: 150mph or Crashing and Burning

What It Looks Like
Going all in on school, work, or responsibilities—pushing through exhaustion, ignoring stress, and overextending until they physically can't anymore. Alternating between being

super productive and completely shut down—either handling everything or struggling to do anything at all. Dissociating or zoning out when overwhelmed—staring at a screen for hours, scrolling mindlessly, or feeling detached from their body and surroundings. Feeling guilty when resting, like they're "wasting time" or "falling behind," even when they're completely depleted.

Their nervous system is either in overdrive (150mph) or completely offline (burnout)—but never balanced.

The Deeper Struggles

In Internal Family Systems (IFS) Parts Work, we see that Good Kids often have two polarized Parts working against each other:

- The Overfunctioning Part: *Go, go, go! Handle everything! Don't let anyone down! Don't let anyone see you sweat!*
- The Underfunctioning Part: *If you're not going to slow down, I'll have to handle this myself and put you into Functional Freeze, or force you into a horizontal position with a Stress Crash (Dorsal Vagal Shutdown).*

These two Parts pull in opposite directions, leaving them trapped in a cycle of extremes. The Overfunctioning Part drives them to achieve, help, and overperform to feel worthy. But when the weight becomes too much, the Underfunctioning Part slams on the brakes. Neither state feels good, but both feel necessary for survival.

This "all or nothing" pattern is deeply tied to the nervous system. Research in Polyvagal Theory shows that when a child experiences chronic stress, shame, or the need to perform for love, their nervous system learns to toggle between Sympathetic Overdrive (Fight/Flight) and Dorsal Vagal Shutdown (Freeze/dissociation)—with little ability to regulate in between.

- Fight/Flight (150mph mode): They push themselves past their limits, trying to stay in control and avoid feelings of inadequacy.
- Freeze (Burnout mode): When they can't keep up anymore, their body shuts down as a protective response, leaving them exhausted, detached, and unable to function.

Because they were never taught how to slow down safely, they only know how to crash. They were conditioned to believe that rest is lazy and worth is earned through accomplishments, so they don't allow themselves to slow down until their body forces them to.

Good Kids were often raised in environments where rest was a reward, not a necessity. They learned that being productive means being "good," (and worthy, lovable and deserving of love) so their nervous system never learned how to exist in neutral. They don't know how to work at a sustainable pace because they were either pushed to achieve or shamed for "slacking off." It's an exhausting cycle of overworking, shutting down, feeling guilty for shutting down, and overworking again.

Where to Start (Parenting a Good Kid)
We have to break these shame-driven cycles of burnout—not just for our kids, but for ourselves. If we are pushing through exhaustion, ignoring stress, and only stopping when our body forces us to crash, our kids learn that they should, too, and that rest is something you have to earn. That the only way to be "good enough" is to push yourself to the edge of collapse.

If we want them to feel safe setting limits and saying, "I can't do that right now" without guilt or feeling ashamed, then our reaction when they set boundaries has to feel like cheering them on, not shaming them.

Model rest as a right, not a reward, and pay attention to how you talk about exhaustion. Do you glorify being overworked?

Do you praise yourself (or others) for "powering through" instead of honoring what your body needs? Show them what it's like to disappoint others in the name of self-care. If we want our kids to be able to tolerate disappointing others without spiraling into shame, they need to see us do it. Let them witness you being brave and saying no, speaking up for what they need, and not over-explaining or apologizing for it.

Instead of saying "I can't take a break, there's too much to do," let them hear you say:

- "I'm feeling drained. I'm going to take a break because I deserve to rest before I hit my limit."
- "My body is telling me I need to slow down, and I am going to listen."
- "I'd love to help our neighbor next week, but I can't take that on right now."

Now, as a parent, when your child says, "I can't do this right now," you might feel frustrated, disappointment, or the urge to push them harder, not because you don't love them, but because you were never given permission to say those words yourself. And now, hearing them from your child feels unfamiliar, maybe even triggering. That's your conditioning talking—it's the Parts of you that believe they need to "motivate" you to be *more lovable* by pushing through.

Instead, when they tell you they've hit a limit in their capabilities, let them see relief in your face, not disappointment. Let them feel that their limits are safe with you and they don't have to fight you to honor what they need. In doing so, you give yourself something you never had: rest, permission to say no, and a guilt- and shame-free boundary.

Because the truth is if we want a different outcome for our kids, we need to get curious and ask them to tell us more when they tell us they can't do something. It's not manipulation. It's not a weakness. They're not being lazy. It's an honest, vulnerable and brave expression of their limits. And our response will teach them one of two things:

- Their limits are valid and deserve to be honored.
- Their limits are unacceptable, and they must override them to be lovable and worthy.

If you feel disappointment creep in, pause and Check Your Expectations.

- Am I expecting them to push through just because I had to?
- Am I projecting my own stuff about hustling and needing to earn rest onto them?
- Am I hearing their "I can't" as an excuse because I was never allowed to say it?

They need to know that their worth is not tied to their productivity, and that when they take care of themselves and honor their capacity, we are going to cheer them on.

"But if I let my kid rest every time they ask, they will just be a lazy bum and never accomplish anything."—Parents everywhere, panicking.

I get it. We don't want to raise kids who give up the second something gets hard. And yes, sometimes we do need to gently nudge them to keep going, to help them stretch outside their comfort zone in a way that builds confidence. But that's not what this is about. Most kids *want* to do things. They want to learn, grow, and accomplish things. They don't want to be lazy. What I'm suggesting here is that we *trust them* and don't default to "They're just being dramatic" or "They're not really that tired". Actually listen. Recognize that pushing through is not always the right lesson. Learning to honor their own limits is just as important as learning to push past them.

When we don't trust them, they learn that other people know better than they do about what they can handle. When their body says *"I need a break,"* they learn to ignore it, that their feelings aren't reliable, and that their limits don't matter.

What They Need to Hear

- "I know saying no is hard, and I'm proud of you for telling me what you need."
- "Thank you for listening to yourself."
- "I love that you're honoring your limits."

Where to Start (Reparenting Yourself)

If you grew up as a Good Kid, you probably weren't taught to trust yourself. So now, as an adult, you work through exhaustion, ignore stress, and only stop when your body forces you to crash. And when you finally slow down? The guilt creeps in. The voice saying, "You should be doing more" and "You haven't worked hard enough today to be this tired" and "You don't deserve to rest yet."

Please hear me when I call such bullshit on this: rest is not failure or laziness. Rest is a *basic human need*. And healing these debilitating and demoralizing cycles of burnout means teaching your nervous system that it is safe now to slow down. You don't have to work yourself into the ground, hustle, and prove your worth. You are enough, even when you're not producing something.

The next time you feel guilt for resting, ask yourself:

- Would I ever expect someone I love to push through like this?
- What am I afraid will happen if I slow down?
- Who benefits from me believing that rest is selfish?

That shame around resting? That voice telling you to "suck it up" and "push through?" That is the voice of the shame-laced system that conditioned you to believe your worth is tied to your accomplishments. It's time to stand up and challenge it.

Practice taking it down a notch and resting before you're fully depleted. Start noticing when you convince yourself you'll rest after everything is done—except everything is never done and you never get that rest. Instead of waiting for a stress crash, practice resting before you hit your limit. Say to yourself, "You deserve to rest before you crash" or "Your body is asking you to slow down, and you are going to listen." At first, this will feel bad and wrong... but lovingly remind yourself: feeling guilty for resting just means you're doing something new that should have always felt safe to do because it is a basic human need.

For so many of us, being good meant being helpful, responsible, hardworking. Our worth felt like it existed in what we could do for others. So now, when we stop, we feel like we are nothing. But your value does not disappear when you slow down.

What Your Inner Child Needs to Hear
- "I love you on your 'laziest' day."
- "It is safe to slow down. I will take care of you."
- "You are lovable when you're productive and you are lovable when you rest."

6. Chronic Overachieving

What It Looks Like
Obsessing over performance and feeling like they have to not just do well, but be *the best* at everything they take on, over-preparing for everything, rehearsing conversations to make sure they "get it right," struggling to celebrate accomplishments and immediately focusing on what they should have done better or what's coming up next. Struggling to enjoy the process—being so focused on proving something through achievement that they miss out on actual fulfillment or joy.

The Deeper Struggles

For Good Kids, overachieving is about proving their worth and value. They've learned that being easy, capable, and self-sufficient is what earns them approval, so they push themselves relentlessly, not just to succeed, but to make it look *effortless*.

Struggling, asking for help, or showing signs of stress or struggle feels like failure because it risks exposing that they're not as "good" and "put together" as everyone believes. Overachievers don't just want to succeed—they feel like failure is not an option. Studies on perfectionism show that high-achievers often push themselves, not because they love the challenge, but because slowing down or failing feels like proof that they're not good enough. Instead of learning resilience, they develop anxiety-driven success—where achievements temporarily soothe the fear of inadequacy, but the cycle always resets and they're back to proving their worth with achievements.

Rest feels undeserved unless they've worked themselves to exhaustion first. Slowing down means facing the feelings they've been avoiding—the self-doubt, the exhaustion, the fear that if they're not constantly proving themselves, they'll fade into the background.

Where to Start (Parenting a Good Kid)

Overachieving looks impressive, but it's often driven not by confidence, but by fear of failure and the terror of being exposed as "not enough." When a child ties their worth to their achievements, they are hustling for approval, safety, and belonging.

If we only praise them for being the best, the smartest, the hardest worker, they internalize the belief that they must keep proving themselves to be worthy, and that their value exists in what they do, not who they are. If we only notice them when they're accomplishing, they learn that their worth disappears when they slow down. And if, when they struggle or fall short, we predictably show up with the energy of "I expected more from you" and "I'm not mad, I'm just disappointed," they will anxiously *hide* their struggles from us and *punish* themselves into succeeding. Not for themselves and their highest good, but out of the crushing fear of disappointing or letting us down. This is how perfectionism and overachieving become their identity—how they learn that rest is weakness, mistakes are shameful, and being anything less than exceptional is *unacceptable*.

Our job is to break these patterns before they become their identity. Focus on praising *the process*. Instead of focusing only on results—highlight how hard they tried, how they pushed through feeling frustrated and stuck, how they creatively problem-solved through it. This helps them build intrinsic motivation—where they value learning and growing *for themselves*, not just to impress others to see you as "good" and "good enough."

We need to make space for mistakes and imperfection. Overachievers fear failure because they believe it will make others see them as less lovable and maybe even exposed as a "fraud." We have to *normalize* and humanize mistakes and help them see that learning is more valuable than being perfect.

When we let our kids be human with human limits, they learn that their worth isn't tied to being perfect, impressive, or constantly achieving. They get to be enough, exactly as they are.

What They Need to Hear

- "I love how you got frustrated and stuck but you steadied yourself and kept going."
- "Do you actually want to do this? It's okay to change your mind."
- "Mistakes mean you're trying and you get to be proud of that, I know I am. What did you learn from this?"

Where to Start (Reparenting Yourself)

Overachieving is a survival strategy. When you grew up earning your worth through success, it felt like the only way to stay safe, loved, and valuable. So now, as an adult, you might not even know who you are without an achievement to chase. Healing means *showing* your nervous system that you are worthy even when you're not proving it.

Start noticing the moments when you feel guilty for resting, or when your brain immediately moves the goalposts after an accomplishment. If achieving something only gives you a brief moment of relief before the pressure resets, ask yourself:

- "What are you afraid will happen if you stop proving yourself?"
- "What does your body actually need right now?"
- "Who are you, outside of what you accomplish?"

At first, these questions might bring up panic, discomfort, or even grief. That's okay. It means you're starting to unlearn the idea that your value is conditional. Yay, you deserve to unlearn that.

You have to make peace with imperfection. If overachieving was your survival strategy, not doing things perfectly and making mistakes feels like it would make *you* a failure. Even small errors might send you spiraling. That's shame talking, making mistakes feel like a personal flaw within *you*. Healing means teaching yourself that you are human, and humans make mistakes sometimes. Your job is to show up and do your best—whatever that looks like—and let your best be good enough.

This is how we break these cycles. This is how we show our Inner Child that they should have never had to earn love. That their worth is not up for debate. That they don't have to hustle for belonging anymore. That *it's safe now* to just be.

What Your Inner Child Needs to Hear

- "I am proud of how hard you tried."
- "You deserve to pause and be proud of what you have done instead of being so focused on what you haven't done yet."
- "You are still lovable and worthy, even when you mess up."

7. Overapologizing (Apologizing Excessively and Fearfully)

What It Looks Like

Saying "I'm sorry" constantly, even when they have nothing to apologize for, apologizing for things that are out of their control, feeling the need to "fix" other people's emotions by apologizing before they're even mad at them.

The Deeper Struggles

When a Good Kid senses someone is upset—especially with them—it feels unsafe. They apologize to restore the connection as quickly as possible because, deep down, they believe that someone can't be mad at them and love them at the same time. They're not just saying sorry for what they did—they're saying sorry for *existing* in a way that may have upset you, trying to prove they're still "good enough" to be loved.

They fear conflict and rejection because they've learned that keeping others happy is the key to staying emotionally safe, so they default to over-apologizing as a way to smooth over tension—even when they've done nothing wrong. Conflict feels like a rejection of them, not just their actions, so they frantically scramble to undo it.

Where to Start (Parenting a "Good" Kid)

When your kid over apologizes—especially after making a mistake—it's a sign they don't know where they stand with you. They're not just seeking forgiveness for the action. They're looking for proof that you still love them. Kids need to know, even when they mess up, even when you're disappointed, even when you're upset—they are still loved, and they still matter to you. When they aren't sure, they fill the gap with apologies, hoping to hear or feel that they're still safe with you.

We need to show them what a healthy apology actually looks like. This teaches them that saying sorry is about accountability—not about erasing their discomfort or begging to be back in someone's good favor.

You have to make it feel safe for them to mess up without disappointing you. They need to hear—and feel—that nothing they do can erase their worth or their connection to us. They need to see that healthy relationships can hold disappointment, frustration, and even anger—without love being taken away, without any conditions. They need to experience this over and over again to reshape their nervous system to see conflict as something manageable and safe, not dangerous.

I'm holding your hand while I put it bluntly: throwing around the threat of our disappointment is being reckless with our impact as parents. It's Relational Shame Trauma. And we must show up to break this cycle for our kids.

Good Kids fear disappointment like abandonment and rejection. When we say, "I'm disappointed in you," they hear, "I didn't like you in this moment." They internalize the belief that being imperfect makes them less lovable. They will overapologize, overperform, and overextend themselves just to stay in our good graces. And when they can't? When they fall short? Shame rushes in. They don't just feel bad about what they did—they feel bad about *who they are*.

If they see a sigh, a shift in your tone, a cold shoulder, or a passive-aggressive comment, their nervous system registers it, and their brain tells them: *You messed up. Fix it fast, make sure they still love you.* So they scramble to get back in your good favor. They override their own feelings to make you okay with them again.

Our disappointment is often born out of unattainable expectations. Just like our parents expected of us... sometimes, we expect them to have self-awareness, emotional regulation, and impulse control far beyond their years. And when they fall short—because they're kids—we sometimes react in ways that make them feel like they are *failing us* and *letting us down*. If our child has to choose between abandoning themselves and disappointing us, they will disappoint themselves every single time. We have to try to make sure they don't have to choose.

We need to Check Our Expectations and ask ourselves:

- Are we expecting emotional maturity that they don't have yet?
- Are we making our disappointment feel bigger than the actual mistake?
- Are we reacting in a way that makes them feel like our approval is on the line?

We have to show them that love is not something they have to keep re-earning. That they are allowed to mess up and still belong. That our feelings about them don't change when they fall short. That their presence and existence does not require constant damage control.

What They Need to Hear

- "I'm frustrated about what just happened but I love you and we're going to work through it together."
- "This mistake does not change how I see you, or how much I love you."
- "What you did was a mistake. Who you are is wonderful."
- "There is nothing you could do that would make me stop loving you."

Where to Start (Reparenting Yourself)

If you were a Good Kid, you overapologized to keep the peace because this meant staying emotionally safe. Now, as an adult, you still feel that panic rise up in your chest when someone seems upset. You still feel the urge to apologize before they even say anything, just in case.

Healing means showing your nervous system that you don't have to fawn and fix your way into being loved. Right now, your body registers disappointment, hostility, and tension as a threat. That's why your Fight/Flight Response kicks in the second you sense conflict. But the truth is: you can survive someone being upset with you. It is most likely not a life or death situation, though I know it feels like it.

Stop apologizing to ease someone else's feelings and learn to sit with the discomfort of someone being mad at you. Overapologizing feels like it makes things better—but really, it trains your brain to believe that you are always the problem. You don't have to take responsibility for things that weren't yours to carry. And every time you sit with this discomfort—every time you let someone be mad and resist the urge to fawn and fix—you show your nervous system that you are safe.

At first, this will feel unbearable, but it's proof that you're healing. Every time you pause before apologizing, every time you let someone be mad without scrambling to fix it, every time you choose self-respect over people pleasing... you are breaking these cycles. You are showing Little You that love is not this fragile. You are teaching yourself that you are worthy—exactly as you are, which is what you always deserved.

What Your Inner Child Needs to Hear

- "You can survive their disappointment."
- "You are still good and worthy, even when someone is unhappy with you."
- "Love is not this fragile. I can hold myself steady, even if they're upset."

8. Being Viciously Self-Critical

What It Looks Like
Beating themselves up for even the smallest mistakes, setting impossibly high standards, feeling deep shame over things most people wouldn't even notice, dismissing accomplishments and feeling like they "should have done better," or immediately focusing on what went wrong instead of celebrating what went right. Feeling haunted by past mistakes, feeling like they have to "earn" their own kindness—only allowing themselves to rest, relax, or feel good if they've worked hard enough to deserve it.

The Deeper Struggles
Self-criticism feels like it protects them from making mistakes that could lead to judgment, disappointment, or punishment. To avoid that pain, their Inner Critic rises up to monitor them at all times. If they could catch their own mistakes before anyone else did, maybe they could avoid criticism altogether. In their mind, it's safer to tear themselves down first than to risk hearing it from someone else.

Good Kids use self-criticism as motivation, believing if they go harder on themselves, they'll avoid making mistakes in the future. But instead of helping them, this keeps them trapped in a cycle of shame, self-doubt, and emotional exhaustion. Their nervous system struggles to self-soothe and regulate from the constant self-criticism and shame.

Their self-worth is conditional; it's tied to being impressive, responsible, or easy to love. Their fragile sense of value was built on external validation instead of an internal belief in their own worth. This means that every mistake, every misstep, every moment of imperfection feels like proof that they're failing and a risk of exposing that they're not as "good" and "put together" as everyone believes.

Self-criticism and perfectionism are besties—research on perfectionism shows that many overachievers push themselves because they're terrified of failure. For Good Kids, being perfect was often the safest way to maintain love and approval—so their brain learned that any failure, no matter how small, was a threat. Instead of seeing mistakes as part of learning, they see them as evidence that they are failing as a person.

Where to Start (Parenting a "Good" Kid)

Our job is to help our kid build a new inner voice—one that isn't cruel, but kind, compassionate and encouraging, one that doesn't tear them down for struggling, but helps them feel safe enough to struggle and learn and grow.

When they spiral into being critical of themselves, don't dismiss their feelings ("You're not stupid! Don't say that!") but also don't agree with them by accident ("You're not bad at math. You just need to work harder"). Instead, help them separate themselves from their Inner Critic. This helps them externalize the harsh voice in their head—so they can start questioning it instead of just believing it.

When I notice my daughter falling into being viciously critical of herself, I have a Circle Back with her where I say, "I think I might be making you feel like nothing you do is good enough—is that how it feels for you? It's safe to tell me if I am. I want to know, so I can own the way I'm impacting you." I give her a context to understand where I was coming from: "I've struggled with feeling like nothing I ever do is good enough and sometimes, especially when I'm stressed out—I accidentally put it on others. I am so sorry I've made you feel this way—it was about me, not you. Thank you for telling me how I've been hurting you."

If we want our kids to be kinder to themselves, we have to show them what that looks like. Model it for them. They need to see us mess up and love ourselves through it, not spiral into shame or beat ourselves up. That way, they start to believe they deserve to treat themselves with kindness in these moments, too.

- Instead of: "Ugh, I'm such an idiot, I forgot my keys again." Try: *"Oops, I forgot my keys. I guess I needed a little more time this morning."*
- Instead of: "I should have done that better." Try: *"I did my best with what I knew at the time."*
- Instead of: "Ugh, I'm the worst at this." Try: *"I'm still learning. I'll get better with practice."*

Next, help them shift their mindset from "I have to be perfect" to "I'm allowed to be in progress" and "This is what my best looks like—and my best is good enough." Every time we let them be human without feeling ashamed of their messy humanity, we teach them that their worth is inherent and not up for debate.

What They Need to Hear

- "It doesn't have to be perfect, just do your best... whatever that looks like today."
- "I see you're feeling frustrated. It's okay to be frustrated with how something goes, but you deserve to Stand By Yourself and be proud of how hard you tried. I know I am."
- "I wonder where that voice comes from. Have I made you feel like mistakes aren't okay?"

Where to Start (Reparenting Yourself)

The way to heal your Inner Critic isn't by thinking your way out of it—it's by experiencing mistakes differently, with self-compassion. Self-compassion isn't about letting yourself off the hook. It's about giving yourself the same grace you give to literally every other person you encounter. It's about teaching yourself that you don't have to be perfect to be loved. And it's about showing your Inner Child that they were never too much, never not enough, and never required to hustle for their worth. They were always lovable. Exactly as they were.

At first, this will feel foreign, maybe even ridiculous. But with time, it will soothe the deepest ache of unworthiness that you've never been able to reach before—the one that taught you that love had to be earned, that mistakes made you unworthy, and that you had to perform to be valuable. And this time, instead of abandoning yourself to meet impossible standards, you'll be the one to Stand By You.

What Your Inner Child Needs to Hear
- "That must have been really hard to feel like you let someone down. I've got you, I will always stand with you."
- "You did your best with what you knew at the time."
- "You are already enough. You don't have to earn your worth."

9. Physical Complaints or Psychosomatic Symptoms

What It Looks Like
Frequent headaches, stomachaches, nausea, and muscle tension before and after social or high pressure situations, losing their appetite during stressful moments or overeating as a way to self-soothe, needing naps or extra rest but still waking up tired, difficulty sleeping, especially during stressful situations, tight shoulders, jaw clenching, restlessness, or feeling "on edge" without knowing why.

The Deeper Struggles
For Good Kids, the emotions they've held don't just disappear—they get stored in the body, showing up as physical symptoms of tension, stress, and exhaustion.

Their body is using so much energy just trying to stay "good" and keep everything under control that they're living in a chronic state of Fight/Flight because their nervous system is stuck in survival mode. When a child is conditioned to be "good" at all costs—prioritizing others, avoiding conflict, and striving for perfection—their body never fully relaxes for a sustained period of time. Even when they seem "fine" on the outside, their nervous system is on high alert, bracing for disappointment, failure, or rejection.

One of the hardest parts of psychosomatic symptoms is that their Inner Critic doesn't just dismiss their pain—it *mocks* it. Because they were conditioned to minimize their struggles and prioritize how others feel, their own suffering feels *invalid* and *embarrassing*. This disconnects them from their own body's signals, making them second-guess whether they're even allowed to be struggling. Instead of listening to what their body needs (rest, support, self-compassion), they override it—until their body has no choice but to shut them down completely.

Where to Start (Parenting a "Good" Kid)

If we want our kids to grow up knowing that their body's signals are trustworthy, we have to model what it looks like to respect those signals ourselves *and* believe them when they come to us saying, "My stomach hurts" or "I don't feel good."

The old way, from our childhoods, meant dismissing, minimizing, or unintentionally gaslighting us with "You're fine," "It's not that bad," or "It's probably just in your head." Let's break these cycles by believing and taking our kids seriously. Because whether their pain is rooted in stress, anxiety, or an actual illness—it's real to them. Instead of trying to convince them it's not a big deal, we can help them get curious about what their body is telling them:

- "I believe you that it hurts that bad. I wonder if your body is trying to tell us something."
- "Let's take a deep breath together and check in—does your body feel tense anywhere else?"
- "Your body sounds like it's holding a lot right now. Let's figure out how to help it feel safe again."

If we brush them off, they will learn to override their body's signals and push through, even when they shouldn't. If we respond with curiosity and compassion, they will learn that their feelings and experiences are valid—and that taking care of themselves isn't something they have to earn or be ashamed of.

We also have to check ourselves—how do we respond when they need rest? Do we see their exhaustion and respect it, or do we unconsciously shame them for "wasting time?" If we want them to feel safe slowing down, we have to make sure our reactions don't reinforce the belief that their value is tied to productivity.

Where to Start (Reparenting Yourself)

The long-term impact of living in Fight/Flight for most of your life doesn't just fade away when the stressor is gone. When your nervous system adapts to chronic stress, your body stays on high alert. Over time, this takes a massive toll on every system in your body—your digestion, your immune system, your sleep, your ability to focus and rest. Your body learned to function in survival mode because, for a long time… it had to.

Your symptoms aren't random. Your body is speaking in the only language it knows: pain, tension, exhaustion. Sometimes, it takes a bit to figure out exactly what it's trying to tell you. The key is learning how to respond with curiosity instead of frustration because the more you listen, the less your body will have to shout at you to get your attention.

This is where IFS (Internal Family Systems) Parts Work can be especially powerful. If a symptom had a voice, what would it say? If the headaches, the exhaustion, the stomachaches could talk—what would they tell you? Are they trying to protect you from slowing down, because rest never felt safe? Are they trying to keep you small and out of trouble? Every symptom, every tension, every ache holds a message from a Part of you that learned a long time ago how to survive. And

Seeing the Signs and Showing Up Differently

just like your younger self, those Parts deserve to be heard, held, understood, and reassured.

At first, slowing down will feel uncomfortable. Guilt will creep in. But healing means learning to challenge and set loving boundaries with your Inner Critic instead of letting it override yourself and what you need.

Your body isn't betraying you. It's been working its ass off to protect you. And now, it's time to show it—it's finally safe to rest, to release everything it's been holding, and to heal and feel safe.

What Your Inner Child Needs to Hear

- "Body, I hear you. I'm not going to ignore you anymore."
- "How can I care for you right now?"
- "It makes sense that you're holding so much—I haven't let you rest."

10. Hidden Self-Soothing Behaviors

What It Looks Like

Emotional eating, restricting eating, biting their nails or cuticles, picking at their scabs or skin, pulling their hair, excessively licking their lips, biting the inside of their mouth until it bleeds, scratching or rubbing their hands or arms until it gets raw, etc.

The Deeper Struggles

When a Good Kid has learned that expressing frustration, sadness, or overwhelm leads to rejection, punishment, or disappointment, they don't stop feeling—they just stop *showing*. Self-soothing behaviors become a quiet way to release tension without risking connection.

Many Good Kids self-soothe as a way to manage their emotions alone. Every time they pick, chew, or restrict, it's not just about the action—it's an attempt to shrink themselves, to feel less, to stay "in control."

Chewing, rubbing, picking, and repetitive motions stimulate the body's proprioceptive system, creating a momentary sense of relief and calm to fill a need for comfort and soothing to regulate. It's a smart survival strategy that helps them cope, even when they're doing their best to pretend the distress isn't there.

> ### Client Story
>
> One of my clients, a teenager named Natalie*, pulled her eyebrows as a way to self-soothe. She had worked incredibly hard to find healthier ways to regulate and she was so proud of herself. But then, life threw something really difficult at her, and her stress level exceeded her ability to cope—so Natalie started pulling again.
>
> Disappointed in herself, Natalie asked if we could bring her mom into a session. Sheepishly, she told me, "Every time Mom catches me playing with my eyebrows, she slaps my hand away."
>
> Cut to the mother–daughter session. As I was explaining what brought all of us here to her mom, Natalie's hand went up to her eyebrows. Without hesitation, her mom looked over and slapped her hand.
>
> I jumped out of my seat. "Okay," I said, staring at the pair of them, "I understand what you're trying to do—obviously, you want to keep Natalie from hurting herself." I took a deep breath. "But what you don't realize is that your reaction is like pouring gasoline on the shame fire already raging inside Natalie—and actually driving the behavior." Her mom seemed to hear me and receive what I said. I then said, "Your reaction is obviously coming from a loving place, but I really need you to commit to trying hard not to slap her like that ever again."
>
> I coached Natalie's mom through a different approach:
>
> 1. Pause. Take five deep breaths. Tell your body, "This is not an emergency."
> 2. Soften. Get curious. Stay warm and loving.
> 3. Instead of slapping her hand, gently wrap yours around it—like giving it a hug.

4. Say: "I see you. I know you're feeling like you need to do that. I'm sorry you're hurting inside right now. I think your body is trying to regulate. Can we bring your hand down gently and find a different way to soothe that doesn't hurt you?"

We brainstormed soothing alternatives:

- A long hug with back rubs
- A satisfying fidget toy
- Cuddling her beloved dog
- Crossing her arms over her chest and rubbing her arms (a butterfly hug).

This was a major turning point for Natalie. I told her I was so proud of her for speaking up and asking for help. And I told her mom I was proud of her too—for listening to the impact she was actually having without getting defensive and for being open to learning what her daughter needed instead.

What Natalie needed wasn't a parent who could stop her from pulling her eyebrows—she needed her mom to look underneath the behavior and see a child who was hurting and trying to cope. She didn't need to be made to feel bad or wrong—because that would only make the shame driving it worse, making it even harder to stop. She needed a patient parent to sit beside her, steady and loving, and help her address the real problem: a nervous system desperately trying to regulate. And most of all, she needed to feel fully loved and supported—not just once she stopped pulling, but through every step of figuring it out. Because when a child feels truly safe and unconditionally accepted, their body doesn't have to scream for relief.

(*not her real name. Shared with the permission and encouragement of this client and her parents.)

A Note About Self-Harm (Non-Suicidal Self-Injury)

If your child is cutting, the most important thing to know is that it's not about attention-seeking or manipulation—it's an attempt to cope with overwhelming emotions, with shame and guilt feeling particularly unbearable. Cutting, a form of non-suicidal self-injury (NSSI), is when someone deliberately harms their own body—often by making small cuts on their skin—as a way to release emotional pain, numb out, or regain some sense of control when everything feels too painful, too scary and too much. It might seem confusing or alarming from the outside, but for many, the physical pain of cutting feels easier to deal with than the emotional pain they're carrying inside.

It's scary to watch your kid hurt themselves, but they need you to be steady, help them feel safe and hold them, emotionally and metaphorically, through the things that feel unbearable right now. If they could just *stop*, they would. Making a child feel ashamed for cutting makes everything worse. Self-harm is often a sign that they don't yet have the tools to process what they're feeling, and punishing or shaming them will only drive them deeper into secrecy and self-loathing. What they need most is your calm, steady presence that says, *I see you, and I will help you with your pain.*

If your child is self-harming, it's important that you reach out to a mental health professional as soon as possible. They need support from someone who isn't also their parent—someone they don't feel pressure to protect, perform for, or reassure that they're okay. They don't need to hold it all together, and they don't have to pretend they're fine. The goal isn't just stopping the behavior—it's helping them find safer ways to release what's too big to carry alone and giving them the tools to regulate through Big Feelings and shame when they hit so they don't need to self-harm to get that relief.

Where to Start (Parenting a "Good" Kid)

If we want to help our kid find safer ways to regulate, our goal is to help them feel safe enough to figure out why they're needing to soothe like that and help them explore alternatives to regulate shame and Big Feelings in ways that don't also harm them. We do that by approaching them with curiosity, connection, and safe alternatives and *without* shame.

Regulate yourself before talking about it. If we come in frustrated or panicked, their nervous system will match our dysregulation and move into shame. If we're disappointed, they will feel that deeply and move into shame. When we respond with calm curiosity, their nervous system will feel safe and they'll be more open to change.

Approach them with curiosity, and don't jump to correct. This makes them feel wrong (which triggers even more shame). Validate them while asking open-ended questions, so they feel seen in this struggle before they'll be ready to hear alternatives. If they're in shame, they will resist alternatives. Focus on seeing that they are hurting and trying to feel better, and there is nothing wrong with wanting to feel better. You've got them and you will figure it out together.

When we prioritize safety, connection, and alternatives, their belief shifts from "My needs are a problem" to "My needs deserve care and so do I."

What They Need to Hear

- "I see you picking at your skin. I wonder if your body is looking for a way to release some tension. Want to try a fidget toy or squeezing your squish cube to see if that helps?"
- "I see you chewing on your sleeve. That makes sense—our mouths sometimes need something to help us regulate. Let's find something safe for chewing, like gum or a chewable necklace."
- "I wonder if your body is craving some deep pressure right now. Want to try a head massage or wrapping up in a blanket burrito instead?"

Your self-soothing behaviors were never random—they were your body's attempt to regulate when no one else was helping you. You weren't being dramatic, weak, or "bad."

You were doing the best you could with the tools you had at the time. I'm proud of your body for finding ways to help you soothe and regulate. Now, you get to give yourself better tools that help you, not hurt you.

Self-soothing isn't something to "fix." It's something to understand. The next time you catch yourself, pause and ask yourself what is really going on. Instead of shaming yourself for these behaviors, get curious about what they're helping you manage. Your body is not against you. It's trying to help you regulate and survive. Just like with a child, you can't rip away the coping strategy before you have something safer in place.

For years, your body has been doing its best to hold it all together for you. It doesn't need more shame. Your body needs a soft place to land. It needs understanding, soothing, empathy, and care. I need you to work on dismantling the shame that makes it hard to believe you deserve those things. You do. You always did. And now you get to finally give that to yourself. Needing that doesn't make you needy or pitiful—think about how wonderful it feels to give other people the understanding, the soothing, the empathy, and the care they need. You deserve to give yourself all of that, too.

Where to Start (Reparenting Yourself)

Some of our hidden self-soothing behaviors—like nail biting, skin picking, emotional eating, overworking, or scrolling for hours—are wired into our nervous system, often passed down through genetics. Research shows that anxiety, impulse control, and how we process stress and reward have a strong genetic component—which is why some of us instinctively reach for sugar when overwhelmed, while others numb out with work. These behaviors are about your brain and body trying to protect and help you regulate the only way they know how. The good news is you're not stuck here. With awareness and the right tools, you can do a lot to rewire these patterns and build self-soothing strategies that actually support you.

But when we see our kids struggling with the same self-soothing behaviors—especially the ones loaded with shame for us—it can be so damn triggering. That deep, buried shame in us flares up, and before we know it, we're shaming them too, thinking we're protecting them from the pain we know too well. But that's exactly what our parents did to us. They weren't trying to be cruel—they just couldn't face their own reflection. Shame tricks us into thinking criticism will "fix" it, but all it does is pass down the same wound: *There's something wrong with me. I'm unlovable. If people knew, they'd leave.* The work isn't forcing our kids to stop—it's healing our own shame first. Because when we do, we break the cycle and show them what it actually looks like to be loved—struggles and all.

What Your Body Needs to Hear
- "Body, what are you needing right now?"
- "What are you feeling that you haven't acknowledged yet?"
- "What would feel good to my nervous system instead?"

The 5 Adjustments

#1 Shift From Critical To Curious
We're often quick to jump to criticism when things aren't going as planned—it takes 2.5 seconds to fall into a knee-jerk reaction like, "You should be able to do this by now!" Criticism triggers shame for kids and shame triggers Fight/Flight. So when we criticize, our kid feels like, "I *do* know how to do this. They shouldn't have to tell me again... what is wrong with me?" it just makes things worse—they are even less able to cooperate and more likely to have an impulse to push back and resist. They'll cope with that Shame Spiral by lashing out

and getting vicious and aggressive, getting defensive, shutting down or getting mad at themselves.

Notice the urge to criticize and instead, ask yourself, "Why are they struggling to do this?" Maybe they're feeling overwhelmed, maybe they need more support, maybe their ability to control themselves has gone offline, or maybe they're just not capable of doing what we're asking at this moment.

Instead of assuming your child is being manipulative if they lie, try shifting to curiosity and ask yourself, "Is there anything I'm doing that's making it hard or scary for them to tell me the truth? How can I make truth-telling feel safer for my kid?"

When we approach our kids with curiosity, they feel seen—like, "My parent knows I'm still in there, they know I'm trying but I've lost control. They want to understand so they can help me." It helps us see them as someone who's struggling, not just "being difficult" or a "problem" we need to fix.

We can break the cycles from our childhood of judging and criticizing kids for what their best looks like right now. Approaching with loving curiosity builds profound trust with our kids and encourages them to lean into their emotions rather than push them down and hide them, which is exactly what we need if we want them to feel safe being their full selves without the pressure to "perform" and please all the time.

Find Your Way To Neutral

Many of us were raised by parents who went cold when they were overwhelmed. Instead of being comforted by our parents after a blow-up—where everyone owned their part and apologized—we got cold, punishing silence. And now, that urge to go cold and ice them out is strong and loud because of course it is. It's what we learned from the people who raised us. I fight this urge regularly and it's okay if you do, too.

When I'm overstimulated, burned out, or triggered, it can feel impossible to stay warm while Parts of me *want* to ice my kid out because it's what I'm used to from my own childhood. I have one vicious Part that tells me to make my kid beg for forgiveness. I was shocked by this at first but then when I thought about it... of course I have that Part—it's still trying to make sense of being made to feel like that by my own mother over and over and over in childhood. That Part of me is not bad, it's trying to help me heal. And it is my responsibility to care for that Part *and* not allow it to hijack me because I am determined to not do that to my kids. So in these moments where I can't find warmth, my goal is to find neutral.

Neutral means not going cold and not forcing warmth. It's staying present, without shutting down or withdrawing. It's holding space, even if we can't do it perfectly and being there, even when we don't have the energy to engage fully.

It's saying, "I need a second," instead of going silent.

It's the energy of, *I'm not going anywhere, I'm going to stay with you even when it's hard,* and, *You are not bad, you are hurting and I will take care of you.*

I sometimes say to my kid, "I am having a lot of Big Feelings right now and I need to take care of myself. So I'm going to go to the other room and will come check on you in five minutes. I love you." And, "It's okay for us to be frustrated with each other. We will work through this together, I love you."

When we find neutral, we give our kids the security we never got. They don't have to wonder if love, affection, and care are being withheld, if they're in trouble just because we're upset. We teach them that people have hard moments, but they don't lose connection because of them. And when we're overwhelmed, we find the neutral and don't ice each other out.

So when you feel yourself slipping into cold mode, remember that you don't have to be warm—just try to find your way to neutral. I sometimes talk myself through it by saying, "Don't go cold, find the neutral. It's okay to be frustrated but don't jerk your love away." Try to stay neutral and connected so they feel safe in your love.

#2 Let Them Resist Without Shame

Kids naturally resist to release to regulate their emotions. When we see our child resisting—whether it's pushing boundaries, acting out, or pushing back—it's easy to do see that as disrespect like our parents did and shut it *down*. But this actually stops their ability to release stress and regulate themselves. Think of it like this: when a balloon is about to burst, it needs to release the pressure. If we shut down their resistance too soon, we shut down their ability to release their emotional tension and regulate.

We can teach kids respect *without* dominating them into submission to us. We can own the hell out of our no *without* taking our kid's reaction personally. We can let our kid be disappointed that we said no *without* feeling like a failure. We can hold our no *and* make it feel safe for our kid to show us they wish we'd said yes. Your kid can be upset about a rule—and still respect it. Breaking these cycles doesn't mean letting our kids walk all over us—it means learning how to lead with respect, not fear and shame. We do this by owning the hell out of our boundaries and letting them resist them without being made to feel ashamed for needing to do so.

Let them resist. It's not a personal attack on you—it's a necessary part of their emotional process. Set and hold strong boundaries and let it be okay for them to have an emotional reaction to your boundary—*of course* they feel sad, mad, or disappointed they have to leave the fun place now. Be their Confident, Loving Leader who lets them flail, push back and feel those intense emotions *without* you taking it personally or escalating to anger and shutting them down. If they get aggressive with their words or body, they need you to set *and* hold strong boundaries, and see that they are not able to control themselves right now. But you're still there for them through all of it, that you're a steady presence they can lean on to help them regulate, no matter how messy it gets.

#3 Check Your Expectations

Let's be real—our parents' expectations of us had little to no consideration for our brain development and what we were actually capable of doing. Remember your parents saying, "I expected more from you" or "I'm not mad, I'm just disappointed?" And how you felt (and probably still feel) like nothing you do is good enough? Yeah, me too.

It's a Capacity Issue, Not a Capability Issue

Brain development fundamentally impacts what our kids are capable of, especially in moments of stress or overwhelm. When kids are dysregulated, their prefrontal cortex—the part of the brain responsible for impulse control, problem-solving, and emotional regulation—goes offline. Their nervous system takes over, prioritizing survival, not logical thinking. So even though they normally can handle a situation calmly, right now, their capacity has changed. If we don't take this into account, we're setting them up to feel like they're failing—and that's when shame takes hold.

Checking Your Expectations is noticing your kid isn't meeting your expectations and reminding yourself, "They're a kid, not a mini adult. They don't need to do everything perfectly, they're allowed to struggle." And when you notice yourself feeling disappointed when your kid isn't meeting your expectations, I need you to ask yourself:

- Are my expectations realistic for where my child is right now?
- Am I expecting them to regulate, think logically and be able to control themselves... when their brain and nervous system literally can't do that right now?

Yes, your child can usually do this without struggle or a meltdown—but right now, they're *showing* you they can't. Yes, they can normally cooperate—but right now, they're *showing* you they can't. This is a really important fork in the road. If we hold rigidly to our expectations, they won't think, *Mom's expectations are too high.* They'll think, *I'm letting them down, I'm such a disappointment.* And that shame doesn't motivate them—it paralyzes them.

If we insist they should be able to meet our expectations anyway, we're setting them up to get smashed by a shame grenade. But when we adjust our expectations accordingly, we create the conditions for growth, emotional safety, and resilience.

Adjusting Expectations *Without* Permissiveness

Checking Your Expectations doesn't mean letting them off the hook or ignoring the impact of their actions. It means meeting them where they are, holding space for their resistance without making them feel ashamed, and then guiding them back into regulation. Once you've Let Them Resist Without Shame, they'll have released the pent-up emotions driving that resistance and they will have the capacity to be able to do the thing you're asking. Their capabilities will come back online. Hold them accountable for their impact, but don't punish them for being overwhelmed.

When we shift from "Why aren't they handling this better?" to "I wonder why they're struggling with this?" we parent with attunement instead of disappointment—one of the most important factors in breaking these cycles.

#4 Stand By Them, No Matter What

In those tough, triggering moments, what our kids are really asking is, "Can you love me... even like this? Even when I'm not perfect? Even when you're mad and disappointed?"

When we react with anger, frustration, or shame, they hear, "No, I don't love you when you're like this." What they need, more than anything, is for us to Stand By Them—no matter what. This doesn't mean standing by their behavior—you can take issue with them lying, being aggressive, saying mean things, etc. We're not letting them off the hook for hurtful behavior.

What I usually say to my kids is, "I don't stand by what you did but I will always Stand By You. I'm right here. You'll need to show up for your impact and we will figure this out together." When we set aside our own frustration, we can hold them accountable for their actions and impact without making them feel like they are a disappointment. Loving them through their messiness and offering them the space to be imperfect helps them feel like we're saying, "Yes, I do love you even like this."

#5 Shift Your Focus

Shifting from Managing *Their* Emotions to Managing *Yours*

As parents now, we can get so focused on trying to help our kids "manage" their Big Feelings that we completely ignore our own. But, when we bottle up our own frustration, anxiety, or overwhelm without addressing it, we end up escalating the situation because we're not dealing with our own emotions as they come up.

It's our responsibility to *turn inward* and manage our own feelings so we can stay regulated—which allows us to have the capacity to be grounded, present, calm, and choose how we want to react. That means noticing inside when *we* are starting to get triggered or overwhelmed, and taking a breath to check in with ourselves before reacting. It also means recognizing the Parts of us that are triggered—those inner voices that push us to shut our kids down because it wasn't safe to act like that when *we* were kids. Our kids need the space to resist and release their emotions without shame. They're doing exactly what their bodies need to do to regulate, and we can help by getting out of the way and *allowing* them to feel and release without shutting it down.

Shifting Back to *Their* Needs and Emotions

Be mindful of when your child is attuning *to you* instead of the other way around—when they're walking on eggshells, worried about making you mad, over-apologizing, or checking in a lot to see if you're happy. If so, it's time to Shift Your Focus back to *their needs and emotions,* not yours. This is going to happen, it happens for me too! Our job is to notice when it's happening and show up to attune back to them.

When we become attuned to our kids' emotions, we stop trying to control or suppress their feelings and instead create a space for them to not be okay, to struggle without feeling judged, to let themselves be real about how it feels inside without worrying about how it will impact us. By doing this, we teach them that their emotions are valid and worthy of being heard, and we can support them in a way that feels safe and loving.

11
Raising Kids Who Don't Have To Recover

A question I have to ask myself sometimes is, "When are you going to stop blaming them for needing help, and actually help them?"

When I've been taking good care of myself—releasing my feelings and stress instead of bottling it all up—I have the capacity and bandwidth to be the warm, loving parent I want to be, the parent that my kids deserve. Spilled something? "No problem honey, it happens to everyone." Disrespectful outburst? "It's okay to be upset. I've got you." I am able to show up with warmth, patience, and empathy, and respond with kindness and understanding because I'm not operating from a place of exhaustion and overwhelm. I have the space to offer *my kids* space to express themselves and resist what I say or my support, without taking it personally.

But some moments are not like this.

Some days, I struggle to take care of myself. I feel that I *don't have time* because I have so much going on. I push the frustration and stress down. Have you ever noticed how our kids push our buttons on days like these? It's like we can't catch a freaking break, and it's coming at us from all sides. But underneath that maddening, "pushing our buttons" behavior is a child who is naturally deeply attuned to our energy, stress level, emotions and mood. They can sense when we're a volcano about to explode, and it makes them feel unsettled, unstable, and unsafe.

On days like this, I can make them feel like they shouldn't be struggling, or they should be able to figure it out on their own. Parts of me feel that they should have to "fend for themselves" the way I had to. But I know deep down that needing help is part of being human. And if I want to teach my kids that they're worthy of support, I have to show them by how I respond—with empathy and patience.

When we shame our kids for struggling, we're not just criticizing their behavior—we're blaming them for their humanity. Struggling is an inevitable part of life, especially when they're learning to navigate big emotions, complex situations, or new challenges. When a child is shamed in these moments, it sends a powerful message that struggling is something to hide, something to be ashamed of. They might internalize the belief that they're broken for feeling what they're feeling, and that their needs are a burden to others.

The truth is, in this situation, we're reflecting our own unresolved shame back onto them. So many of us were raised in environments where our parents responded to our emotional struggles with criticism or dismissal. Now, we often find ourselves repeating this pattern because it's how we learned to cope. We feel uncomfortable with our child's distress, not because they are doing anything wrong, but because it reminds us of our own unresolved struggles.

But when we allow ourselves to confront this discomfort and truly support our kids in their struggle, we break that cycle. We teach them that it's okay to ask for help, that they are worthy of support, and that struggling doesn't make them unworthy of love or care.

Our kids' behavior is an extension and reflection of their emotional well-being and nervous system regulation. When they act out, shut down, or withdraw, it's often a sign that their nervous system is dysregulated—something we need to help them with, not shame them for. When we blame them for needing help, we dismiss their inner turmoil as something they should just "get over" on their own. But their struggles are an invitation for us to show up, listen, and provide the support they need.

So when you realize that you're blaming your kid for needing support, remind yourself that they need your help right now, and do your best to show up to help them without making them feel ashamed for needing the help. Remind yourself that as parents, we are the ones who have the power to create a safe space for our kids to feel what they feel without judgment. The impact of showing up with empathy, instead of blame, can transform their emotional world and, ultimately, their entire life. We owe it to them—and ourselves—to break the cycle and teach them that it's okay to need help, that it's okay to struggle, and that their worth is not defined by their ability to do it all on their own.

Reality Checks for Our Parent's Misguided Beliefs and Expectations

We're all walking around with our parents' old school, misguided, utterly impossible expectations living inside us. When our child's behavior triggers our frustration, that's often a sign that those old, unattainable standards from our childhood are getting in the way. It's on us to pause and reality-check these misguided beliefs. One of the biggest reasons we struggle when kids misbehave and have a hard time being "good" is because, deep down, we expect them to act more like adults than they're actually capable of. We don't mean to do this. We just project maturity onto them based on how "good" they *usually* are… just as our parents did with us. They knew how to do this yesterday; why are they struggling today? They seem so grown-up in some ways; why are they melting down over something small?

But here's the thing: kids aren't tiny adults. They're constantly in flux, with brains that are still under construction. The mistake we often make—especially with Good Kids—is assuming that because they act mature in some ways, they *should* be able to handle more than they actually can.

When we Check Our Expectations, we start seeing kids for who they actually are—not who we think they "should" be. Instead of getting frustrated that they're struggling with something they "should" be able to handle, we can remind ourselves: *They're not capable of that right now because they don't have much capacity left.* Their development isn't a straight line, and our expectations shouldn't be either. When we meet our kids where they are, instead of where we expect them to be, we stop seeing their struggles as defiance or failure—and start recognizing them as growth.

Misguided Belief: A Parent's Worth Is Tied to Their Child's Good Behavior and Achievements

Reality check: Expecting a child to always be respectful, well-behaved, and perfectly in control is not just unrealistic—it's physiologically impossible. Kids are human beings with developing brains and nervous systems, not miniature adults. They experience stress, frustration, exhaustion, and overwhelm, just like we do. And yet, many of us were raised to believe that "good" parenting meant shaming, scaring, or punishing a child into shutting down those natural responses. But that's not teaching emotional regulation—that's teaching emotional suppression.

The truth is, a parent's worth has nothing to do with their child's behavior or achievements. A parent's actual job is to parent the child they have—not the fantasy child they imagined, not the "easy" child they wish they had, not the child that would make them look good. Kids are not accessories to prove a parent's worthiness. A parent's job is to guide, support, and nurture their child into becoming their fullest, most authentic self—not mold them into whatever version of "successful" and "acceptable" will win the most approval from others.

Misguided Belief: Respect Is Earned Through Fear, Punishment, and Control

Reality check: We didn't obey and behave out of respect—we did it out of *fear*... and that's not the parenting flex our parents think it is. It is messed up, harmful, and abusive to intimidate a child into obedience, to make them so afraid of punishment, rejection, or humiliation that they shove their needs, emotions, and mistakes deep down. It's also not raising respectful kids—it's dominating a child into submission, expecting instant compliance and blind obedience and calling it respect.

Punishments aren't about accountability. They're about control, born out of the belief that kids deserve to suffer. They don't. Shame doesn't build character—it annihilates it. It doesn't make kids better—it makes them believe they are bad, inherently defective, and only pretending to be good. Shame is poison, and there is no safe dose of poison.

The discipline kids actually need teaches them about their impact without shame. It's about holding them accountable while still believing in their inherent goodness, even when they mess up—not convincing them that deep down, they're selfish, bad, and unworthy of love unless they earn and prove it through obedience and good behavior. Because when we shame kids into behaving, we're raising kids who are terrified that their worth is conditional, who carry that fear into every relationship they have for the rest of their lives.

Dominating a child looks like, "You do what I say, when I say it, no questions asked." That child thinks, "I have to obey or I'll get in trouble." What I'm suggesting instead is teaching our kids to be respectful by treating them with respect, which looks like, "The answer is no (final answer)—and you're allowed to have feelings about it." That child thinks, "I follow this rule because I trust and understand you."

Misguided Belief: Emotions Should Be Suppressed to Maintain Control and Order

Reality check: It is messed up to withdraw love, attention, affection, and care in the name of "teaching a child to control their emotions," especially when the adults demanding this control can't even regulate their own. How many of us were told to "stop overreacting and get a hold of yourself" by parents who slammed doors, yelled, sulked in silence, or weaponized their disappointment? That's not emotional regulation—that's being reckless with your impact.

You don't teach kids emotional regulation by forcing them to suppress their emotions—you teach them by *allowing them to experience them*. Expecting a kid to instinctively "control" their emotions without practice is like tossing them a unicycle and expecting them to ride it perfectly on the first try without ever seeing anyone do it well and mocking them when they fall. When we make kids feel ashamed for their Big Feelings, their ability to feel emotions isn't just suppressed—it's denied altogether. This is what Relational Shame Trauma does—it wires a child's brain and nervous system to see emotions as dangerous, to shut them down before they even fully register.

And all emotional energy gets trapped in our body. It turns into chronic tension, stomachaches, headaches, fatigue, and an underlying sense of unease we can't quite explain. It seeps into our relationships, where we struggle to express or even know what we need, feel overwhelmed by conflict, and fear being "too much" for others. The result is a lifetime of disconnection from ourselves, from our own inner world, from the full range of our human experience.

Instead of shaming our kids for struggling, we need to model regulation, co-regulate with them, and guide them through the big emotions they are still learning to navigate. A child should never have to wonder if they are still lovable just because they are having a hard time.

Misguided Belief: Vulnerability Is Weakness

Reality check: When parents refuse to help their kids because "they should know by now" or "I shouldn't have to tell you again," it doesn't teach independence or build confidence—it teaches the child to feel ashamed for needing help. Kids don't walk away from that thinking, Wow, I guess I just need to try harder! They walk away thinking, I'm annoying. I'm a burden. I should be able to handle this on my own. What is wrong with me? That belief follows them into adulthood, where they'll overextend themselves, refuse to ask for support even when they're drowning, and beat themselves up for needing anything from anyone. Sound familiar?

Let's call bullshit on the idea that kids should only need to be told once and then magically be able to do something perfectly. Learning is messy. Growth takes time. Expecting a kid to "just know better" after one correction and never struggle again is a wild take.

The difference between a child who grows up trusting themselves or a child who doubts their own worth often comes down to how their parent handles conflict and what comes next. A parent who Circles Back and says, "Hey, I got frustrated earlier, I made you feel like you shouldn't need help. I want you to know it's always okay to ask for help and I will work on showing you that," raises a kid who believes their needs are valid. A parent who "apologizes" but still makes it the child's fault—"I guess I'm sorry, but if you had just listened the first time, I wouldn't have had to get that upset"—raises a kid who learns that love is conditional on getting everything right and not upsetting others. One creates security. The other creates a lifetime of silent suffering.

Mistakes Are Part of Being Human

If perfection is the standard, shame is the only method. The fear of being a disappointment doesn't create resilience—it creates crippling self-doubt, anxiety and a deep fear of ever being seen as less than perfect. And it doesn't motivate kids to improve... it makes them afraid to even try in the first place, because shame-laced failure isn't just about what they did—it's already who they believe they are. They become adults who can't celebrate their wins because they're already focused on what they should have done better. Spiraling over tiny mistakes, replaying them on a loop in their heads and paralyzed by procrastination because they might now do it perfectly. Adults who base their entire self-worth on their performance, productivity, and ability to meet impossible standards.

Breaking the Cycle of "I'm Not Mad, I'm Disappointed"

We spent our whole childhood avoiding disappointing our parents, and now, as adults, we panic at the thought of our kids being disappointed in *us*. We bend over backwards to make sure they're happy. We rush to smooth things over, to make them feel better, to avoid feeling *their* disappointment because it still triggers our wounds.

But, the way we handle our kid's disappointment is the way we teach them how to handle their own. If we shut down their feelings with, "I'm not mad, I'm just disappointed," we are passing down the same Relational Shame Trauma that made us so afraid of it in the first place. We're teaching them that disappointment is something to be ashamed of, something that threatens love and connection. But if we can be brave and let our kids feel it—if we sit with them in their frustration, if we show them that it's safe to be disappointed, to not always get what they want, to be human—we break the cycle. We teach them that disappointment is just a feeling, not a reflection of their worth. And in doing so, we give ourselves permission to let go of the fear, the bracing, the perfectionism. We start to heal the part of us that still feels like a letdown every time we have a human moment.

We teach our kids what we needed to learn:

- You don't have to be perfect to be lovable.
- Disappointment doesn't mean you've failed—it means you care.
- No feeling can take away your worth.

"But... I *Am* Disappointed in My Child."

Disappointment is a reaction to an *expectation,* and if we're being honest, we were raised by parents who had some pretty outrageous expectations. And even though we know how damaging that was, we still feel that deep pang of disappointment when our own kids struggle to meet *our* expectations.

Here's the hard truth: sometimes, our expectations are unreasonable. Our child's capacity drives their capabilities, which means their capacity must *also* drive our expectations.

If a child is dysregulated, their impulse control has gone offline. Expecting them to "just do better" or making them ashamed for falling short teaches them that something is wrong with them for struggling. And when we let our disappointment show, it's a shame grenade. Instead of thinking, "This expectation isn't fair," they think, "I should be able to do this. What's wrong with me?" Instead of learning resilience, they learn self-loathing. They stop feeling like they are struggling and start believing they are defective.

If our disappointment is coming from the fact that our kid isn't behaving the way we think they should—but they are showing us loud and clear that they can't—then we are the ones with the problem. Not them. They need us to see that they are struggling, not scold them for struggling incorrectly. They don't need us to pile more shame onto an already overwhelming moment. They need us to show up with regulation, guidance and a desire to understand where they are coming from.

Because if we don't Check Our Expectations, *they* will take the blame. Not in a logical "I should have handled that better" way, but in a deep "I am bad for disappointing my parent" way. A heartbreaking number of child *and* adult counseling clients have said some version of that and I have seen firsthand the way that sticks and shapes their inner world—emboldening their already relentless Inner Critic, their fear of failure, the crushing pressure to always be in control. The worst part? Once kids internalize that shame, we don't even have to say we're disappointed anymore. They take the baton and do it for us.

So next time you feel that wave of disappointment rising up, pause. Check Your Expectations, and ask yourself:

- Was this expectation actually reasonable, given their current capacity?
- Did my child ever agree to this expectation?
- Am I making their struggle about my feelings, instead of about what they need?

Because if our disappointment is rooted in an expectation they never agreed to or don't currently have the capacity to meet—then it's not on them to change. It's on us.

Shame and Children

The child's brain, especially the prefrontal cortex (responsible for reasoning and regulating emotions), isn't fully developed. This makes it harder for them to rationalize or understand that "Mom or Dad is just upset right now—it doesn't mean they don't love me." Instead, the amygdala, the brain's fear center, takes over, flooding their body with stress hormones like cortisol and making the situation feel overwhelming or even terrifying.

Shame Spirals in Kids

Even though we do our best, sometimes we wind up shaming our kids because we're at the end of our rope after a bad day or because we don't realize we're doing it or just because shit happens. I get it. I do it, and *you* don't need to feel ashamed about doing it too as long as you're committing to showing up for your impact and repairing the relationship after you make a mistake.

A child's brain and nervous system are wired for survival, and their primary source of safety is their caregiver. This means that a parent's anger, disapproval, or disappointment doesn't just feel bad—it can feel dangerous. Not because the child is overreacting or being dramatic, but because their developing brain is scanning for threats to their connection, security, and belonging. When a parent reacts with withdrawal, harsh criticism, or shame-based discipline, the child internalizes messages about their worth. And when shame is activated without repair or support, the child enters a Shame Spiral—a dysregulated state where they feel unworthy, unlovable, and disconnected from the people they need most.

Kids enter a Shame Spiral when they feel like they are bad, like there is something fundamentally wrong with them. Unlike guilt—which focuses on what they did—shame makes it about who they *are*.

When many of us experienced this as kids, our Shame Spiral was seen as "attention-seeking" or manipulation. The very moment we needed love, connection, and guidance the most, our parents often doubled down—withdrawing even further, shutting us down, or punishing us for our distress. It was like pouring gasoline on an already raging fire. Not only were we paralyzed by shame, but we also learned to feel ashamed of our shame. We internalized the belief that needing help to regulate was a weakness, that struggling made us unworthy of love.

Fast forward to today, and if this was your experience, it's likely that you are absolutely brutal with yourself when you mess up. Your Inner Critic took the baton from your parents, so they don't even need to say they're disappointed anymore because your brain automatically fills in the gaps. And if you're like most recovering Good Kids, you may even insist that you were the one who held yourself to impossible standards, you were the one who was always disappointed in yourself. But where do you think you learned that?

The Science

Shame is so overwhelming that our body treats it like a threat—so it activates the nervous system into Fight, Flight, Freeze, or Fawn. People in a Shame Spiral—kids *and* adults—often react in predictable ways and understanding this helps us to know how to support our kids and be the water, not gasoline on their fire.

Lashing Out in Anger (Fight Response)

Shame is so painful that sometimes the nervous system flips into Fight Response to deflect attention from the shame. Instead of feeling small and powerless, the child lashes out at others—because even though they don't want to be "bad," it feels better than feeling helpless.

Shutting Down (Freeze/Flight Response)

When the shame feels too big to bear, the body shuts down to escape it. The child may physically shrink, avoid or be unable to make eye contact, or disappear into another room—not because they're "pouting," but because their nervous system is trying to protect them from overwhelming pain.

Getting Defensive (Fight/Fawn Response)

Defensiveness comes from the desperate attempt to prove they're not bad. When someone points out a mistake, it feels like they're saying, "You're unworthy of love"—so the brain and body react by putting up walls, trying to escape the unbearable feeling of rejection and abandonment.

Emotional Outbursts (Fight/Flight Response)

Shame is so big and overwhelming that sometimes the body explodes with it—leading to crying, yelling, or other intense reactions. The child isn't trying to be dramatic or attention-seeking. They literally don't know how else to regulate their nervous system and their body facilitates a release of the pent-up emotions and pressure.

Perfectionism and Over-Apologizing (Fawn Response)

Many Good Kids respond to shame by doubling down on perfectionism—trying to never mess up, never make mistakes, never be a burden. And when they do make a mistake? They apologize excessively, desperately trying to fix things and make sure they are still loved.

How to Minimize Shame Spirals

While it's normal to feel frustrated or disappointed as a parent, there are ways to minimize the impact of these emotions on your child's nervous system.

Regulate Yourself First

Before responding, take a moment to calm your own nervous system. Take a deep breath, ground yourself, and approach the situation from a place of calm rather than reactive anger or frustration. Your regulated nervous system can help regulate theirs.

Avoid Shame-Laced Language

Statements like "What's wrong with you?" or "I'm so disappointed in you" can be deeply wounding for kids. Shift Your Focus to their behavior, not their worth. Try, "I'm not going to let you throw toys. Are you able to stop or do you need my help?," while staying as curious as you can. If you can't be emotionally warm, find neutral and avoid going cold.

Stay Connected, Even in Conflict

Reassure your child verbally and nonverbally that you Stand By Them and your love and connection are unwavering, even when there's conflict, misbehavior, and messy moments. Phrases like, "I'm frustrated right now, but it's okay for us to be frustrated with each other. I love you, even when it's hard," or "It's okay to make mistakes—we'll figure this out together," help maintain that sense of safety.

Show Them How to Regulate

Show your child that big emotions can be managed safely. Narrate your process: "I'm feeling upset right now, so I need to get my feelings out and then when you're ready, we can talk about what happened. We can be frustrated with each other and still love each other. I love you."

Circle Back to Repair After Conflict

If you've reacted in a way that scared or upset your child, repair the relationship by acknowledging your behavior, taking accountability, and reassuring them. For example: "I raised my voice earlier, and I'm sorry if that scared you. I love you, and I'm here to help you through this."

Provide Safe Boundaries

Your kid needs you to be their Confident, Loving Leader in a way that feels safe and predictable. A calm and firm "I'm not going to let you hit your brother, but it's okay to feel mad" provides structure, stability and maintains connection.

Children thrive in environments where they feel safe, seen, and loved—even when they're being corrected or disciplined. They'll never admit it to you, but I can't tell you how many times I've had a child counseling client who tells me how close they feel with their parent after their parent learns how to be their Confident, Loving Leader. Their parent's rules make them feel loved and safe. Learning how to stay connected and shift from Critical to Curious and finding the neutral helps their nervous system feel secure and teaches them that relationships can handle mess ups and mistakes with repair and relational safety.

Shame-Prone vs. Guilt-Prone Self-Talk

The way a parent responds to their child's mistakes—whether with connection or shame—shapes whether the child becomes shame-prone or guilt-prone.

Guilt-Prone Self-Talk → "I did something bad."

Guilt is uncomfortable, but it's adaptive. It helps us reflect on what we did, take responsibility for it, and be inspired to show up to do better next time.

Shame-Prone Self-Talk → "I am bad."

Shame, on the other hand, is paralyzing. It doesn't help the child learn from their mistakes—it makes them feel like *they* are the mistake. It makes it harder for them to believe they can do better in the future because they see *themselves* as the problem.

The research on this is crystal clear: longitudinal studies show that kids with Shame-Prone Self-Talk are far more likely to experience anxiety, depression, low self-worth, and self-destructive behaviors. The strongest predictor of whether a child develops Shame-Prone vs. Guilt-Prone Self-Talk is parenting style. It happens in the little moments where we reinforce the shame or the guilt. We are going to fall into shaming sometimes. When we do—we Circle Back to own that, challenge the shame they're feeling and help them refocus their Shame-Prone Self-Talk back to Guilt-Prone Self-Talk:

"I know I made you feel like I was disappointed in you for doing that, and I'm sorry I made you feel like you were bad. I was upset in the moment, I lashed out, and I hurt you. It's important to me that you know I don't think you're bad. What you did is something we need to talk about, and I may not stand by what you did—but I will always Stand By You. We will figure this out together."

From Shame to Accountability

The way we respond to our kids when they make mistakes is everything. When we react with shame, we might think we're teaching them an important lesson—but all we're really teaching them is to fear us and our reaction, to fear their mistakes, and to fear themselves. So how do we change this? We Check Our Expectations. We remember that a child's capacity drives their capabilities—and their capacity must also drive our expectations of them, in real time. If a child is acting out, their impulse control has already gone offline.

Instead of shaming them, we step in as their Confident, Loving Leader and help them regain it. We separate *who they are* from *what they did*. We shift from "What is wrong with you?" to "You're having a hard time, not giving me a hard time." We replace "You should be ashamed of yourself" with "Those actions hurt someone. Let's make it right." We show them that making a mistake doesn't mean they're unlovable, that their worth isn't something that can be lost.

Kids don't learn to do better from shame. They learn to hide their mistakes, bury their feelings, and turn their anger inward. But when they feel safe enough to face their mistakes without losing connection? That's when real growth happens. That's the power of parenting without shame.

Allie on the Playground

When my daughter, Allie, started preschool at four, her class started each day on the playground. A few days into that first week, her teacher told me that each morning, instead of playing with the other kids on the playground, my daughter stood with her.

I was shy as a kid. I so badly wanted Allie to have lots of friends. But my wise, Higher Self was there too—unworried. Proud of her for doing what felt comfortable for her. With a deep, unshakeable determination that hit me like a lightning bolt—to show up as her mom in a way where this would get to be an experience of *feeling proud of herself*. Instead of an experience where she was struggling to do something she "should" have been able to do, not meeting expectations and... disappointing me. You know how sometimes as parents, something random feels deeply significant and you feel like you need to try to get this one right? That's how it felt for me.

That first week, when I asked her, "How do you like playground time?" and she said she hadn't played, I replied, "I'm so proud of you for doing what feels good for you." As Allie's head snapped up, her eyes going wide with surprise, I continued, "I'm glad you feel good standing with Ms. Tania. One day, you might feel ready to go play with the other kids. Your job is to listen inside and do that when *you* are ready. Thank you for taking care of yourself."

As time went on, she would tell me on the way to school, "Mommy, today I'm going to go play!"

I was so careful with how I responded. I would say, "If that's what feels right for you, then yay I hope you enjoy it. And if you're not quite ready yet, that's okay too. You get to be loyal to you."

Allie ended up standing with Ms. Tania for weeks and weeks. Thankfully, none of the other kids made a big deal about it. Eventually, she asked me why this was so hard for her. "Is it weird that I don't play with the other kids?" Of course, I interpreted this as her asking, *What is wrong with me?* I told her, "Everyone needs different things and our job is to listen inside for what we need and do it, even if other people don't understand. So no, I don't think it's weird—I think it's wonderful that you're doing what feels right for you."

Then one day at pick-up... she walked up to me with the biggest smile on her face and proclaimed, "Mommy, I played today!" She was so proud of herself. And that's what made it beautiful—not that she finally did something she "should" have been able to do, not that she had been letting me down and finally stopped. It was beautiful because *she did it in her own time, when she was ready*. And in that moment, her pride was hers—not about meeting an expectation, but about trusting *herself*.

As parents, we have such an incomprehensibly profound impact on our kids while carrying such deep wounds ourselves. It's so tricky trying to figure out what our role needs to be and how to support them when they're struggling. In these moments, meet them where they are right now. Get curious instead of critical. Keep encouraging them to listen inside and do what feels good for *them*. Cheer so loudly when they choose themselves—especially when that comes with being misunderstood and letting other people down. Say, "I trust you to know what you need" and, "Thank you for telling me what feels good for you." There are few things more magical than watching a kid feel cheered on for taking care of themselves.

When We're Ashamed

Sometimes, after a messy moment where we yell or shut our kid down, our Inner Critic swoops in with some really brutal lines—things like, "You should have never had kids. You're a failure and a bad parent." My Inner Critic likes to gut punch me with, "Your kids deserve a better mom." It feels paralyzing, I see you.

In those moments, it can be hard to continue to breathe, let alone remember you're not actually a monster. According to research on shame resilience, our Shame Spirals are our mind's way of handling guilt by transforming it into shame—attacking your whole identity instead of focusing on the one mistake. Under all that viciousness is genuine guilt and heartbreak over how we might have hurt our child when we lost our temper and snapped at them.

We can notice our Inner Critic pushing us into shame and pivot back to guilt, bringing the focus back to the thing that happened instead of *what this all means about me as a person*. Recognizing that difference—"I made a mistake" (Guilt-Prone Self-Talk) vs. "I am a mistake" (Shame-Prone Self-Talk)—is everything. When you notice your Inner Critic firing off lines like, "You're a failure," try saying to yourself: "You are a good parent who had a hard moment. You can Circle Back, own your behavior, and repair with your child."

Of course we will make mistakes all the time. I know I do. But I also show up to be brave enough to *notice* that shame, work through it and pivot back to guilt about my impact. And Circle Back to repair with my child. All we can do is our best—whatever that looks like at that moment—and show up for our impact by apologizing when we hurt our kids.

I talk myself through moments like this by saying things like:

- "You are a good parent who had a hard moment. You need to Circle Back and show up for the impact you had and you will. Apologizing makes you a good parent."
- "A hard moment does not make you a bad parent, I see you trying so hard."

- "Breaking generational cycles of trauma is not about never messing up—it's about breaking the damaging cycles of sweeping stuff under the rug and making kids feel responsible for setting their parents off. Just by Circling Back to repair, you're breaking countless cycles. You're a really good mom."

Parenting Is Freaking Hard

We need to make it feel safe for parents to say, "Parenting is freaking hard sometimes"—*out loud, without shame and with a full chest*—without everyone chiming in, "But you chose this!" or "But it's worth it." Yes, of course it's worth it, but telling parents that in the moment doesn't magically remove the exhaustion, triggering anxiety, resentment, or the longing to hide in the bathroom for five damn minutes where nobody needs us.

When you keep that frustration bottled up, it just festers and makes things even harder to bear. Research on Relational Shame and stress shows that resentment we bottle up and suppress doesn't magically disappear—it seeps into your interactions, potentially threatening and poisoning the connection you have with your kids. It's like carrying an overfilled balloon around—sooner or later, it goes *pop!* You might go *pop!* at your child over small stuff or give off a vibe that something's "wrong" without saying why. Kids pick up on that so quickly, and they start tiptoeing around, afraid they'll set you off.

You're stuck in a Shame Spiral, thinking, "I'm a bad parent for resenting my own kid," which only makes you more tense and shut down emotionally. This tension blocks you from seeing your child as inherently good, deep down inside. It makes it extremely hard to see and believe they're doing their best. This keeps us stuck in survival mode. Over time, that stress makes it harder to trust your child and connect in a genuine way, and they struggle to feel safe being their real, messy, wonderful selves around you.

Bottling that resentment also robs you of the joyful moments. It's tough to truly feel delight in the little things—like a spontaneous hug or a precious, silly dance—when your mind is crowded with suppressed guilt and frustration. Research on parent–child relationships shows that even when we think we're hiding our frustration, our kids pick up on the tension and hostility, sensing that something's "off." This is why doing a Circle Back to reconnect and repair after hard moments is so crucial because if we don't own the way we bit our kid's head off when they asked us a question and help them understand that we've been bottling up our feelings and exploded, they can start to feel like *they* are the problem. And the more we bottle up our feelings and move into resentment, the more *we* start to believe they're the problem. Many of us know this well from childhood ourselves.

For me personally, as someone who bottled everything up until I finally learned how to feel my feelings at 29 in therapy—if I don't regularly talk through and release my feelings, I move into a dark headspace pretty quickly. It starts with being vicious with myself and moves into being vicious with everyone else. And it's very easy to fall into a trap where I'm hijacked by Parts of me that believe my kid is manipulating me and is an obnoxious, selfish, spoiled brat. Then I enter a Shame Spiral because I feel like a horrible mom for being vicious with everyone else, in my thoughts and in real life—so I am more vicious with myself. And the cycle continues. The key to breaking out of this, every single damn time, is to release the air from the balloon and say the things out loud to someone who can hold me and love me through it.

Completing the Stress Cycle

When the feelings run deep—so deep I can't quite put them into words or make sense of them—I remind myself that my body knows how to let them go, if I just get out of the way and let it do its job. According to research on embodied healing and trauma release, using our body to physically move through heavy, intense emotions can help us release them. Sometimes, the stress that's getting stirred up at a deep level is stored in our body and can't be expressed through an emotional release right now.

Think about recruiting your body for help and saying, "Body, I'm handing this off to you. Help me release it." Fascinating and groundbreaking research on stress and the body shows that physically activating and engaging your musculoskeletal system—through things like walking, air squats, wall push-ups, stretching, or even dancing—helps you complete the stress cycle by burning off leftover bottled-up feelings and stress hormones. This sends powerful signals to your nervous system that you have now moved away from the threat, are no longer in danger and can move out of the stress cycle and Fight/Flight. Try this. It's incredibly powerful to trust your body to show up for you and do what it's biologically wired to do.

Bringing It Out into the Light

By bringing these feelings into the light, whether with a trusted friend, therapist, or someone else who really sees you, you're giving yourself permission to unload the shame you feel for even having these thoughts. That honesty doesn't disqualify your love for your kids; it actually protects it because you're dealing with the feelings that already exist. Over time, letting your frustration be heard (instead of pretending it's not there) frees up space for genuine enjoyment. You can show up with your heart still in it, more present, more compassionate, and less weighed down by the unspoken "shoulds" that keep you from soaking in the good stuff.

I've held space for so many counseling and coaching clients to say the things we're not "supposed" to say out loud about parenting and witnessed the profoundly healing impact it has. Here are a few things my clients have said:

- "Parenting is so much harder than I thought it would be."
- "I straight up hate parenting sometimes. Don't get me wrong, having kids is the best thing I have ever done but… parenting is exhausting and unrelenting and sometimes… I just hate it."
- "I just wish I got breaks as a parent. Never getting a break and them always, always, always needing me sometimes makes me feel like a caged animal—the rage. Then I feel like a monster for having the rage."

According to research on Relational Shame Trauma, hiding these "unacceptable" emotions only fuels the sense that we're unworthy of connection. But saying them out loud—in a safe, non-judgmental space—can be the key to unloading that resentment and the shame you feel for having it. Safe relationships where we feel held and loved through helps to remind us we're not monsters for feeling anger, rage, exhaustion, or resentment… we're just human beings with human limits.

We need to see these feelings for what they are: signals that we are not getting enough extra support, rest, or empathy—not proof that we're failing. Being real about how you feel does not disqualify your love for your kids. It allows you to deal with the feelings that, like it or not, are already there. It's so important to let those feelings have their moment and help the Parts of you that are struggling feel seen and validated. That honesty can be the very thing that helps you show up for your kids with your heart still in it.

12
Big Feelings Shouldn't Equal Big Trouble

Anger

We're terrified that if we let our kids express their anger, it will spiral out of control—that they'll turn into adults who can't manage their emotions. But the exact opposite is true. It's not feeling anger that creates an "anger problem." It's being made to feel ashamed of it, punished for it, and never learning how to process it in a healthy way. So we push it down, pretend we're fine, and hope for the best. Sound familiar? That's exactly what so many of us do—we bottle it up until we explode like a volcano, feel terrible, and swear we won't do it again… until we do.

So how are we supposed to teach our kids to manage anger if we were never taught how to manage our own? If your kid explodes like a volcano or bottles everything up and pretends they're fine, they're showing you what they've learned about anger so far. And that's where you come in.

Resistance Is Regulation

Our parents told us to "control" our anger, but what they actually meant was don't have it at all. They didn't want to see the tears, hear the yelling, or deal with the mess of our emotions. By "control," they meant bottle it up, shove it down, and act like everything is fine. But suppression isn't control—it's avoidance. And pushing anger down doesn't make it go away. It buries it deeper, where it festers, creating a pressure cooker that eventually explodes.

Our parents' expectations weren't based on child development or emotional health. They were based on their own unresolved shame and discomfort with big emotions—ours and their own. No one showed them how to process anger in a healthy way, so they passed that fear and avoidance onto us. That's how our nervous system learned to associate anger with danger, punishment, abandonment, and rejection. Instead of seeing it as a normal, healthy part of being human, we saw it as something to fear.

Think of anger like a dropped soda can. If you keep shaking it, the pressure builds until it explodes the second it's opened. But if you slowly release the pressure over time, it doesn't blow up—it just fizzes out safely. Anger works the same way.

Letting our kids feel their anger and work through it in a safe, supported way teaches them how to regulate and manage their emotions. Shutting it down is the recipe for a lifetime of bottling, exploding, and feeling ashamed about both.

Resistance isn't defiance—it's a biological process. When kids push back, they're not just testing us, they're trying to move through their emotions. If we shut that resistance down, we also shut down their ability to release pent-up anger, stress and emotions. They don't learn how to move through anger—they learn how to stuff it. And what happens to Good Kids who bottle their anger? They turn it on themselves. It festers as self-doubt, people pleasing, perfectionism, and resentment. They don't stop feeling anger—they just stop believing they're allowed to feel it.

The research is clear on the long-term cost. When kids are shamed out of releasing their anger through Fight Response, they are more likely to experience chronic stress-related illnesses, difficulty advocating for themselves, and an increased risk of anxiety and depression. But kids who are allowed to access and integrate their anger in a healthy way, through Fight Response—especially in stressful environments—develop greater resilience, emotional regulation, and self-advocacy skills. Fight Response isn't a problem; it's a crucial regulation tool.

Why It Feels So Scary to Let Our Kids Be Mad at Us

Let me ask you something: on a scale from totally comfortable to absolutely terrifying... did it feel safe to be mad at your parents?

For many of us, when conflict happened, we were made to feel like a monster and sent away, shut down, or punished. Our parents, likely overwhelmed themselves, never Circled Back to talk things through, apologize, or give us space to say "That scared me, and I need to know we're okay now." We learned that anger wasn't just unacceptable and dangerous—it was a threat to our connection. According to research on Relational Shame Trauma, childhood dynamics like these teach us that conflict is dangerous and any moment we lose control means we risk losing the relationship altogether.

So *of course*, now that we're parents, when our kids get mad at us, it hits something really deep. It triggers the very same fear we were conditioned to have: *What if their anger means I'm failing? What if it means they don't love me?* And because we were never given a safe way to process our own anger, their emotions feel like something we need to shut down—not because we don't love them, but because we never learned how to sit with anger without feeling terrified by it.

Frustration

Frustration can be so triggering for us, especially if we grew up in a home where our parents couldn't handle seeing us upset. But frustration is just another emotion. Research on child development and co-regulation shows that frustration can help kids (and parents) unload built-up stress—both from the present moment and from past situations we've bottled up. When your child hits that irritated, "This isn't fair!" point, it's not some moral failing, it's a sign they need a safe outlet to let the air out of the balloon before it goes *pop!* It feels messy—and based on our parenting, unnecessary—but allowing ourselves to be frustrated when frustrating things happen is a crucial part of learning to handle life's curveballs.

Challenge the Parts of you that think, "Oh no, frustration is bad and unsafe—I need to make it stop immediately." Keep breathing into your belly and talk yourself through it. Remind yourself that it's okay for them to be frustrated, and you want them to get that frustration out. My own personal mantra for allowing my kids to be frustrated has been, "Tolerate the struggle."

Say this to them—and yourself, too:

- "It's okay to be frustrated when frustrating things happen."
- "Wow, that looks hard, it's okay to be frustrated."
- "I see you, you keep trying even though that's frustrating."

If they explode, good! They needed to release some stuff. Let them freaking *blow*.

Even if it feels like you're both dangling over an emotional cliff for a minute—this can remind us of childhood when we got shut down *and* when our parent's temper was flaring. Remind yourself that this is their body's way of releasing stress they've been holding onto. It can feel like life or death to our nervous system. But they can survive it and so can you! And everyone is better for it.

You want them to build a tolerance for frustration. I'm convinced that allowing ourselves to be freaking frustrated when frustrating things happen is utterly *life changing*. It was for me. And it has been for so many of my child and adult counseling clients.

Hurt

When our kids are hurt, they need to feel seen in how they're feeling, in real time, not rushed, not "fixed," not reality checked and not told why they *shouldn't* feel the way they do. Kids don't need to find the damn silver lining right now. They don't need to be reminded that it's "not that bad." They don't need to be nudged toward "being grateful because it could be worse" when they're in pain.

What kids need—what any human in pain needs—is **for someone to see them hurting and choose to stay**—to see them, to sit next to them with their pain, and to trust that it hurts the way they say it hurts.

I see this all the time in therapy. The moment when someone, maybe for the first time in their life, tells the truth about how much something hurts, and instead of being told to "see the bright side" or that they're "making a big deal out of nothing," someone just *sees* them. And my goodness, the way they react is so heartbreakingly beautiful. They break down, often in deep relief, because for the first time, someone isn't trying to minimize what happened to them or how much it hurt.

Growing up, maybe they were called "dramatic" or "having a pity party" and felt shamed for feeling deeply, like they should have been able to "handle it." And now—if we're not careful—we can end up repeating that cycle with our own kids. Not because we mean to, but because we were taught to believe that emotions are something to fix, rather than something to feel.

When your kid is hurting, try this:

"I see you. It's okay to be____(sad, frustrated, overwhelmed)."

Then *stop talking*. Just hold space. Let them be in it without making them feel like they need to rush to the part where they "feel better." Or make it sound less hard, less painful, more palatable.

Critical Steps Before Trying "Name It To Tame It"

The parenting world loves the whole "name it to tame it" thing. Here are my issues with that and why I don't recommend it when kids are deep in their emotions.

Kids need to stay in a feeling place, not be rushed into a thinking place. They also need *us* to stay in the feeling mode and resist moving into thinking mode (fixing it, intellectualizing it). When we jump in too soon with, "You're feeling angry because your friend didn't invite you" or "You're sad because you lost the game"—we're unintentionally trying to pull them out of their emotional experience and into logic and reason. But emotions aren't logical or reasonable.

Moreover, we often get it wrong: The Thing is *not* The Thing. The Thing it all *seems* to be about at the surface isn't often the actual issue. So you might see anger at the surface, but what's underneath? What seems like frustration might actually be grief and shame. So now, instead of feeling understood, they feel even more alone and misunderstood—like, "You don't get it." And when they feel unseen in their pain, the shame deepens. The hardest part for kids usually isn't just the feeling itself—it's the feeling that they *shouldn't* feel this way. Underneath the sadness, the anger, the fear—there's often a deeper shame. They're thinking, *Why am I like this? Why can't I handle this better? Other kids wouldn't feel this way.*

The shame under the feeling is often harder and more debilitating than the feeling itself. And kids need us to notice that shame and help them with it. Use these simple, grounding statements without rushing to name it:

- "I see you. It's okay to be upset."
- "It's so hard to feel this way. I see you."
- "I'm so sorry you're hurting right now. I'm here with you."

And if you sense they're spiraling into shame, go deeper with these Life Preserver Scripts to help them with the shame:

- "Are you feeling bad about yourself? You're not bad. I know you, and deep down, you are good. I love you."
- "Are you feeling like something is wrong with you? It's so hard to feel that way. There is nothing wrong with you. I love you."
- "I'm not disappointed in you, and you don't need to feel ashamed of yourself. It's okay to make mistakes. I will always, always love you."

Later, when they're more regulated and have worked out of the Shame Spiral, you can Circle Back to talk about making things right, taking responsibility, and understanding their emotions with more clarity. In the moment, they don't need a lesson… they need *you*. They need to know you see them, you still love them and you Stand By Them—even when they're *like this.*

No fixing. No over-explaining. Just seeing them, staying with them, Standing By Them. That's what helps them regulate overwhelming emotions and the shame underneath them.

When They Say Something That Cuts Deep

"Nobody likes me."

"I'm so stupid / ugly / fat."

"I'll never be happy again!"

Do not reality check them when they say these things. I know it's tempting to feel like you need to rescue them from their distress. But—saying, "That's not true! You have so many friends! You're beautiful! You're so smart!" doesn't land the way you think it does.

When we rush to correct their feelings with logic, what they hear isn't comfort—it's dismissal. They think, *You don't get it. I shouldn't feel this way. I'm all alone right now.*

That's the kind of aloneness that turns pain into shame. That's how they start believing that big emotions make them "too sensitive" and "too much," that struggling makes *them* unlovable, that they have to *hide* what they're feeling to be acceptable. Shame is sneaky like that; it twists our most loving efforts into what feels like proof that they're wrong for feeling the way they do.

When your child is in the emotional storm, remind yourself:

- Their feelings in that moment might not be rational, but they are real.
- They're not trying to be dramatic. This is how it feels to them right now.
- There's a part of them that is hurting intensely, and they don't need us to argue with it.

Try saying:

- "It's so hard to feel like that."
- "That sounds really painful. I'm so sorry you feel this way."
- "I know this feeling is so big right now. I'm here with you."

That's it. That's the magic. Stand By Them. Let them feel without shame.

This is so damn tricky for us. My Inner Critic likes to crush me with, "This shouldn't be so hard for you. They deserve a mom who doesn't struggle like this." And I hear you, but we are all learning how to feel our feelings as full-grown adults, alongside our kids without ever having a parent (or maybe anyone) do this for us! We're navigating all the shame that gets stirred up for *us* because of how our parents rejected, abandoned and *shut down* our feeling selves. Please be gentle and patient with yourself.

You're going to feel like a newborn giraffe, trying to stand up for the first time. You're going to mess this up because of course you are. You're going to want to crawl out of your skin sometimes. You're going to want to jump in and rescue them. You're going to hold space for a while then feel like they've "had enough time and now it's time to move on." But when it feels awkward and cringey, keep going. When you're at the end of your rope, hold the hell on. Keep going.

Do This for Yourself, Too

It's not just our kids who need this. You need this, too.

When you've got the Big Feelings—notice when you default to intellectualizing your feelings—when you're analyzing, explaining, or trying to make sense of them instead of simply honoring and letting them be. Notice when you rush to tell yourself why it's "not that bad" or why you "shouldn't" be feeling the way you do. Notice when you work to justify your emotions. Notice when you explain them away. Notice when you try to rush to the part where you see the bright side or find the lesson.

You need what every human in pain needs: someone to see you hurting and choose to stay. Because that's what reparenting really is. It's learning how to Stand By Yourself in the moments you feel most unlovable, no matter what. It's saying:

- "This is so painful for you. I see you."
- "You don't have to rush through this. I'm here."
- "You make sense and this makes sense."
- "I see you. I've got you. I love you." (The Magic 9 Words All Humans In Struggle Need)

Meltdowns

You've probably heard from well-meaning mental health professionals that allowing kids to express their anger will only make them more aggressive. But here's the thing: many studies making this claim fail to account for shame as a confounding variable in aggression—they don't consider the role that shame plays in fueling reactive aggression. When kids are made to feel ashamed for being mad, their nervous system registers that shame as a deep threat. For some kids, shame triggers an intense Fight Response—leading to more explosive, reactive aggression.

So it's not allowing kids to be mad that makes them aggressive—it's shaming them for being mad that creates that pattern. Research shows that shame is one of the most potent drivers of reactive aggression because it's such a deeply painful, intolerable emotion.

When kids feel ashamed of their anger, they don't learn how to regulate it; they learn that anger is dangerous and must be fought against, denied, or exploded out, and never learn how to move through it safely. If we truly want to raise kids who can handle their emotions in a healthy way, we have to stop treating anger like a problem that needs to be shut down and start seeing it for what it is: a normal, necessary emotion that, when given space and guidance, can be processed safely—without shame, without punishment, and without fear. Anger is an emotion that our kids will experience consistently throughout their lifetimes, so they need those tools for the rest of their lives.

A Confident, Loving Leader

Goodness, these moments when our kid is angry can feel so triggering. I need you to remind yourself that their anger was *already in there*, building up as frustration, overwhelm and stress they'd been stuffing down. You don't want them to push it back inside and pretend everything's fine—you want them to release it so their body can regulate down. You can say, "You're mad that I said no, and it's okay to be mad at me. The answer is still no."

Anger isn't the problem. Not knowing how to process it safely is. And that's where we come in. Give them what so many of us never got—the ability to feel, to fight for themselves, and to know that even when they're mad, they are still completely and utterly loved.

"It's okay for you to be mad at me."

That's it. That one sentence. You'll be amazed at the magic that happens when you offer this simple reassurance. It's like a weight is lifted—off both of you. You've shown them that their feelings are valid, and they've been given the safe space to process those emotions. It's a game-changer. Let's start letting our kids be mad—without taking it personally and without making it mean we're failing.

We think that we need to take an active role in the meltdown, help them name their feelings or orchestrate things. But, really, your job is to stand back and let them *blow*. Your child's anger isn't something to control, fix, or stop. Your job is to guide them through their messy humanity and show them that they can release it in healthy ways.

Trust that they are blowing up because they *need to* release some stress and Big Feelings. We want a controlled explosion with strong boundaries around the aggression. Say, "You can be mad, but I'm not going to let you hurt me."

Hold the Boundary

Their resistance isn't going to wear your no down into a yes—the answer still needs to be no. They can be mad about it. They can be frustrated about it. They don't have to like it. And they can express that anger or frustration to help themselves calm down. Sticking to your boundaries while they resist shows them that emotions aren't something to be feared or suppressed.

We allow the resistance, but we don't let them hurt themselves, others, or things. They can push against the boundary, but the boundary doesn't change. That's what it means to be their Confident, Loving Leader.

Encourage them to *release* it instead of suppressing it. They can scream into a pillow, say all the things they want to say into a pillow, stomp their feet, tear up paper, throw a stuffed animal, punch a pillow. Sometimes they'll do it if we do it with them. Research on child development and co-regulation shows that kids often release bottled-up stress to regulate their nervous system. Sometimes their body needs to physically resist to release to regulate.

Try This:

- "I see that you are really mad right now. It's okay to be mad. I'm not going to let you hurt yourself, anyone else, or anything, but you are allowed to be mad."
- "Your Big Feelings do not scare me. I am right here. I've got you."
- "It's okay to push back. It's okay to feel this all the way through. I will help you find a way to let it out that doesn't hurt anyone."

You may need to hold their hands or legs and say, "You're having a hard time controlling yourself right now. When you're able to control yourself again and stop trying to hurt me, I will let go of your arms." This is not about overpowering and intimidating them into submission by showing them we are bigger and stronger than them. This is about seeing that they've lost control and needing something—or someone—to physically resist. It can feel like wrestling an angry alligator, but we want them to walk away feeling like, "My mom helps me when I lose control by holding me until I calm down." Not, "My mom overpowers me and gets scary mad, so I shut down and pretend I'm calm so she'll stop." Hold the boundary and remember they're still in there asking, "Can you love me... even like this?"

Allowing anger doesn't mean allowing aggression. They need strong, stable boundaries, and they actually want them. Their anger makes them feel unstable—when you hold the boundary, it helps them feel safe.

Impulse Control

When your child is struggling to control themselves, please don't say, "I can't trust you right now." That message plants a devastating Relational Shame wound because it doesn't just say, "you made a mistake"—it says, "***You** are untrustworthy.*" Over time, that message doesn't just make them question your trust in them—it chips away at their ability to trust themselves, something they'll carry long after this moment has passed.

Impulse control isn't about trust. It's about the brain and nervous system being overwhelmed. Even as adults, we struggle to regulate ourselves when stress, exhaustion, big emotions, overstimulation, blood sugar crashes, or shame take over our system. Nobody—child nor adult—can "just control themselves" when their impulse control is being actively undermined by dysregulation. And as kids grow, factors like hormones and brain development make self-regulation even harder.

Instead, say: "You're having a hard time controlling yourself right now. I've got you." Then, step in to help them until their impulse control comes back online. This isn't about labeling them as "out of control"—it's about recognizing that they are momentarily physiologically impaired and guiding them back to regulation.

Try not to take their words or actions personally when they're dysregulated. Just like us, they'll say and do things they wouldn't under normal circumstances. But instead of making this a moment where they feel ashamed for struggling—something we, as adults, still struggle with—help them through it. Because learning how to regulate with support is how they eventually learn to do it on their own.

I need you to operate from a place of belief in their inherent goodness. Even when—especially when—they've lost control. See through the triggering behavior at the surface to the Real Them, underneath—the precious child beneath the chaos at the surface. Finding your way out of criticism into curiosity, out of coldness into warmth. Grounding yourself into the truth that if they *could* control themselves right now, they *would*. Reminding yourself that kids truly just want to make their parents happy, they don't want to frustrate, annoy or enrage them.

It doesn't feel good to act like this; it feels scary, like running with scissors. They don't like how this is playing out either... and yet, their brain is unable to facilitate self-control right now until they get regulated. This is them resisting to release to regulate.

Your job is to learn how to not take their dysregulation personally. Be steady, hold the rope, and keep believing in them.

Parental Anger

Our kids are always watching us, absorbing not just what we say but what *we* do. So when it comes to anger, I need you to pause and ask yourself: *What am I teaching them about anger?* If you struggle with bottling and then exploding, they're likely picking up on that—whether you mean for them to or not. And I don't have to tell you how confusing and frustrating it is to have a parent insist that you "should be able to" handle something perfectly when they can't do it themselves.

Many of us, as recovering Good Kids, have spent our entire lives suppressing anger, only for it to leak or explode out of us in ways that feel out of control. We have to learn how to handle our anger—often right alongside our kids. And that's okay. It's not too late. The real power is in showing them that emotional regulation is a learned skill, not an innate trait, and that it's a process, not a performance.

Be brave enough to get curious about your own relationship with anger. When you have those moments where you bottle and explode, don't just sweep them under the rug—Circle Back and talk to your kid about it. Own it. Tell them, "I'm sorry I lost my temper. Did I scare you or hurt your feelings? I'm still learning how to handle my Big Feelings. I don't want to bottle and explode, and I'm practicing how to handle my anger in healthier ways that don't hurt others." Show them that learning to regulate emotions takes time, that no one gets it right every time, and most importantly, teach them how to Circle Back and repair when they do lose it. Model what it looks like to own your impact—how to take responsibility for your outburst, how to apologize, how to reconnect.

Debriefing for Clarity on What's Bothering You

Years ago, in a desperate attempt to be able to see the anger explosions coming and not hurt my daughter, I created a password-protected document that I still use to this day, called my Debrief. I dump all of the swirly, whirly trauma and overwhelming heaviness from these moments to try to get to the deeper pain that had been set off. Sometimes I Debrief after I have moved the Big Feelings out of my body and have my feet under me, to figure out what that was all about. Other times, when I can't figure what is bothering me, I use to Debrief to help me release what my body was refusing to release.

I See You Trying

It's okay if motherhood or parenthood has triggered rage for you. You've spent a lifetime bottling your feelings, walking on eggshells and made to feel ashamed for not meeting unattainable expectations. So now, as a parent, when the pressure builds and the responsibility of it all feels crushing, inevitably that exhaustion, overstimulation, and chronic dismissal of your own needs would lead to rage. How could it not? Please hear me when I say this: there is nothing wrong with you. And there is *so much* wrong with how you were raised.

As Cycle Breakers, we are *going* to get triggered. A whole lot. The goal is *not* to never get triggered. The goal is to break the damaging cycles around how we handle getting triggered—not making it our kid's fault for setting off our temper, owning our impact instead of making them feel responsible for our emotions and well-being. It's about giving them the apology they deserve instead of doubling down on making them feel ashamed. The lesson we want our kids to take away is, "My parent is human and when they mess up, they make it right." Not, "It's my fault for setting them off."

13

When They Don't Push Back—And That's the Problem

Punishments Are Not the Answer

We were raised by parents who had misguided beliefs that children needed to suffer in order to learn. That punishments "toughen kids up," that suffering "builds character," that fear leads to respect. If a child misbehaved, the solution wasn't to understand what was going on beneath the behavior—it was to shut it down and make them feel afraid of what would happen if they did it again. Punishments laced with shame and fear that demanded compliance or *else*.

Our parents didn't know any other way. Like their parents before them, they didn't know how to consider our emotional needs, our brain development, or our capacity to actually meet their expectations. And when we couldn't meet their expectations, instead of adjusting those expectations, we were punished. We were told we *should* be ashamed. We were made to feel that our worthiness of love and connection depended on how "good" we were.

Fear laced with shame doesn't create respect. Fear and shame create compliance, self-doubt, and eventually, resentment. When a child learns to fear punishment, they aren't developing an internal moral compass—they're learning how to avoid consequences. Shame then takes that fear a step further, teaching them that making mistakes isn't just bad—it makes *them* bad. Over time, this creates a child who performs goodness out of fear, while internally struggling with self-worth. And when that fear fades—as it inevitably does—kids don't suddenly develop a deep respect for their parents. Instead, they either withdraw, distance themselves, or begin pushing back in rebellion. If the goal is to raise a child who listens out of trust, respect, and connection—not out of fear of punishment—then punishment will never be the answer.

When we say, "My kid doesn't listen to me," what we're really saying is, "My kid isn't afraid of what will happen if they don't." And because many of us were raised to believe that obedience means respect, we see that as a problem. If we don't check these patterns in ourselves, we will repeat them. Because what we don't heal, we pass down.

So if punishments aren't the answer, what is?

When a child makes a mistake, they don't need to be made to feel worse about themselves—they need to learn how to make things right. They need to know that they are still good, still loved, still worthy of belonging even when they mess up. Because that's what actually teaches accountability—knowing that they are safe enough to take responsibility instead of being afraid to own up to their actions.

- Get curious instead of critical. Ask how things fell apart for them, not what's wrong with them.
- Talk through the impact of their words and actions without attacking who they are.
- Help them take responsibility and apologize for their impact without making them feel like they're bad or unworthy of forgiveness.

Real respect isn't something you can force—it's something that is built through mutual respect and trust, by being *in a relationship* with our kids, by showing them that we see them, hear them, and love and value them *and treat them with respect* even when they mess up.

You deserved that as a child. Accountability and respect don't come from making kids suffer. They come from showing them, over and over again, that even in their hardest moments, they are still worthy of love.

Time Out

I don't recommend Time Out. Yes, I am familiar with the scientific literature that concludes that it is safe and effective in managing and reducing unwanted behavior—specifically aggression and noncompliance. For me, as a licensed mental health clinician who focuses on Relational Shame and trauma, the question isn't "Is Time Out safe?" The questions are, "When will someone study Time Out and consider the way it induces relational shame for kids? And can we conclude that Time Out is safe if we're not considering the emotional and relational consequences of the relational shame Time Out induces?"

Kids are wired to seek us out for co-regulation and support when they're dysregulated to help them meet their core needs. When we say, "You're in Time Out. Go sit over there and think about what you've done"—that's us withdrawing and withholding love, attention, affection, and support and forcing them to be separate from us when their body is screaming at them to seek us out.

Another huge part of my concern about Time Out is that kids' impulse control often goes offline when they're dysregulated, so how can we expect a dysregulated child who is already showing you they can't control themselves... to sit still? And when they can't do what we order them to, why would we escalate the punishment? This makes them feel like there is something wrong with them, and we're disappointed in them for not being able to control themselves (Relational Shame)—when they already showed us they can't control themselves right now.

I'm a fan of the Time In concept. In Time Ins, we offer our dysregulated kids the stable, consistent boundaries they need and *stay with them* to offer support and co-regulation.

We owe it to our kids to learn how to spot a Shame Spiral, so we can throw them that life preserver and love them through it, when shame is telling them that nobody loves them. And we help them feel safe to get their feelings out with us so they can regulate down. I think we need to honor when kids ask for space and to be left alone, if we can (if they're not going to be destructive, for example).

The Silent Treatment

As we've discussed many times before, it is traumatic and confusing for a child to get the silent treatment from their parent. The child's brain and nervous system really struggle to make sense of their parent loving and caring for them one minute then the next, angrily acting like they don't exist.

The Silent Treatment vs. Needing Space

However, sometimes, we understandably get triggered and need space. I'm often asked about how to take a minute to regroup without it feeling like the silent treatment for our child.

I don't know about you but, sometimes, if I'm triggered in just the right way, I feel like I'm suddenly feral. I go into complete survival mode. I'm a little girl again, just trying to make it through. It's really inconvenient because it's my job to take care of *both* myself *and* my child. But I'm not in a place where I can hold space for my child's emotions and help them feel safe again.

Instead, find your way to be as neutral as you can. Give them some sense of what's going on without putting it on them. Go out of your way to say in words that they matter to you, and it matters to you that they are not okay. Tell them you see they need you right now, and you will be able to be there for them in a few minutes, but, right now, you need to take care of yourself and your Big Feelings, *and then* you'll be able to take care of them and theirs.

If you feel like a caged animal in these moments—I see you. When my kids were a toddler and a baby, nothing triggered me into yelling like trying to walk away to get my feelings out and my toddler refusing (really unable) to give me two minutes in the next room. It was such a hard time for both of us. Lots of volcanic eruptions and lots of Circling Back to repair. We do our best and show up for our impact.

Breaking the Silent Treatment Cycle

I have Parts of me that sometimes *want me* to give my child the silent treatment. These Parts are loud and vicious, demanding my child *suffer* and *beg for forgiveness* just like I had to as a kid. When this first started happening, I felt really ashamed. I felt like a terrible mom. But it's actually a completely understandable reaction to getting the silent treatment as a kid and being a parent trying to break that cycle.

It was impossible for our brains to reconcile our parents being a caregiver *and* a threat, and it was impossibly confusing and scary for our parents to be warm and loving with us one minute… then cold and ignoring our existence the next. These Parts of us are still trying to figure all of that out—by putting the shoe on the other foot and stepping into the parent role, as they understood it from our childhood. These Parts of us are not bad. They are trying to protect us, make some sense of what happened back then *and* keep us from getting hurt again like that.

And we must be responsible for our impact on our kids. It's our responsibility to manage these Parts of us—noticing when they're getting loud and wanting us to withdraw from our kids. Setting strong boundaries with them and pushing through the discomfort to connect with your child and stay warm or at least neutral, instead of going cold.

"I see you're upset. I'm a little overwhelmed with my Big Feelings, too. I'm going to go into this room and get some of my feelings out and then I'll come find you so we can reconnect and talk about what happened. Remember, it's safe for us to be frustrated with each other. I love you."

Then Circling Back to these Parts of us when the dust settles and getting curious, asking them, "What are you afraid will happen if I don't ice my kid out?" and "How old do you think I am?"

How People Pleasing Shows Up in Parenting

If you struggle with people pleasing in parenting, there is nothing wrong with you. I've struggled with it too—how could we not? When our kids push back, when they're upset with us, when they don't like the choices we've made, it hits something deep inside us. It makes us want to fix it, soften it, smooth things over so we don't have to sit with the awful feeling of disappointing them. This is Relational Shame Trauma playing out in real-time. It's why we struggle to say no and hold our boundaries because the thought of disappointing them feels like rejection.

We brace when our kids have Big Feelings about our boundaries. Our lived experience tells us that when people get mad at us, they don't love us. So we bend our own rules, cave when we know we shouldn't, walk on eggshells, trying to avoid setting them off. We exhaust ourselves managing their emotions, as if their feelings are our responsibility. Sound familiar? Our body interprets their reaction as a threat and before we know it, we're softening our no, over-explaining, or backing down completely just to avoid the discomfort of their pushback. Not because we don't want to hold the limit, but because we were never taught that pushback is safe.

But if we want to raise kids who don't feel like they have to people please their way through life—who know they can disagree, push back, have Big Feelings, and still be fully loved—then we *must* do this work. And I know it's hard. I know it feels unnatural. But the fact that you're even here, reading this, trying to do better—that is brave as hell. It matters. You are already changing everything for your kids.

People pleasing in parenting isn't just freaking exhausting; it makes us wobbly planks on their Boundaries Bridge. And when we're wobbly, they keep testing because they need us to be steady. Holding your boundary isn't mean or cruel. It's what makes them feel safe and loved and held steady.

Over-Explaining Your Boundaries

You say no, but then immediately feel the urge to explain, justify, soften the boundary so your kid won't be mad at you. Before you know it, you're in a full-on TED Talk about why ice cream before dinner isn't a good idea, hoping if you say it just right, they'll understand and accept it without a fight. I see you. It's okay that this is hard for you. Many of us grew up in homes where "no" meant shame, disapproval, or punishment, so now, we over-explain to protect ourselves from that same feeling. But the truth is, they just need to see and feel that you're steady and confident in your no.

Say no clearly and with warmth. "I know you really want ice cream, and the answer is no. It's okay to be disappointed." Then stop talking. They don't need a PowerPoint presentation—they need to see that you're confident in your no, a stable plank on their Boundaries Bridge.

Caving When They Push Back

You start strong, holding the boundary... but the whining starts, or the tears, or the "please, please, pleeease," and your resolve starts crumbling. Your chest gets tight, your brain is screaming, "I can't take this," and then—you've given in. And blamed them for it (just like our parents did). The discomfort of their disappointment can feel unbearable sometimes. When they push back, it can feel like you're doing something wrong, when really, this is exactly what their brain is wired to do—to test for stability to make sure you'll hold steady even when they resist. And the wildest part? They actually need and *want* you to hold steady, so they can resist to release to regulate. They're not trying to break you down. They're trying to release bottled-up feelings so they can feel regulated and safe.

Expect the pushback. It's normal and their brain is wired to test for stability, hoping and needing you to hold to what you said and allow them to resist. Remember, kids resist when they need to release bottled-up emotions so they can release and regulate. Instead of seeing their resistance as a problem, hold steady and let them get all of that out. "I hear you. The answer is still no."

Letting Guilt Make Your Decisions

Saying no makes you feel like a bad parent. Their sad face, their disappointment—it all hits something deep in you that says, "You're being too harsh. Just let them have this one." So you say yes, even when you don't want to. This comes from being made to feel as kids that upsetting others made us bad.

Check in with yourself: *Am I saying yes because I want to... or because I feel guilty?* Remind yourself, discomfort is not the same as harm. Kids need loving limits and a steady leader who isn't afraid of upsetting them. And boundaries actually make kids feel safer—even when they don't like them.

Walking on Eggshells Around Their Moods

They wake up cranky, or they start spiraling into a meltdown, and you feel it immediately in your body—you tense up, you hold your breath, and suddenly, you're in emotional damage control mode. Your brain is scanning for how to keep the peace, how to avoid setting them off, how to prevent this from escalating. You need to hear this: it is not your job to absorb their moods or make them okay. It was never supposed to be your job to do that for your parents, as a kid either. I know this is hard because you were taught that managing other people's emotions was what made you "good."

But your kid doesn't need you to tiptoe around their feelings—they need you to be steady and okay, even when they're not. Instead of managing their mood, manage *your* own frustration, anxiety, and energy. What works for me is saying to myself, "That is your child, not your parent. You're not a little kid anymore. Your kid is having Big Feelings and it needs to be okay for them to not be fine. It's not your job to make this better, your job is to take care of you right now."

Your job isn't to make sure they're never upset—it's to show them that it's okay to not pretend to be fine all the time and that emotions are safe and not a threat to the relationship.

Taking Their Emotions Personally

They're mad at you, and the rejection, the anger, the frustration—it all feels so personal, so unbearable. And I know how deep this runs because so many of us were raised to believe that upsetting someone meant we were bad. But this isn't about you. This is your moment to show up with this energy: *You don't have to make me happy to be loved here. I can handle your Big Feelings. I am not going anywhere. I will stay with you.*

Say to yourself: "That is your child, not your parent. You're not a little kid anymore. It needs to be okay for them to be mad at you. They need you to be their parent right now. This isn't personal, let them thrash on the other end of the rope and love them through it."

Separate their feelings from your worth. Their disappointment is a normal human emotion and says nothing about you as a parent. Their frustration doesn't mean you're failing. They are allowed to have Big Feelings, and they need you to hold your boundary and let them resist it to release to regulate, while Standing By Them.

Trying to Be "the Fun Parent"

You want them to have a happy childhood—to look back and remember joy, laughter, connection. So the thought of being the one who says no, the one who sets the rules, the one they push against feels... awful. You'd rather keep things fun and light so they'll love being around you. You are trying so hard to give them the warmth and ease you didn't get. But kids don't actually need a parent who is always fun—they need a parent who is steady and stands by them. Fun and connection matter, but so do boundaries, structure, and a loving leader who isn't afraid to disappoint them sometimes. Because that's how they learn that love doesn't go away when things aren't easy.

You are their Confident, Loving Leader, not their cruise director. Playfulness and connection matter, but boundaries make kids feel safer *and* loved by you. Kids don't need us to be fun all the time—they need us to be steady.

Feeling Responsible for Their Happiness

You see them struggling, and before you even think about it, you're scanning for how to fix it. How to cheer them up, how to make it better, how to get them back to "fine" as quickly as possible. And this makes sense, y'all—so many of us grew up in families where emotions weren't just ours to carry. We absorbed our parents' stress, felt responsible for managing their moods, and learned that peace meant keeping everyone happy and okay. So now, when our kids are struggling, we panic. Their discomfort triggers our old wiring that says any unhappiness is a problem to be solved.

But the truth is happiness is not the default state of being human. Neutral is. Life moves between ups, downs, and long stretches of just okay—and that's normal. When we try to fix, we're not just taking on a job that isn't ours, we're making them feel like they "should" be fine—which subtly sends them a damaging message we're all intimately familiar with: "You should feel better. What is wrong with you?" and makes them feel ashamed. Let's not do that to our kids. Let's work toward being a parent who makes it feel like emotions are meant to honored, felt and moved through us—not stuffed down, numbed, or compulsively rushed away.

Try being an empathetic witness. Instead of fixing, try validating. "It's okay to be upset" or "That's really frustrating, huh?" Let them sit with it. Let them feel it. Let them be. They don't need you to hide or remove their frustration—they need to move through it in their own time. Don't project an artificial time limit and expect them to be through it "by now" like our parents did. When we stop trying to force happy, we teach them something so much bigger: All feelings are safe. Even the messy ones.

Bracing Yourself for Their Reaction

Before you even say "No," you're already bracing for impact—bracing for the whining, the arguing, their disappointment, their anger, for love to be withdrawn. Your shoulders creep up, your jaw locks, your breath gets shallow, and you scan the room. Our nervous system reads these body cues and tension as evidence of a threat and keeps us stuck in Fight/Flight.

And because our body is already in self-protection mode, we become more likely to be a wobbly plank—to backpedal, over-explain, or cave altogether.

It was wild when I started noticing this in myself. Bracing wasn't just something I did in high-stress moments—it was my default state as recently as last year. I kept catching myself gently settling back into bracing throughout the day. My work now is to notice it with loving curiosity (usually I notice my shoulders and neck are tight first) and I say to myself: "Oh, I'm bracing again." And if I have the time, I ask: "Body, what are you bracing for? What are you afraid will happen? How can I care for you right now to help you feel safe?"

Then I speak to my body in its native language—*regulation*. I consciously complete the stress cycle by activating my muscles to signal to my body that *we have moved away from the threat*.

The next time you feel yourself bracing for their reaction, notice it with curiosity, compassion and love. It's not "Ugh I'm doing it again." It's "Oh, I'm noticing I'm bracing again. I make sense and this makes sense. Body, let me help you feel safe again." Drop your shoulders. Relax your jaw. Holding a boundary is an act of love—you're showing them that relationships can handle honesty and limits.

Seeking Their Approval

We want to be the "good" parent—the one who is fair, reasonable, calm, and lovable in our kids' eyes, the one who explains things so well that they *see our side and agree with us*. Because deep down, their approval feels like proof that we're doing a good job. And if they're upset with us? It can feel like we've failed.

But, we have come into parenting with completely backwards alarm bells. Right now, our alarm bells go off when our kids disagree with us because, when we were kids, it wasn't safe for *us* to disagree with our parents.

But those are the wrong alarm bells. The proper alarm bell here is one that sounds when a child *doesn't feel safe to disagree with us*. When a child stays silent, swallows their frustration, shuts down instead of pushing back. Because that's not a sign of a well-behaved child—that's a sign of shame and fear.

So when our kids resist, when they challenge, when they push back, we're actually getting the very thing we needed most as kids. We're showing them that our love is steady enough to hold their big feelings. They can be mad, upset, and disappointed without losing us. They can trust us and our love.

Remind yourself that you get to give them the parent they deserve who understands that your job is to lead, not to be liked. Work on settling into the idea that you don't need your child to approve of your decisions—you need to trust *yourself* in them. When you feel yourself bracing for their reaction, remind yourself: "This is my child, not my parent. Their disagreement is not rejection. Their pushback is not disrespect. It is safe for them to be upset." Then hold yourself through it and Stand By Them while they feel what they need to feel.

This is doing such powerful things for you—it's rewiring your alarm bells. *Let disagreement be safe. Let pushback be expected. Let their anger, frustration, and resistance be met with steadiness and love, not fear.* Because when we stop bracing for their emotions and start making room for them, we show them that they don't have to be easy or agreeable to keep our love—we will Stand By Them, no matter what.

I see you trying. I know this work is hard. I know there are days when it feels like too much, too big, not in the cards for you. But this isn't about doing it perfectly—it's about continuing to show up. It's about noticing when you're slipping into people pleasing with your kid; noticing when their disappointment makes you panic; noticing when you start to over-explain or bend your boundary just to keep the peace. And then, instead of shaming yourself for it, using that moment to course correct. Because your kid doesn't need you to be perfect—they just need you to be as steady as you can, show up for your impact, and Stand By Them. And I really need you to hear this you don't have to be ashamed that this is hard for you. You get to be proud of yourself for how hard you are trying.

Relational Colostrum: Why Circle Backs Are Liquid Gold

I like to call Circle Backs "Relational Colostrum" because they're that powerful, healing "liquid gold" in our relationships with our kids, especially when we have triggering, tense moments and conflict.

Why are we all so freaking terrified of conflict, you ask? Why will we twist ourselves into a pretzel to avoid conflict? Well, we grew up in homes where something would go wrong—someone would yell, someone would cry, someone would get their feelings hurt—and then... nothing. No one talked about it, no one said sorry. Just a hostile silence nobody acknowledged, then everyone expected to just act like it never happened and move on. Many of us learned to be the one who apologized, even if we weren't the one who caused the hurt. We blamed ourselves to keep the peace. But our bodies remember the part our parents left out. The repair part.

Conflict doesn't have to mean swallowing unseen, unacknowledged, unhealed hurt and pain. Conflict doesn't have to mean pretending it didn't happen just to get them to stay close. It doesn't have to mean bracing for love to be pulled away the second we show on the outside how much it hurt us on the inside. We get to rewrite that story—for Today Us, Little Us and our kids.

Because healthy conflict—the kind where we come back together to talk about what happened—doesn't ruin relationships. It actually makes them stronger by teaching our kids (and Little Us) that even when things get hard, love doesn't have to disappear. When we show up to say things like, "That was a tough moment. I'm sorry I hurt you. Can we talk about it?"—that small but powerful moment builds deep relational trust with our kids. It teaches them so many profound things that we all needed but didn't get: that it's safe to be honest about how something hurts you. That we can mess up and still be and feel loved. That when things get hard, we come back to each other. That they are worthy of an apology when someone hurts them. All while modeling and *SHOWING THEM* exactly how to start and navigate that messy, vulnerable awkward conversation.

This is why I refer to the process of Circling Back as "Relational Colostrum"—because they are liquid gold for our relationship with our child. They nourish and nurture the relationship with everything our nervous systems were starving for: safety, accountability and repair, and proof that love doesn't get jerked away when shit gets hard and we're lovable even when we mess up. They say what we ached to hear growing up—"I still love you even though that just happened. I'm not going anywhere. Let's work through it together."

During a meltdown, kids can't really hear us. They're completely dysregulated, and there's no point in trying to get them to "see the light." They can't understand why you said no, and that it actually makes sense why they can't do the thing. In these moments, I recommend using The Magic 9 words that all kids need to hear when they're in struggle— "I see you. I've got you. I love you." This shows them that you see them in there, under their emotional storm, and assures them that they're safe, even in the emotional chaos.

Try to stay warm and engaged instead of getting icy and withdrawing from them emotionally. Focus on holding the boundary and allowing them to resist it, so they can resist to release to regulate down. We hold space for the messy Big Feelings, and we keep reminding ourselves that they're dysregulated right now but *they're still in there* and once they release they will regulate down and come back to us.

After the blow-up, when everyone's calmer, we do a Circle Back. If it's tense and hostile, where everyone has gone to their respective corners of the home, we show up as their Confident, Loving Leader and break the stalemate—showing up to start the awkward conversation. That might look like, "Hey, things got intense just now and I wanted to talk about what happened and reconnect. Are you ready to talk or do you need more time?" We lead this conversation, acknowledging that something went down—maybe we got mad, maybe they got scared, maybe we both said things we regret. Then we show them they're loved and held through the conflict.

When we Circle Back with our kids, we are breaking so many cycles of generational trauma that taught us that when someone is mad at us, they stop loving us. And we should sweep conflict under the rug and pretend nothing ever happened. Conflict is emotional chaos, especially for kids—they need a framework to help them make sense of big arguments and scary blowups—especially if we scared them with our anger.

How to Do a Circle Back and Repair
- Own what you said.
- Own *and* see how you made them feel.
- If needed, give them a context to understand what happened.
- Give a genuine apology (no "I'm sorry, but you...").

Examples of Circle Backs
- "I got really frustrated with you, and I yelled and lost control. Was that scary for you? Did I hurt your feelings? It's safe to tell me if I scared or hurt you. I want to know

so I can own the way I made you feel and give you the apology you deserve."

Or:

- "I see you. We've been having a tough time with each other. I've got you, I want to talk about what happened so we can repair. I love you, even when things are hard, and I'm not going anywhere."

With words like those, you're proving that love doesn't go away just because tempers flared and things got tense. Research on Relational Shame Trauma shows that kids who experience healthy repair with their caregivers learn to expect it in their other relationships moving forward. So by Circling Back, you're not only showing your child *how* to start that awkward conversation after conflict to own your behavior and apologize when you hurt someone, but they start to believe, "I deserve someone who will say sorry when they hurt me."

Again, we didn't get that kind of repair, which made us think that's just how relationships work. So, when we do meet people who want to talk things through, it can feel unfamiliar, maybe even unsettling because our nervous system learned a different "normal." By Circling Back with our kids now, we're not only healing them, we're also gently retraining our own nervous system to see honest repair as safe and loving, rather than threatening or awkward.

And that's the real magic, showing your child (and your own Inner Child) that even when there's conflict and Big Feelings flying around, you can keep showing up for each other and love each other through the hard moments. Over time, these moments don't just repair the relationship; they actually make it stronger—it's like relational liquid gold when we love each other through our "worst" moments, refusing to give up on each other and apologizing when we hurt each other.

Bringing It All Together: Disrespect and Refusing To Cooperate

"Time to take a shower, guys!," I said.

My then six-year-old said, "No, I am not going to take a shower! I hate showers!" and laid down on the kitchen floor.

Our parents would have called this "disrespect" because she was disobeying me. She had an overwhelming impulse to resist me in that moment. To refuse to go shower. She didn't even know why. It was not about the shower—she *loves* showers. The "disrespect" was actually telling me she was dysregulated and needing an emotional release. She was *resisting to release to regulate*—with a stress level of 9.8ish out of 10. Her nervous system pushed her into resistance *so* she could release and regulate.

I gave her a minute and said, "I hear you honey, you don't want to take a bath or shower, but that's what we're going to do. Let's go—can you stand up on your own or do you need my help?"

I held my breath and waited for the explosion. Sure enough, she started screaming and thrashing around on the floor, hooting and hollering about how much she hates showers and she wasn't doing it.

Still, I felt *relieved* when she exploded. I wasn't disappointed or trying to avoid the explosion. I didn't think she was being a brat... I held the boundary knowing that would give her something to *resist* so she could get the release she needed and regulate down.

The Thing that this seemed to be about was not The Thing it was actually about—I did not need to try to convince her why it was important to keep our bodies clean, or why showers are so fun or make it a game to get her to cooperate—because it was never about the shower, y'all. She needed me to see that her body was in resistance. And she needed me to hold the boundary and let her blow.

All this stuff exploding out of her is what was overwhelming her before. She resisted getting in the shower, *so* I would hold that boundary, *so* she could resist it, *so* she could unload. And unload she did. An intense meltdown for like two minutes.

I always have to talk myself through the meltdowns because it reminds Little Me of being screamed at. One of my OG mantras in these moments is, "Tolerate the struggle." My job right now is to tolerate that she needs to have this struggle right now with resisting the shower. To show up as her Confident, Loving Leader who can hold the boundary and let her blow—without taking the resistance personally. Keeping my Perspectacles on, trying to see and connect with The Real Her under that "disrespect" and "defiance."

I held space for her, I didn't make her feel ashamed of herself for needing to resist the shower. I stayed warm and loving through the moments of darkness and thrashing. I held her leg when she tried to kick me, and I told her, "You've lost control, and you're trying to hurt me with your anger. It's okay to be mad, but I'm not going to let you hurt me. I'm here, and I love you." Aggression comes from a place of shame so she was in shame, asking me, "Can you love me... even like this?" She needed me to show her that yes, I will love you through your darkest, messiest moments. And yes, I've got you when you lose control and kick me—I know you don't want to kick me but your body and impulses have taken over.

She needed me to give her some solid ground to feel stable and safe while allowing her to resist me and release all of this. She needed me to remember that once she releases, she will regulate down and come back to me as her calm, sweet, cooperative self. And she did. She said she was sorry for yelling at me and trying to kick me. Then she happily sang, "Let's scrub our bodies and get clean" on the way to the bathroom. She had a wonderful shower *and* her self-worth and connection were nurtured through this experience.

Our Parents Would Call That "Soft" Parenting. They're Wrong.

Regulating myself to stay calm and loving when my kid is spiraling isn't weak. Resisting the overwhelming urge to shut them down isn't weak. Seeing through the screaming and flailing to The Real Them inside isn't weak. And choosing to not pass down the fear-based, shame-laced discipline that wrecked me isn't weak. It's all strong as hell. And this way raises kids who don't need years of therapy to believe they're inherently lovable.

Parenting is so much less maddening and triggering this way. When we can see that the resistance *is* the release. Because without this knowledge, we see this as our child "disobeying" us. We think they're just pulling a stunt, and they could just choose to shut this all down and suddenly be willing to cooperate. That's how our parents saw us. When we see these moments like that—as attention-seeking and manipulative—then the next step is to overpower the child, shutting this down and punishing them, making them feel like they were being ridiculous and owe you an apology for putting you through this.

If we shut down any and all disrespect and defiance, then we *also* shut down our kid's ability to release stress and regulate down. Meltdowns are not my favorite thing—they can be super triggering, especially when I haven't managed my stress and emotions well and I'm a 9 out of 10! I can go from Mary Poppins to Cruella de Ville real quick. But in a weird way, it feels sacred and special to be able to let my kid feel safe *letting it all hang out*, knowing I will love them no matter what. Knowing they can push me away and show what we believe are our "worst sides" and I will hold them right through it. Trusting I've got them and I'll hold the boundary they're pushing against, and I'll hold space for their Big Feelings.

Because that's what they need most in those moments—not punishment, not rejection, and definitely not shame. Feeling safe trusting that they have nothing to fear when they have messy, overwhelming emotions—and their meltdowns and misbehavior don't make them "bad" or unworthy. And when they fall apart and see me stay steady and loving, it sends them a powerful message to answer their question: "Yes, I can love you even like this—you don't have to hide your struggles from me. I'm here. You're safe. You're loved—exactly as you are, even when it's hard."

When we send that message, love stops being attached to their ability to "behave" and "be good." That child starts to believe they are *inherently* worthy of love because they don't have to earn it first by being "good" anymore. And... that child starts to love and trust themselves, too. It's not freaking easy, but giving them that soft spot to land feels like the most important work I'll ever do in my whole life.

Most of us never had that and our lives and our relationships with our parents would be really different if we had. Our parents see us allowing our kids to have their Big Feelings and say we're "coddling" them and they will be "entitled" and "spoiled." Y'all, they have no idea what they're talking about. The scientific literature says otherwise. Meeting kids' emotional needs doesn't make them entitled or spoiled—it helps them to feel safe, seen and loved. Punishments are awful teachers; we don't learn much when we're stressed out from the shame and fear; we're in survival mode.

The truth is, kids need *and want*, I would argue, to be held accountable for their behavior and taught about the impact of their actions. And we can do all of that while still making them feel deeply loved, supported, and understood.

Conclusion

This is the beginning of your softest, strongest, most healing chapter yet. This is the part of the story where you start belonging *to yourself*, the part where you start being loyal *to yourself*. This is the part when you stop asking, "Am I 'too much'?" and start whispering, "I don't have to prove anything to anyone. I've got me."

Trust yourself.

You've spent so long trying to be good, earn your place, hold everything together, be easy, and be lovable. But now, *you get to rest*. Be messy. Practice taking up space and having needs, preferences and opinions—without apologizing. Stop shapeshifting and start coming home to who you really are.

You're unlearning the Good Kid rules that tamed you with shame and fear.

You're listening to the Parts of you that were silenced and abandoned. You're learning to recognize the shame—it's like glitter, isn't it? It's freaking *everywhere*. You're learning how to stay with yourself when things get painful.

I know it's hard. Keep going, you deserve to heal this.

Take what you've learned. Notice when you're getting critical with yourself and shift into curiosity. Let Yourself Feel Without Shame. Recognize when you're holding yourself to unattainable standards and Check Your Expectations. When you're scrambling to please and perform and do everything perfectly, Shift Your Focus back to yourself, what you need, what you deserve. And work on Standing By Yourself, No Matter What.

Finally start to *give yourself* all the support, the understanding, the patience and the love without conditions that you give to everyone else. Practice loving who you've become. Practice loving yourself fiercely, ferociously, relentlessly and without conditions—the way you always deserved.

When your Inner Critic shows up with those old stories, trying to pull you back, remind yourself: you're not that scared little kid anymore. You're the one who came back for them.

You don't have to keep dragging around all that shame and self-doubt. You really don't. When it feels uncomfortable, when it would be easier to slip back into old habits of people pleasing and hypervigilance and performing for love—remind yourself that *you deserve better than survival mode.*

I'm so proud of you I can hardly stand it. I'm beaming from ear to ear thinking about the way you're showing up and doing your best—whatever that looks like each day. That choice quietly but profoundly changes everything. For you. For the people lucky enough to know you now. And for generations to come. I hope you can feel how profound and world-changing that really is.

Please be gentle with yourself as you do this sacred, freaking hard work. Keep reminding yourself that you are unlearning a lifetime of conditioning and bullshit that taught you to shrink, to please, to perform. Of course the new way feels awkward and uncomfortable. Of course it's hard. That doesn't mean you're failing—it means you're being brave. It means you're stepping into territory you were never shown how to navigate—and healing in the ways you've always deserved. Keep going. You're doing something extraordinary.

I hope this book is helping you believe at the deepest level that you always were a story worth loving, exactly as you are. I'm cheering you on as you come home to yourself. Thank you for letting me be a part of your healing journey.

Acknowledgments

Matt. Thank you for being the first person to love all of me, without conditions. You showed me and helped me believe I did actually deserve love. Thank you for teaching me how to love myself with such tenderness. I could have never dreamed of such a happy, warm home, marriage and life like the one we've created together. You have always believed I was made to do great things. Thank you for the many, many ways you have held down the fort with our family so I could have the space to write this book. Getting to love you and be loved by you is the best thing.

Sharon. Thank you for holding space for me all these years. For believing in my own inherent worth long before I could. For teaching me how to feel my feelings and be freaking gentle with myself. For meeting me with such stunning, unwavering patience, understanding and encouragement. For guiding me back to myself, over and over again.

Anne and Logan. Thank you for the way you love and hold me – all of me – and lovingly…demand that I always consider what I need and take really good care of myself. I don't quite know how to put into words how it feels for you to cheer loudest when I show up as full-on Me. Our friendship has healed me in profound ways. And I'm so grateful I get to mother my kids with both of you by my side.

Camp Lovable fam. It is such an honor to guide you and witness your healing. Thank you for sharing your stories with me, some of which I'm so proud to share in this book. I am endlessly inspired by you and your healing.

Eli. Thank you for your epic pep talk before I started writing this book, I referenced back to it so many times. Thank you for believing in me, in this book, and in the heart behind every single page. Your words make me feel seen and held and set up the rest of the book so beautifully. Nobody does Attachment like you, friend.

Brené Brown, Ph.D., LMSW. Thank you for putting shame on the map for me. Your work and the way you put words to all of the most profound life things continues to absolutely astound me and facilitate healing at the deepest levels. I humbly but proudly stand on your shoulders with my work and this book. Thank you for being you.

Richard Schwartz, Ph.D. Thank you, from all of my Parts. It is not an exaggeration to say that your work changed my entire life and continues to give me a way to make sense of myself in a way nothing else ever has. You and your work helped me stop feeling broken and start feeling beautifully complex. I am endlessly grateful and honored to include your work in this book.

Rachel. Thank you for believing in me and my work and seeing the path ahead with this book. Thank you for your guidance and relentless support throughout this process. I'm so proud of what you've helped me create with this book.

References

Chapter 1: The Good Kids Aren't Alright

Brown, B. (2006). "Shame resilience theory: A grounded theory study on women and shame." *Families in Society*, 87(1), 43–52.

Brown, B. (2006). *The Gift of Imperfection: Let Go of Who You Think You're Supposed to Be and Embrace Who You Are*. Hazelden Publishing.

Brown, B. (2008). *I Thought It Was Just Me (But It Isn't): Making the Journey from "What Will People Think?" to "I Am Enough."* Avery.

Flett, G. L., & Hewitt, P. L. (2002). "Perfectionism and maladjustment: An overview of theoretical, definitional, and treatment issues." In G. L. Flett & P. L. Hewitt (Eds), *Perfectionism: Theory, Research, and Treatment* (pp. 5–31). American Psychological Association.

Gibson, L. C. (2015). *Adult Children of Emotionally Immature Parents: How to Heal from Distant, Rejecting, or Self-Involved Parents*. New Harbinger Publications.

Gilbert, P. (2009). *The Compassionate Mind: A New Approach to Life's Challenges*. New Harbinger Publications

Huang, Y., Pan, J., & Zhang, R. (2024). "A review of the impact of parenting styles on adolescents' self-esteem." *Journal of Education, Humanities and Social Sciences*, 26, 869–873.

Hughes, D. A. (2004). *Building the Bonds of Attachment: Awakening Love in Deeply Troubled Children*. Jason Aronson Inc.

Miller-Day, M., & Lee, J. W. (2001). "Communicating disappointment: The viewpoint of sons and daughters." *The Journal of Family Communication*, 1(2), 111–131.

Perry, B. D., Pollard, R. A., Blakley, T. L., Baker, W. L., & Vigilante, D. (1995). "Childhood trauma, the neurobiology of adaptation, and 'use-dependent' development of the brain: How 'states' become 'traits.'" *Infant Mental Health Journal*, 16(4), 271–291.

Qian, G., Wu, Y., Wang, W., Li, L., Hu, X., Li, R., Liu, C., Huang, A., Han, R., An, Y., & Dou, G. (2022). "Parental psychological control and adolescent social problems: The mediating effect of emotion regulation." *Frontiers in Psychiatry*, 13, 995211.

Schwartz, R. (2021). No bad parts: Healing trauma and restoring wholeness with the internal family systems model. Sounds True.

Shafran, R., Cooper, Z., & Fairburn, C. G. (2002). "Clinical perfectionism: A cognitive–behavioural analysis." Behaviour Research and Therapy, 40(7), 773–791.

Shaver, P. R., & Mikulincer, M. (2019). *Attachment in Adulthood: Structure, Dynamics, and Change* (2nd ed.). The Guilford Press.

Sofrona, E., & Giannakopoulos, G. (2024). "The impact of parental depressive, anxiety, and stress symptoms on adolescents' mental health and quality of life: The moderating role of parental rejection." *Children*, 11(11), 1361.

Stoeber, J., & Otto, K. (2006). "Positive conceptions of perfectionism: Approaches, evidence, challenges." *Personality and Social Psychology Review*, 10(4), 295–319.

Van der Kolk, B. A. (2015). *The Body Keeps the Score: Brain, Mind, and Body in the Healing of Trauma* (1st ed.). Penguin Books.

Chapter 2: Good Kid Biology

Bowlby, J. (1969). *Attachment and Loss: Volume I—Attachment*. Basic Books.

Cassidy, J., & Mohr, J. J. (2001). "Unsolvable fear, trauma, and psychopathology: Theory, research, and clinical considerations related to disorganized attachment across the life span." *Clinical Psychology: Science and Practice*, 8(3), 275–298

Cozolino, L. (2014). *The Neuroscience of Human Relationships: Attachment and the Developing Brain* (2nd ed.). W.W. Norton & Company.

Crittenden, P. M. (2006). *The Dynamic-Maturational Model of Attachment and Adaptation*. W.W. Norton & Company.

Gilbert, P., & Procter, S. (2006). "Compassionate mind training for people with high shame and self-criticism: Overview and pilot study of a group therapy approach." *Clinical Psychology & Psychotherapy: An International Journal of Theory & Practice*, 13(6), 353–379.

Huang, Y., Pan, J., & Zhang, R. (2024). "A review of the impact of parenting styles on adolescents' self-esteem." *Journal of Education, Humanities and Social Sciences*, 26, 869–873.

Labanski, A., Langhorst, J., Engler, H., & Elsenbruch, S. (2020). "Stress and the brain-gut axis in functional and chronic-inflammatory gastrointestinal diseases: A transdisciplinary challenge." *Psychoneuroendocrinology*, 111, 104501.

Mikulincer, M., & Shaver, P. R. (2019). "Attachment orientations and emotion regulation." *Current Opinion in Psychology*, 25, 6–10.

Nagoski, E., & Nagoski, A. (2019). *Burnout: The Secret to Unlocking the Stress Cycle*. Ballantine Books.

Perry, B. D., Pollard, R. A., Blakley, T. L., Baker, W. L., & Vigilante, D. (1995). "Childhood trauma, the neurobiology of adaptation, and 'use-dependent' development of the brain: How 'states' become 'traits.'" *Infant Mental Health Journal*, 16(4), 271–291.

Porges, S. W. (2007). "The polyvagal perspective." *Biological Psychology*, 74(2), 116–143.

Porges, S. W. (2011). *The Polyvagal Theory: Neurophysiological Foundations of Emotions, Attachment, Communication, and Self-Regulation*. W.W. Norton & Company.

Schore, A. N. (2003). *Affect Regulation and the Repair of the Self (Vol. 2)*. WW Norton & Company.

Schwartz, A. (2020). *A Practical Guide to Complex PTSD: Compassionate Strategies to Begin Healing from Childhood Trauma*. Sourcebooks, Inc.

Shaver, P. R., & Mikulincer, M. (2002). "Attachment-related psychodynamics." *Attachment & Human Development*, 4(2), 133–161.

Shaver, P. R., & Mikulincer, M. (2019). *Attachment in Adulthood: Structure, Dynamics, and Change* (2nd ed.). The Guilford Press.

Van der Kolk, B. A. (2015). *The Body Keeps the Score: Brain, Mind, and Body in the Healing of Trauma* (1st ed.). Penguin Books.

Van der Hart, O., & Horst, R. (1989). "The dissociation theory of Pierre Janet." *Journal of Traumatic Stress*, 2(4), 397–412.

Walker, P. (2013). *Complex PTSD: from Surviving to Thriving: A Guide and Map for Recovering from Childhood Trauma*. Azure Coyote, Lafayette, CA.

Chapter 3: "You Should Be Grateful."

Brown, B. (2006). "Shame resilience theory: A grounded theory study on women and shame." *Families in Society*, 87(1), 43–52.

Brown, B. (2006). *The Gift of Imperfection: Let Go of Who You Think You're Supposed to Be and Embrace Who You Are*. Hazelden Publishing.

Brown, B. (2008). *I Thought It Was Just Me (But It Isn't): Making the Journey from "What Will People Think?" to "I Am Enough."* Avery.

Cicchetti, D., & Toth, S. L. (2009). "The development of depression in children and adolescents." *American Psychologist*, 64(2), 165–174

Flett, G. L., & Hewitt, P. L. (2002). "Perfectionism and maladjustment: An overview of theoretical, definitional, and treatment issues." In G. L. Flett & P. L. Hewitt (Eds), *Perfectionism: Theory, Research, and Treatment* (pp. 5–31). American Psychological Association.

Gibson, L. C. (2015). *Adult Children of Emotionally Immature Parents: How to Heal from Distant, Rejecting, or Self-Involved Parents*. New Harbinger Publications.

Gilbert, P. (2009). *The Compassionate Mind: A New Approach to Life's Challenges*. New Harbinger Publications

Gilbert, P., & Procter, S. (2006). "Compassionate mind training for people with high shame and self-criticism: Overview and pilot study of a group therapy approach." *Clinical Psychology & Psychotherapy: An International Journal of Theory & Practice*, 13(6), 353–379.

Gottman, J. M., & Declaire, J. (1997). *The Heart of Parenting: How to Raise an Emotionally Intelligent Child*. Simon & Schuster.

Hooper, L. M., L'Abate, L., Sweeney, L. G., Gianesini, G., Jankowski, P. J., & Hooper, L. (2014). "Parentification." *Models of Psychopathology: Generational Processes and Relational Roles*, 37–54.

Hughes, D. A. (2004). *Building the Bonds of Attachment: Awakening Love in Deeply Troubled Children*. Jason Aronson Inc.

Kim, S., Thibodeau, R., & Jorgensen, R. S. (2011). "Shame, guilt, and depressive symptoms: A meta-analytic review." *Psychological Bulletin*, 137(1), 68.

McMahon, T. J., & Luthar, S. S. (2007). "Defining characteristics and potential consequences of caretaking burden among children living in urban poverty." *American Journal of Orthopsychiatry*, 77(2), 267–281.

Mikulincer, M., & Shaver, P. R. (2019). "Attachment orientations and emotion regulation." *Current Opinion in Psychology*, 25, 6–10.

Neff, K., & Germer, C. (2018). *The Mindful Self-Compassion Workbook: A Proven Way to Accept Yourself, Build Inner Strength, and Thrive.* Guilford Publications.

Perry, B. D., Pollard, R. A., Blakley, T. L., Baker, W. L., & Vigilante, D. (1995). "Childhood trauma, the neurobiology of adaptation, and 'use-dependent' development of the brain: How 'states' become 'traits.'" *Infant Mental Health Journal*, 16(4), 271–291.

Reid, R. C., & Crisanti, A. S. (2020). "The enduring effects of parental alcohol, tobacco, and drug use on child well-being: A multilevel meta-analysis." *Development and Psychopathology*, 32(2), 765–778.

Shaver, P. R., & Mikulincer, M. (2019). *Attachment in Adulthood: Structure, Dynamics, and Change* (2nd ed.). The Guilford Press.

Schore, A. N. (2003). *Affect Regulation and the Repair of the Self (Vol. 2)*. WW Norton & Company

Schwartz, A. (2020). *A Practical Guide to Complex PTSD: Compassionate Strategies to Begin Healing from Childhood Trauma*. Sourcebooks, Inc.

Tangney, J. P., Burggraf, S. A., & Wagner, P. E. (1995). "Shame-proneness, guilt-proneness, and psychological symptoms." In J. P. Tangney & K. W. Fischer (Eds), *Self-Conscious Emotions: The Psychology of Shame, Guilt, Embarrassment, and pride* (pp. 343–367). Guilford Press.

Tangney, J. P., Stuewig, J., & Mashek, D. J. (2007). "Moral emotions and moral behavior." *Annual Review of Psychology*, 58(1), 345–372.

Treeby, M., & Bruno, R. (2012). "Shame and guilt-proneness: Divergent implications for problematic alcohol use and drinking to cope with anxiety and depression symptomatology." *Personality and Individual Differences*, 53(5), 613–617.

Van der Kolk, B. A. (2015). *The Body Keeps the Score: Brain, Mind, and Body in the Healing of Trauma* (1st ed.). Penguin Books.

Chapter 4: The Voice That Says It's All Your Fault

Bennett, D. S., Sullivan, M. W., & Lewis, M. (2005). "Young children's adjustment as a function of maltreatment, shame, and anger." *Child Maltreatment*, 10(4), 311–323.

Brown, B. (2006). "Shame resilience theory: A grounded theory study on women and shame." *Families in Society*, 87(1), 43–52.

References

Brown, B. (2006). *The Gift of Imperfection: Let Go of Who You Think You're Supposed to Be and Embrace Who You Are*. Hazelden Publishing.

Brown, B. (2008). *I Thought It Was Just Me (But It Isn't): Making the Journey from "What Will People Think?" to "I Am Enough."* Avery.

Flett, G. L., & Hewitt, P. L. (2002). "Perfectionism and maladjustment: An overview of theoretical, definitional, and treatment issues." In G. L. Flett & P. L. Hewitt (Eds), *Perfectionism: Theory, Research, and Treatment* (pp. 5–31). American Psychological Association.

Gibson, L. C. (2015). *Adult Children of Emotionally Immature Parents: How to Heal From Distant, Rejecting, or Self-Involved Parents*. New Harbinger Publications.

Gilbert, P. (2009). *The Compassionate Mind: A New Approach to Life's Challenges*. New Harbinger Publications

Gross, J. J., & John, O. P. (2003). "Individual differences in two emotion regulation processes: Implications for affect, relationships, and well-being." *Journal of Personality and Social Psychology*, 85(2), 348.

Huang, Y., Pan, J., & Zhang, R. (2024). "A review of the impact of parenting styles on adolescents' self-esteem." *Journal of Education, Humanities and Social Sciences*, 26, 869–873.

Hughes, D. A. (2004). *Building the Bonds of Attachment: Awakening Love in Deeply Troubled Children*. Jason Aronson Inc.

Mikulincer, M., & Shaver, P. R. (2019). "Attachment orientations and emotion regulation." *Current Opinion in Psychology*, 25, 6–10.

Miller-Day, M., & Lee, J. W. (2001). "Communicating disappointment: The viewpoint of sons and daughters." *The Journal of Family Communication*, 1(2), 111–131.

Neff, K., & Germer, C. (2018). *The Mindful Self-Compassion Workbook: A Proven Way to Accept Yourself, Build Inner Strength, and Thrive*. Guilford Publications.

Peng, B., Hu, N., Yu, H., Xiao, H., & Luo, J. (2021). "Parenting style and adolescent mental health: The chain mediating effects of self-esteem and psychological inflexibility." *Frontiers in Psychology*, 12, 738170.

Perry, B. D., Pollard, R. A., Blakley, T. L., Baker, W. L., & Vigilante, D. (1995). "Childhood trauma, the neurobiology of adaptation, and 'use-dependent' development of the brain: How 'states' become 'traits'." *Infant Mental Health Journal*, 16(4), 271–291.

Porges, S. W. (2011). *The Polyvagal Theory: Neurophysiological Foundations of Emotions, Attachment, Communication, and Self-Regulation*. W.W. Norton & Company.

Qian, G., Wu, Y., Wang, W., Li, L., Hu, X., Li, R., Liu, C., Huang, A., Han, R., An, Y., & Dou, G. (2022). "Parental psychological control and adolescent social problems: The mediating effect of emotion regulation." *Frontiers in Psychiatry*, 13, 995211.

Schwartz, R. (1997). *Internal Family Systems Therapy*. Guilford.

Schwartz, R. (2021). *No Bad Parts: Healing Trauma and Restoring Wholeness with the Internal Family Systems Model*. Sounds True.

Shafran, R., Cooper, Z., & Fairburn, C. G. (2002). "Clinical perfectionism: A cognitive–behavioural analysis." *Behaviour Research and Therapy*, 40(7), 773–791.

Shaver, P. R., & Mikulincer, M. (2019). *Attachment in Adulthood: Structure, Dynamics, and Change* (2nd ed.). The Guilford Press.

Sofrona, E., & Giannakopoulos, G. (2024). "The impact of parental depressive, anxiety, and stress symptoms on adolescents' mental health and quality of life: The moderating role of parental rejection. *Children*, 11(11), 1361.

Tangney, J. P., Burggraf, S. A., & Wagner, P. E. (1995). "Shame-proneness, guilt-proneness, and psychological symptoms." In J. P. Tangney & K. W. Fischer (Eds), *Self-Conscious Emotions: The Psychology of Shame, Guilt, Embarrassment, and Pride* (pp. 343–367). Guilford Press.

Tangney, J. P., Wagner, P., Fletcher, C., & Gramzow, R. (1992). "Shamed into anger? The relation of shame and guilt to anger and self-reported aggression." *Journal of Personality and Social Psychology*, 62(4), 669.

Tangney, J. P., Wagner, P. E., Hill-Barlow, D., Marschall, D. E., & Gramzow, R. (1996). "Relation of shame and guilt to constructive versus destructive responses to anger across the lifespan." *Journal of Personality and Social Psychology*, 70(4), 797.

Tangney, J. P., Stuewig, J., & Mashek, D. J. (2007). "Moral emotions and moral behavior." *Annual Review Psychology*, 58(1), 345–372.

Treeby, M., & Bruno, R. (2012). "Shame and guilt-proneness: Divergent implications for problematic alcohol use and drinking to cope with anxiety and depression symptomatology." *Personality and Individual Differences*, 53(5), 613–617.

Van der Hart, O., & Horst, R. (1989). "The dissociation theory of Pierre Janet." *Journal of Traumatic Stress*, 2(4), 397–412.

Van der Kolk, B. A. (2015). *The Body Keeps the Score: Brain, Mind, and Body in the Healing of Trauma* (1st ed.). Penguin Books.

Walker, P. (2013). *Complex PTSD: From Surviving to Thriving: A Guide and Map for Recovering from Childhood Trauma*. Azure Coyote, Lafayette, CA.

Chapter 5: You Didn't Want To Be "A Burden"

Bowlby, J. (1969). *Attachment and Loss: Volume I—Attachment*. Basic Books.

Deci, E. L., & Ryan, R. M. (2000). "The 'what' and 'why' of goal pursuits: Human needs and the self-determination of behavior." *Psychological Inquiry*, 11(4), 227–268.

Gilbert, P. (2009). *The Compassionate Mind: A New Approach to Life's Challenges*. New Harbinger Publications

Miller-Day, M., & Lee, J. W. (2001). "Communicating disappointment: The viewpoint of sons and daughters." *The Journal of Family Communication*, 1(2), 111–131.

Neufeld, G., & Maté, G. (2013). *Hold On to Your Kids: Why Parents Need to Matter More than Peers*. Vintage Canada.

Peng, B., Hu, N., Yu, H., Xiao, H., & Luo, J. (2021). "Parenting style and adolescent mental health: The chain mediating effects of self-esteem and psychological inflexibility." *Frontiers in Psychology*, 12, 738170.

Qian, G., Wu, Y., Wang, W., Li, L., Hu, X., Li, R., Liu, C., Huang, A., Han, R., An, Y., & Dou, G. (2022). "Parental psychological control and adolescent social problems: The mediating effect of emotion regulation." *Frontiers in Psychiatry*, 13, 995211.

Perry, B. D., Pollard, R. A., Blakley, T. L., Baker, W. L., & Vigilante, D. (1995). "Childhood trauma, the neurobiology of adaptation, and 'use-dependent' development of the brain: How 'states' become 'traits'." *Infant Mental Health Journal*, 16(4), 271–291.

Van der Kolk, B. A. (2015). *The Body Keeps the Score: Brain, Mind, and Body in the Healing of Trauma* (1st ed.). Penguin Books.

Chapter 6: The Part Where You Stop Being Mad At Yourself

Atlas, G. (2021). *Emotional Inheritance: A Therapist, Her Patients, and Their Stories of Trauma*. W.W. Norton & Company.

Barrett, L. F. (2017). *How Emotions are Made: The Secret Life of the Brain*. Pan Macmillan.

Bowlby, J. (1969). *Attachment and Loss: Volume I—Attachment*. Basic Books.

Brown, B. (2006). "Shame resilience theory: A grounded theory study on women and shame." *Families in Society*, 87(1), 43–52.

Brown, B. (2006). *The Gift of Imperfection: Let Go of Who You Think You're Supposed to Be and Embrace Who You Are*. Hazelden Publishing.

Brown, B. (2008). *I Thought it was Just Me (But it isn't): Making the Journey from "What will people think?" to "I am enough."* Avery.

Damasio, A. R. (1999). *The Feeling of What Happens: Body and Emotion in the Making of Consciousness*. Houghton Mifflin Harcourt.

Flett, G. L., & Hewitt, P. L. (2002). "Perfectionism and maladjustment: An overview of theoretical, definitional, and treatment issues." In G. L. Flett & P. L. Hewitt (Eds), *Perfectionism: Theory, Research, and Treatment* (pp. 5–31). American Psychological Association.

Gottman, J. M., & Declaire, J. (1997). *The Heart of Parenting: How to Raise an Emotionally Intelligent Child*. Simon & Schuster.

Gross, J. J. (2002). "Emotion regulation: Affective, cognitive, and social consequences." *Psychophysiology*, 39(3), 281–291.

Hughes, D. A. (2004). *Building the Bonds of Attachment: Awakening Love in Deeply Troubled Children*. Jason Aronson Inc.

Labanski, A., Langhorst, J., Engler, H., & Elsenbruch, S. (2020). "Stress and the brain-gut axis in functional and chronic-inflammatory gastrointestinal diseases: A transdisciplinary challenge." *Psychoneuroendocrinology*, 111, 104501.

Porges, S. W. (2011). *The Polyvagal Theory: Neurophysiological Foundations of Emotions, Attachment, Communication, and Self-Regulation*. W.W. Norton & Company.

Rosenberg, S. (2017). *Accessing the Healing Power of the Vagus Nerve*. North Atlantic Books.

Schwartz, R. (1997). *Internal Family Systems Therapy*. Guilford.

Schwartz, R. (2021). *No Bad Parts: Healing Trauma and Restoring Wholeness with the Internal Family Systems Model*. Sounds True.

Severs, L. J., Vlemincx, E., & Ramirez, J. M. (2022). "The psychophysiology of the sigh: I: The sigh from the physiological perspective." *Biological Psychology*, 170, 108313.

Van der Kolk, B. A. (2015). *The Body Keeps the Score: Brain, Mind, and Body in the Healing of Trauma* (1st ed.). Penguin Books.

Chapter 7: You Carry Your Childhood Into Every Relationship

Beattie, M. (2022). *Codependent No More: How to Stop Controlling Others and Start Caring for Yourself* (First Spiegel & Grau edition). Spiegel & Grau.

Bowlby, J. (1969). *Attachment and Loss: Volume I—Attachment*. New York.

Gilbert, P. (2009). *The Compassionate Mind: A New Approach to Life's Challenges*. New Harbinger Publications

Hayes, S. C. (2005). *Acceptance and Commitment Therapy: The Process and Practice of Mindful Change*. The Guilford Press.

Phillips, C. (2022). Let them [Unpublished viral poem]. Shared publicly via Facebook.

Porges, S. W. (2011). *The Polyvagal Theory: Neurophysiological Foundations of Emotions, Attachment, Communication, and Self-Regulation*. W.W. Norton & Company.

Robbins, M., & Robbins, S. (2024). *The Let Them Theory: A Life-Changing Tool that Millions of People Can't Stop Talking About*. Hay House.

Schore, A. N. (2003). *Affect Regulation and the Repair of the Self (Vol. 2)*. W.W. Norton & Company.

Schwartz, A. (2020). *A Practical Guide to Complex PTSD: Compassionate Strategies to Begin Healing from Childhood Trauma*. Sourcebooks, Inc.

Shaver, P. R., & Mikulincer, M. (2002). "Attachment-related psychodynamics." *Attachment & Human Development*, 4(2), 133–161.

Shaver, P. R., & Mikulincer, M. (2019). *Attachment in Adulthood: Structure, Dynamics, and Change* (2nd ed.). The Guilford Press.

Van der Kolk, B. A. (2015). *The Body Keeps the Score: Brain, Mind, and Body in the Healing of Trauma* (1st ed.). Penguin Books.

Chapter 8: Giving Yourself What They Couldn't

Bennett, D. S., Sullivan, M. W., & Lewis, M. (2005). "Young children's adjustment as a function of maltreatment, shame, and anger." *Child Maltreatment*, 10(4), 311–323.

Broekhof, E., Bos, M. G. N., & Rieffe, C. (2021). "The roles of shame and guilt in the development of aggression in adolescents with and without hearing loss", *Research on Child and Adolescent Psychopathology*, 49, 891–904.

Brown, B. (2006). "Shame resilience theory: A grounded theory study on women and shame." *Families in Society*, 87, 43–52.

Brown, B. (2006). *The Gift of Imperfection: Let Go of Who You Think You're Supposed to Be and Embrace Who You Are*. Hazelden Publishing.

Brown, B. (2008). *I Thought it was Just Me (but it isn't): Making the Journey from "What will People Think?" to "I am enough."* Avery.

Carter, C. S. (2009). *The Influence of Oxytocin in Relationships: Partners, Friends, Parents, and Others*. The Guilford Press

Cozolino, L. (2014). *The Neuroscience of Human Relationships: Attachment and the Developing Brain* (2nd ed.). W.W. Norton & Company

Ford, J. D., & Courtois, C. A. (2009). *Treating Complex Traumatic Stress Disorders: An Evidence-Based Guide*. Guilford Press.

Gross, J. J., & John, O. P. (2003). "Individual differences in two emotion regulation processes: Implications for affect, relationships, and well-being." *Journal of Personality and Social Psychology*, 85(2), 348.

Hughes, D. A. (2004). *Building the Bonds of Attachment: Awakening Love in Deeply Troubled Children*. Jason Aronson Inc.

Neff, K. D. (2011). *Self-Compassion: The Proven Power of Being Kind to Yourself*. William Morrow.

Rogers, C. R. (1995). *On Becoming a Person: A Therapist's View of Psychotherapy*. Houghton Mifflin Harcourt.

Tangney, J. P., Wagner, P., Fletcher, C., & Gramzow, R. (1992). "Shamed into anger? The relation of shame and guilt to anger and self-reported aggression." *Journal of Personality and Social Psychology*, 62(4), 669.

Tangney, J. P., Wagner, P. E., Hill-Barlow, D., Marschall, D. E., & Gramzow, R. (1996). "Relation of shame and guilt to constructive versus destructive responses to anger across the lifespan." *Journal of Personality and Social Psychology*. 70(4), 797.

Tangney, J. P., Stuewig, J., & Mashek, D. J. (2007). "Moral emotions and moral behavior." *Annual Review of Psychology*, 58(1), 345–372.

Chapter 9: Facing Your Stuff So Your Kids Don't Have To

Cozolino, L. (2014). *The Neuroscience of Human Relationships: Attachment and the Developing Brain* (2nd ed.). W.W. Norton & Company.

Carter, C. S. (2009). *The Influence of Oxytocin in Relationships: Partners, Friends, Parents, and Others.* The Guilford Press.

Damasio, A. R. (1999). *The Feeling of What Happens: Body and Emotion in the Making of Consciousness.* Houghton Mifflin Harcourt.

Doidge, N. (2007). *The Brain That Changes Itself: Stories of Personal Triumph from the Frontiers of Brain Science.* Viking.

Gilbert, P. (2009). *The Compassionate Mind: A New Approach to Life's Challenges.* New Harbinger Publications

Gottman, J. M., & Declaire, J. (1997). *The Heart of Parenting: How to Raise an Emotionally Intelligent Child.* Simon & Schuster.

Gross, J. J. (2002). "Emotion Regulation: Affective, Cognitive, and Social Consequences." *Psychophysiology,* 39(3), 281–291.

Hughes, D. A. (2004). *Building the Bonds of Attachment: Awakening Love in Deeply Troubled Children.* Jason Aronson Inc.

Lansbury, J. (2024). *No Bad Kids: Toddler Discipline Without Shame.* Rodale Books.

Neff, K. D. (2011). *Self-Compassion: The Proven Power of Being Kind to Yourself.* William Morrow.

Perry, B. D., Pollard, R. A., Blakley, T. L., Baker, W. L., & Vigilante, D. (1995). "Childhood trauma, the neurobiology of adaptation, and 'use-dependent' development of the brain: How 'states' become 'traits'." *Infant Mental Health Journal,* 16(4), 271–291.

Shaver, P. R., & Mikulincer, M. (2019). *Attachment in Adulthood: Structure, Dynamics, and Change* (2nd ed.). The Guilford Press.

Siegel, D. J., & Bryson, T. P. (2021). *The Power of Showing Up: How Parental Presence Shapes Who our Kids Become and How Their Brains Get Wired.* Ballantine Books.

Van der Kolk, B. A. (2015). *The Body Keeps the Score: Brain, Mind, and Body in the Healing of Trauma* (1st ed.). Penguin Books.

Chapter 10: Seeing the Signs and Showing Up Differently

Brown, B. (2006). *The Gift of Imperfection: Let Go of Who You Think You're Supposed to Be and Embrace Who You Are.* Hazelden Publishing.

Flett, G. L., & Hewitt, P. L. (2002). "Perfectionism and maladjustment: An overview of theoretical, definitional, and treatment issues." In G. L. Flett & P. L. Hewitt (Eds), *Perfectionism: Theory, Research, and Treatment* (pp. 5–31). American Psychological Association.

Gilbert, P. (2009). *The Compassionate Mind: A New Approach to Life's Challenges.* New Harbinger Publications

Gross, J. J., & John, O. P. (2003). "Individual differences in two emotion regulation processes: Implications for affect, relationships, and well-being." *Journal of Personality and Social Psychology,* 85(2), 348.

Hesse, E. (1999). "The adult attachment interview: Historical and current perspectives." *Handbook of Attachment: Theory, Research, and Clinical Applications*, 2.

Klonsky, E. D. (2007). "The functions of deliberate self-injury: A review of the evidence." *Clinical Psychology Review*, 27(2), 226–239.

Lanius, R. A., Vermetten, E., & Pain, C. (2010). *The Impact of Early Life Trauma on Health and Disease*. Cambridge UP.

Neff, K. D. (2011). *Self-Compassion: The Proven Power of Being Kind to Yourself*. William Morrow.

Neufeld, G., & Maté, G. (2013). *Hold on to Your Kids: Why Parents Need to Matter More than Peers*. Vintage Canada

Perry, B. D., Pollard, R. A., Blakley, T. L., Baker, W. L., & Vigilante, D. (1995). "Childhood trauma, the neurobiology of adaptation, and 'use-dependent' development of the brain: How 'states' become 'traits'." *Infant Mental Health Journal*, 16(4), 271–291.

Porges, S. W. (2007). "The polyvagal perspective." *Biological Psychology*, 74(2), 116–143

Porges, S. W. (2011). *The Polyvagal Theory: Neurophysiological Foundations of Emotions, Attachment, Communication, and Self-Regulation*. W.W. Norton & Company.

Schore, A. N. (2003). *Affect Regulation and the Repair of the Self (Vol. 2)*. WW Norton & Company.

Shafran, R., Cooper, Z., & Fairburn, C. G. (2002). "Clinical perfectionism: A cognitive–behavioural analysis." *Behaviour Research and Therapy*, 40(7), 773–791.

Shaver, P. R., & Mikulincer, M. (2019). *Attachment in Adulthood: Structure, Dynamics, and Change* (2nd ed.). The Guilford Press.

Siegel, D. J., & Bryson, T. P. (2011). *The Whole-Brain Child: 12 Revolutionary Strategies to Nurture Your Child's Developing Mind*. Delacorte Press.

Stoeber, J., & Otto, K. (2006). "Positive conceptions of perfectionism: Approaches, evidence, challenges." *Personality and Social Psychology Review*, 10(4), 295–319.

Van der Kolk, B. A. (2015). *The Body Keeps the Score: Brain, Mind, and Body in the Healing of Trauma* (1st ed.). Penguin Books.

Chapter 11: Raising Kids Who Don't Have To Recover

Brown, B. (2006). "Shame resilience theory: A grounded theory study on women and shame." *Families in Society*, 87(1), 43–52.

Gilbert, P. (2009). *The Compassionate Mind: A New Approach to Life's Challenges*. New Harbinger Publications

Huang, Y., Pan, J., & Zhang, R. (2024). "A Review of the Impact of Parenting Styles on Adolescents' Self-Esteem." *Journal of Education, Humanities and Social Sciences*, 26, 869–873.

Miller-Day, M., & Lee, J. W. (2001). "Communicating disappointment: The viewpoint of sons and daughters." *The Journal of Family Communication*, 1(2), 111–131.

Nagoski, E., & Nagoski, A. (2019). *Burnout: The Secret to Unlocking the Stress Cycle*. Ballantine Books.

Peng, B., Hu, N., Yu, H., Xiao, H., & Luo, J. (2021). "Parenting style and adolescent mental health: The chain mediating effects of self-esteem and psychological inflexibility." *Frontiers in Psychology*, 12, 738170.

Porges, S. W. (2007). "The polyvagal perspective." *Biological Psychology*, 74(2), 116–143.

Porges, S. W. (2011). *The Polyvagal Theory: Neurophysiological Foundations of Emotions, Attachment, Communication, and Self-Regulation*. W. W. Norton & Company.

Qian, G., Wu, Y., Wang, W., Li, L., Hu, X., Li, R., Liu, C., Huang, A., Han, R., An, Y., & Dou, G. (2022). "Parental psychological control and adolescent social problems: The mediating effect of emotion regulation." *Frontiers in Psychiatry*, 13, 995211.

Shafran, R., Cooper, Z., & Fairburn, C. G. (2002). "Clinical perfectionism: A cognitive–behavioural analysis." *Behaviour Research and Therapy*, 40(7), 773–791.

Smiley, P. A., Rasmussen, H. F., Buttitta, K. V., Hecht, H. K., Scharlach, K. M., & Borelli, J. L. (2020). "Parent control and child shame: Associations with children's task persistence and depressive symptoms in middle childhood." *Parenting*, 20(4), 311–336.

Sofrona, E., & Giannakopoulos, G. (2024). "The impact of parental depressive, anxiety, and stress symptoms on adolescents' mental health and quality of life: The moderating role of parental rejection." *Children*, 11(11), 1361.

Sroufe, L. A., Egeland, B., Carlson, E. A., & Collins, W. A. (2005). *The Development of the Person: The Minnesota Study of Risk and Adaptation from Birth to Adulthood*. Guilford Press

van Eickels, R. L., Siegel, M., Juhasz, A. J., & Zemp, M. (2025). "The parent–child relationship and child shame and guilt: A meta-analytic systematic review." *Child Development*, 1–23.

Van der Kolk, B. A. (2015). *The Body Keeps the Score: Brain, Mind, and Body in the Healing of Trauma* (1st ed.). Penguin Books.

Chapter 12: Big Feelings Shouldn't Equal Big Trouble

Ford, J. D., & Courtois, C. A. (Eds). (2013). *Treating Complex Traumatic Stress Disorders in Children and Adolescents: Scientific Foundations and Therapeutic Models*. Guilford Press.

Gilbert, P. (2009). *The Compassionate Mind: A New Approach to Life's Challenges*. New Harbinger Publications

Lemerise, E. A., & Arsenio, W. F. (2000). "An integrated model of emotion processes and cognition in social information processing." *Child Development*, 71(1), 107–118.

Neufeld, G., & Maté, G. (2013). *Hold on to Your Kids: Why Parents Need to Matter More Than Peers*. Vintage Canada.

Perry, B. D., Pollard, R. A., Blakley, T. L., Baker, W. L., & Vigilante, D. (1995). "Childhood trauma, the neurobiology of adaptation, and 'use-dependent' development of the brain: How 'states' become 'traits'." *Infant Mental Health Journal*, 16(4), 271–291.

Porges, S. W. (2007). "The polyvagal perspective." *Biological Psychology*, 74(2), 116–143

Porges, S. W. (2011). *The Polyvagal Theory: Neurophysiological Foundations of Emotions, Attachment, Communication, and Self-Regulation.* W.W. Norton & Company.

Siegel, D. J., & Bryson, T. P. (2011). *The Whole-Brain Child: 12 Revolutionary Strategies to Nurture Your Child's Developing Mind*. Delacorte Press.

Sroufe, L. A., Egeland, B., Carlson, E. A., & Collins, W. A. (2005). *The Development of the Person: The Minnesota Study of Risk and Adaptation from Birth to Adulthood*. Guilford Press.

Tangney, J. P., Wagner, P., Fletcher, C., & Gramzow, R. (1992). "Shamed into anger? The relation of shame and guilt to anger and self-reported aggression." *Journal of Personality and Social Psychology*, 62(4), 669.

Tangney, J. P., Wagner, P. E., Hill-Barlow, D., Marschall, D. E., & Gramzow, R. (1996). "Relation of shame and guilt to constructive versus destructive responses to anger across the lifespan." *Journal of Personality and Social Psychology*, 70(4), 797.

Tangney, J. P., Stuewig, J., & Mashek, D. J. (2007). "Moral emotions and moral behavior." *Annual Review of Psychology*, 58(1), 345–372.

Chapter 13: When They Don't Push Back – And That's the Problem

Brown, B. (2006). "Shame resilience theory: A grounded theory study on women and shame." *Families in Society*, 87(1), 43–52.

Brown, B. (2006). *The Gift of Imperfection: Let Go of Who You Think You're Supposed to Be and Embrace Who You Are*. Hazelden Publishing.

Brown, B. (2008). *I Thought It Was Just Me (But It Isn't): Making the Journey From "What Will People Think?" to "I Am Enough."* Avery.

Gilbert, P. (2009). *The Compassionate Mind: A New Approach to Life's Challenges*. New Harbinger Publications

Gilbert, P., & Procter, S. (2006). "Compassionate mind training for people with high shame and self-criticism: Overview and pilot study of a group therapy approach." *Clinical Psychology & Psychotherapy: An International Journal of Theory & Practice*, 13(6), 353–379.

Gottman, J. M., & Declaire, J. (1997). *The Heart of Parenting: How to Raise an Emotionally Intelligent Child.* Simon & Schuster.

Hughes, D. A. (2004). *Building the Bonds of Attachment: Awakening Love in Deeply Troubled Children.* Jason Aronson Inc.

Kim, S., Thibodeau, R., & Jorgensen, R. S. (2011). "Shame, guilt, and depressive symptoms: A meta-analytic review." *Psychological Bulletin,* 137(1), 68.

Neff, K., & Germer, C. (2018). *The Mindful Self-Compassion Workbook: A Proven Way to Accept Yourself, Build Inner Strength, and Thrive.* Guilford Publications.

Perry, B. D., Pollard, R. A., Blakley, T. L., Baker, W. L., & Vigilante, D. (1995). "Childhood trauma, the neurobiology of adaptation, and 'use-dependent' development of the brain: How 'states' become 'traits'." *Infant Mental Health Journal,* 16(4), 271–291.

Schwartz, A. (2020). *A Practical Guide to Complex PTSD: Compassionate Strategies to Begin Healing from Childhood Trauma.* Sourcebooks, Inc.

Shaver, P. R., & Mikulincer, M. (2002). "Attachment-related psychodynamics." *Attachment & Human Development,* 4(2), 133–161.

Shaver, P. R., & Mikulincer, M. (2019). *Attachment in Adulthood: Structure, Dynamics, and Change* (2nd ed.). The Guilford Press.

Siegel, D. J., & Bryson, T. P. (2011). The Whole-Brain Child: 12 Revolutionary Strategies to Nurture your Child's Developing Mind. Delacorte Press.

Tangney, J. P., Burggraf, S. A., & Wagner, P. E. (1995). "Shame-proneness, guilt-proneness, and psychological symptoms." In J. P. Tangney & K. W. Fischer (Eds), *Self-Conscious Emotions: The Psychology of Shame, Guilt, Embarrassment, and Pride* (pp. 343–367). Guilford Press.

Tangney, J. P., Stuewig, J., & Mashek, D. J. (2007). "Moral emotions and moral behavior." *Annual Review of Psychology,* 58(1), 345–372.

Treeby, M., & Bruno, R. (2012). "Shame and guilt-proneness: Divergent implications for problematic alcohol use and drinking to cope with anxiety and depression symptomatology." *Personality and Individual Differences,* 53(5), 613–617.

Van der Kolk, B. A. (2015). *The Body Keeps the Score: Brain, Mind, and Body in the Healing of Trauma* (1st ed.). Penguin Books.

Index

4 S's (Drs. Daniel Siegel and Tina Payne Bryson) 185

Abandonment, 26, 36, 40, 51, 52, 55, 65, 75, 77, 84, 113, 114, 120, 133, 134, 155, 157, 167, 188, 189, 208, 224, 225, 259, 278
  Abandonment wounds, 135
  Emotional abandonment, 42
  Self-abandonment, 20, 88, 130, 138, 139, 143, 149, 189, 230
Abuse, 4, 6
  Substance abuse, 44, 52–53
  Emotional abuse, 41, 67
  See silent treatment
Accountability, 12, 44, 59, 71, 86, 114–116, 126–127, 168, 178, 179, 196, 224, 244, 245, 251, 260, 262, 288, 301, 307
Aggression, 17, 29, 163, 165, 186–187, 240, 242, 245, 279–280, 283, 289, 305
Amygdala, 18, 111, 161, 256
Anger, 29, 32, 38, 43, 45, 47, 65, 64, 76, 77, 121, 136, 155, 160, 163–166, 181, 183, 186, 194, 198, 199, 200, 210, 224, 242, 245, 257, 258, 259, 262, 269, 271–273, 276, 279, 280, 281, 283, 284, 295, 297, 305
  Our parents' anger, 16, 17, 48, 80, 81, 86, 89, 93, 95, 100, 103, 115, 150, 257
  See also: rage
Anxiety, 7, 9, 24, 26, 28, 48, 49, 54, 74, 77, 106, 110, 132, 145, 147, 148, 157, 162, 192, 195, 199, 210–213, 220, 221, 231, 238, 245, 254, 261, 266, 272, 295
Apologies, 5, 7, 11, 20, 24, 32, 41, 42, 44, 60, 61, 87, 91, 95, 119, 154, 155, 162, 179, 183, 205, 206, 216, 224, 240, 265, 273, 286, 288, 300, 301, 303
  Over apologizing, 20, 52, 65, 124, 155, 156, 201, 203, 204, 216, 223–226, 246, 259

Performative apologies, 61, 253
Approval, 8, 68, 69, 84, 109, 128, 146, 152, 149, 195, 202, 207 210, 220, 225, 228, 251, 298
  Our parents' approval 4, 7, 16, 20, 28, 29, 39, 73–74, 93, 95, 122, 123
Attachment figures, 23, 126
Attachment issues, 37
Attachment Theory, 20, 23, 147
Attachment patterns, 23
  Anxious / preoccupied attachment, 24
  Avoidant / dismissive attachment, 23
  Insecure attachment, 23
  Disorganized attachment, 23, 25
  Secure attachment, 25–26, 185
Attunement, 4, 23, 50, 81, 116, 117, 130, 244, 246, 247
  Hyper-attunement, 18, 20, 48, 50, 52, 67, 113

Bad Kids, 28–29
Big Feelings, 15, 19, 20, 29, 34, 35, 36, 45, 47, 58, 101, 102, 104, 110, 181, 185, 187, 186, 198, 210, 236, 241, 245, 252, 279, 281, 282, 285, 291, 292, 293, 295, 296, 299, 302, 303, 306, 307
Belonging, 5, 25, 63, 64, 69, 75, 86, 88, 91, 101, 114, 118, 121, 123,127, 167, 195, 210, 220, 222, 225, 257, 288
Blame, 7, 17, 45, 48, 50, 51, 52, 60, 68, 86, 87, 88, 92, 93, 95, 114, 115, 155, 164, 169, 172, 247, 248, 249, 256, 294, 300
Bottling it up, 49, 77, 170, 186, 245, 247, 266
  Bottling anger, 163, 166, 271–272, 284–285
  Bottling feelings, 9, 11, 48,104, 106, 177, 180, 188, 198, 262, 267, 268, 285, 294

327

Bottling emotions, 34, 38, 47, 77, 94, 199, 207–210, 294
Bottling stress, 103, 104, 274, 282
Boundaries 52, 81, 94, 122, 134, 162, 191, 192–194, 196, 201, 204, 206, 216, 242, 260, 281–282, 283, 290, 292, 293, 294, 296, 298, 299, 301, 304, 305, 306
   Boundary pushing, 15, 104, 149, 242
   Boundary setting 11, 81, 128, 134, 149, 152, 161, 168, 194, 215, 233, 291
   Setting boundaries with yourself, 168–169
   Boundaries Bridge, 192–193, 293
Breathwork, 132, 274
Burnout, 5, 82, 85, 99, 214–215, 218, 240
Butterfly tapping 111, 151, 200

Capacity, 51, 52, 53, 61, 81, 85, 184, 217, 243, 244, 245, 247, 250, 255, 256, 262, 287
Circle Back, 47, 87, 132, 148, 179, 183, 228, 253, 260, 261, 265, 266, 267, 273, 277, 285, 291, 292, 300–303
Challenging authority, 72, 73, 178
Childhood development, 183–185
   Nervous system development, 15–21
Code of How to Be Valuable, 120
Codependency, 54, 128, 158
Conflict, 18, 24, 26, 78, 90, 102, 144, 146, 179, 192, 203, 205, 223, 224, 226, 252, 253, 260, 273, 300, 302, 303
Connection, 17, 18, 20, 21, 23–26, 31, 37, 55, 59, 63–64, 65, 66, 75, 78, 87, 88, 90–91, 101–103, 105, 111 113, 118, 121, 123, 125, 126, 131, 132, 134, 144–145, 146, 168, 172, 201, 202, 204, 223, 224, 237, 241, 242, 254, 257, 260, 261, 262, 266, 267, 269, 273, 287, 288, 292, 296, 305
   Connection with ourselves, 150, 161
   Disconnection, 18, 19, 24, 26, 64–65, 69, 124, 147, 179, 231, 257

Disconnection from ourselves, 77, 80, 252
Conditional love, 4, 24, 43, 57, 75, 95, 114, 118, 123, 129, 143, 147, 149, 195, 197, 253
Confident, Loving Leader, 164, 191, 242, 260, 261, 280, 282, 296, 302, 305
Consequences, 26, 32, 40, 75, 89, 102, 137, 178, 196, 287, 289
Compassion, 19, 91, 113, 115, 118, 125, 126, 127, 128, 129, 132, 133, 134, 135, 144, 154, 158, 162, 166, 170, 172, 201, 213, 228 232, 268, 298
   Self-compassion, 115, 126, 131, 168, 202, 229, 231
Core Needs, 185–200, 289
Cortisol, 161, 256
Criticism, 16, 23, 33, 36, 38, 65, 69, 90, 91, 113, 114, 119, 120, 121, 130, 135, 144, 166, 168,186, 187, 189, 227, 239, 240, 248, 257, 264
   Self-criticism, 5, 11, 68, 75, 121, 124, 133, 227–230, 309
   Inner Critic, 7, 90, 96, 114, 120–127, 129, 131, 133, 153, 168, 206, 227, 228, 229, 231, 233, 256, 258, 264, 265, 278, 310
Curiosity, 119,125, 127, 128, 133, 135, 139, 151, 154, 173 183, 201, 206, 209, 211, 212, 232, 232, 237, 240, 260, 298
   Get Curious, 45, 65,125, 129, 130, 133–134, 138, 148, 155, 158, 168, 204, 216, 231, 234, 238, 264, 285
   Critical to Curious, 134, 191, 200, 239–242, 284, 288
Cycle Breaking, 26, 45, 47, 56, 58, 61, 92, 116, 134, 157, 170, 172, 179, 183, 185, 186, 187, 191, 196, 208, 222, 224, 226, 231, 239, 240, 242, 244, 248, 249, 254, 266, 286, 291, 302

Defiance, 56, 101, 105, 177, 190, 198, 250, 272, 305, 306
Depression, 28, 199, 261, 272, 272
Digestive issues, 21–22, 198
   See stomachaches

Index

Disappointment, 9, 12, 16, 17, 24, 38, 40, 65, 87, 106, 114, 122, 124, 151–153, 155–156, 186, 195, 196, 204, 207, 210, 217, 225, 226, 226, 227, 231, 242, 244, 245, 255, 256, 258, 263, 277, 292, 293, 294, 296, 297, 299, 304
   "I'm not mad, I'm just disappointed", 28, 33, 41, 66, 76, 79, 221, 243, 254
   Disappointment in our kids, 206, 216–217, 224–225, 243, 254–256, 262, 289
   Our parents' disappointment, 33, 45, 49, 57, 67, 75, 76, 79, 80, 82, 84, 92, 99, 100, 106, 169, 187, 204 225, 252, 254, 256, 257
Disapproval, 40, 151, 153, 156, 293
   Our parents' disapproval, 18, 33, 100, 257
Discipline, 28, 32, 33, 34, 37, 40, 41, 43, 91, 99, 100, 101, 102, 104, 126, 177, 182, 251
   "Don't come home if" discipline, 43–44
   See punishment
Dissociation, 17–18, 19, 67, 71, 138, 214
Dopamine, 161

Eating disorders, 5, 199
Emotional detachment, 157–158
Emotional distance, 24, 147
Emotionally reactive parents, 47–50
   Narcissistic and borderline parents, 50–52
   Parents with substance use disorder, 52
Emotional needs, 34, 38–39, 69, 94, 115, 117, 149, 162, 185, 287, 307
Emotional outbursts, 26
Emotional suppression, 5, 20, 22, 28, 32–33, 35, 39, 47, 52, 77, 80–81, 100, 106, 110, 114, 117, 123, 131, 197, 198, 199, 201, 240, 246, 250, 251, 252–253
   See bottling emotions
Emotional withdrawal, 17, 28, 41, 50, 71, 74, 76, 84, 88

Emotional wellbeing, 28, 50, 101, 157, 162, 178, 248
Emotional wounds, 35–37
Empathy, 51, 126, 172–173, 178, 238, 247, 248, 249, 269
Endorphins, 22
Enmeshment, 80
Expectations, 13, 33–34, 43, 58, 65, 68, 71, 72, 83, 90, 95, 99, 109, 133, 190, 225, 250, 255, 262, 263, 285, 287
   Check Our Expectations, 191, 217, 243–244, 250, 256, 262
   Our parents' expectations, 225, 243, 249, 250, 271

Failure, 38, 48, 68, 74–76, 80, 82, 113, 115, 170, 171, 177, 180, 185, 201, 218, 220, 222, 227, 228, 231, 242, 243, 265, 273, 274, 281, 296, 298
Fear, 23–26, 31, 40, 45, 66, 94, 102, 120, 128, 141–143, 148, 150, 153, 161, 172, 179, 183, 191, 192, 195, 206, 210, 211, 212, 242, 273, 276, 280, 281, 299, 307
   Fear of/avoidance of abandonment, 33, 51, 58, 63, 64, 65, 91, 125, 162, 207, 224
   Fear of/avoidance of conflict, 5, 7, 8, 9, 17, 18, 20, 28, 37, 49, 52, 65, 67, 78, 90, 91, 109, 120, 122, 160, 201, 223, 231, 300
   Fear of/avoidance of criticism, 91, 114
   Fear of/avoidance of disappointment, 193, 224
   Fear of/avoidance of failure, 4–5, 12, 19, 74–76, 89, 91, 124, 201, 220, 253, 256
   Fear of/avoidance of rejection, 18, 26, 38, 58, 63, 65, 91, 125, 162, 207, 223, 224, 251
   Fear of/avoidance of punishment, 91, 207, 251, 287
Feeling Beings, 130, 178, 197–200
Feeling like a burden, 9, 26, 32, 39, 46, 55, 64, 65, 76, 77, 79, 82, 83, 88, 91, 99–107, 113, 122, 131, 132, 138, 143, 144, 198, 204, 205, 248, 253

Feeling not enough, 5, 7, 9, 11, 37, 39–40, 55, 57, 64, 70, 71, 76, 89, 93, 120, 123, 129, 133, 136, 152, 171, 210, 215, 228, 229
Feeling your feelings, 137–138, 153, 199
Feeling like you're too much, 10, 11, 38, 39–40, 45, 70, 77, 88, 92, 93, 96, 114, 122, 136, 137, 143, 166, 193, 197, 199, 205, 209, 210, 211, 229, 252, 278, 309
Fight/Flight, 20, 48, 67, 88, 110–111, 130–131, 143, 156, 181, 199, 204, 214–215, 226, 230, 232, 239, 259, 268, 297
  Fawn response, 16–20, 27–28, 50, 65, 101, 103, 149, 151, 156, 259
  Flight response, 5, 16–20, 28, 65, 103, 160, 258
  Fight response, 5, 16, 17, 27–29, 49, 101, 177, 199, 258, 272, 280
  Freeze response, 65, 101, 103, 214–215, 258
  Functional freeze, 214
Frustration, 32, 38, 47, 76, 101–102, 104, 182, 190, 192, 193, 198, 199, 200, 205, 207, 209, 210, 216, 224, 225, 229, 232, 237, 245, 247, 249, 250, 253, 254, 259, 260, 266, 267, 268, 273–274, 280, 281, 284, 295, 296, 297, 299

Gaslighting, 61, 179, 231
Grief, 61, 71, 115, 116, 167, 222, 276
Gonzalez-Mena, Janet, 192
Grounding techniques, 112
Guilt, 5, 61, 63, 81, 84, 134, 154, 186, 192, 214–215, 216, 218, 219, 222, 233, 257, 261, 265, 267, 294
  Guilt-prone self-talk, 261–262, 265
  Guilt trips, 27
Gut-Brain Axis, 21–23

Headaches, 55, 113, 198, 199, 230, 232, 252
Healing, 7–8, 11, 12, 23, 29, 36, 44–45, 59, 86, 89, 112, 123, 125, 126, 128, 129, 130, 132, 134, 135, 146, 148, 155, 157, 161, 162, 178, 183, 199, 202, 206, 218, 222, 226, 269, 288, 300, 303

Embodied healing, 268
Healing childhood trauma, 160
Healing attachment, 26
Healing from shame, 58, 65
Healing Relational Shame, 172
Healing Relational Trauma, 109–110, 151–152, 207
Healing Relational Shame Trauma, 22, 113–120, 189
High achieving, 5, 13, 37, 54–55, 73, 74, 99, 109, 220
  See overachieving
Holding space, 8, 20, 95, 116, 187, 188, 191, 212, 241, 244, 275, 279, 290, 302, 306
Humiliation, 38, 41, 251
Hurt, 275
Hypervigilance, 9, 11, 18, 28, 40, 48, 51, 53, 64, 84, 110, 113, 117, 124, 161, 210–213
Hyper-aware, 54, 67, 117

Independence, 32, 52, 59, 79, 82–83, 100, 253
Inner Child, 10, 124, 154–155, 161–162, 200, 203, 206, 207, 210, 212, 213, 219, 222–223, 226, 229, 233
Intellectualization, 137, 279
Internal Family Systems (IFS) 127–129, 133–134, 168, 214, 232
  Self, 127, 133, 153
  Parts, 127–130, 132, 134–135, 138, 148, 159, 161, 167, 168, 197, 214, 216, 232–233, 241, 245, 267, 269, 291, 292
  Protector Parts, 127, 138
Intimidation, 27–28, 186
  Physical intimidation, 27
  Emotional intimidation, 28
Isolation, 41, 65, 83, 15
  See also Time Out

Lansbury, Janet, 192
Let them, 152, 153, 154, 156, 157, 207, 210, 229, 242–243
Life Preserver Scripts, 277
Laziness, 19, 33, 82, 121, 196, 215, 218, 219
Low confidence, 26
Lying, 245

Index

Magic 9, 209, 279, 301
Meltdowns, 200, 207, 244, 279–280, 295, 301, 305, 306, 307
Misbehavior, 15, 100, 102–103, 105, 177, 249, 260, 287, 307
Misguided beliefs, 31–44, 72–86, 177, 249, 287
Mistakes, 19, 33, 38, 40, 57, 58, 67, 68, 72, 74, 75, 76, 78, 80, 91, 92, 120, 125, 126, 127, 129, 144, 167, 185, 186, 188, 195, 201–203, 207, 210–211, 221, 222, 223, 225, 227, 228, 229, 230, 250, 251, 254, 257, 258, 259, 260, 261, 262, 265, 277, 287, 288
Movement, 110-100, 132

Nagoski, Drs. Emily and Amelia, 20
Need suppression, 28, 33, 58, 78, 80, 85, 117, 123, 149, 251, 286
Neediness, 10, 25, 46, 52, 59, 114, 181
Neglect, 6, 49, 67, 92, 99, 114, 146, 147, 161
    Emotional neglect, 23, 52, 67
    Self-neglect, 85
Nervous system, 15–28, 35, 37, 46, 49–50, 54, 63–65, 71, 86–89, 93, 95, 100, 103, 105, 110, 113, 114, 119, 121, 123–126, 132, 135, 143, 144–145, 147–151, 152, 156, 161, 181, 186, 190, 198, 199, 203, 206, 209, 210, 211, 212, 213, 214, 222, 224, 226, 227, 230, 231, 232, 237, 243, 248, 250, 252, 257, 258–259, 268, 272, 274, 280, 282, 283, 290, 297, 303, 304
    Parasympathetic nervous system, 22, 23, 111, 199
    Sympathetic nervous system, 14, 22, 110, 111, 199, 214
    Ventral vagal system, 111
    Vagus nerve 111
Numbing, 5, 17, 18, 55, 67, 77, 197, 207, 236, 238, 297

Obedience, 4, 37, 38, 72, 102, 109, 155, 177, 251, 288
    Disobedience, 43
Overachieving, 75, 219–223, 228

Over functioning, 5, 75, 214
Overperforming, 114, 124, 138, 214, 224
Overthinking, 19, 138
Overwhelm, 17, 19, 25, 77, 80, 83, 84, 88, 130, 130, 137, 161, 162, 182, 188,190, 205, 206, 209, 211, 213, 214, 233, 240, 241, 243, 244 245, 247, 250, 256, 259, 273, 280
Oxytocin, 161

Parentification, 54, 79
People pleasing, 5, 9, 11, 19–20, 28, 40, 54, 57, 64, 68, 81, 85, 148–150, 154, 160, 201, 203–207, 213, 226, 253, 272
    People pleasing in parenting, 292, 299
Perfectionism, 7, 9, 11, 13, 19, 39, 54–55, 68, 73, 74–76, 83, 123, 133, 179, 190, 201, 220, 228, 231, 255, 259, 272
Physical harm, 41, 67
    See: spanking
Physiological sigh, 111, 151, 156, 200
Polyvagal theory, 20, 147, 214
    Dorsal Vagal Shutdown, 17, 67, 214
Prefrontal cortex, 18, 161, 243, 256
Procrastination, 19, 254
Punishment, 15, 17, 27, 29, 31–33, 35–42, 44, 47, 65, 71, 75, 89, 91–92, 95, 100–103, 106, 119, 120, 126, 144, 149, 165, 177, 178, 186, 191, 194, 198, 208, 227, 236, 250, 251, 257, 271, 273, 280, 287–292, 293, 306, 307
    See discipline
Pushing back, 15, 27, 29, 100–103, 105, 149, 204, 206, 242, 282, 288, 292, 293, 299

Rage, 46–48, 50–52, 101, 186, 269
Red flags, 100, 147–148
Rejection, 4, 16, 23–24, 36, 40, 45–46, 52, 58, 64–65, 69, 74–77, 84, 113, 114, 120, 121, 147, 192, 193, 194, 198, 209, 223, 231, 259, 278, 292, 295, 299, 307
    Emotional rejection, 18

Regulation, 21, 87, 89, 92,105, 112, 115, 131–132, 151, 156, 157, 160, 186, 189, 194, 198, 199, 200, 206, 209, 211, 212, 227, 234, 236, 237, 238, 242, 243, 244, 245, 246, 257, 259, 260, 272, 277, 280, 283, 284, 298, 305
    Co-regulation, 49, 132, 186, 200, 211, 252, 273, 282, 289, 290
    Dysregulation, 67, 103, 105–106, 112, 115, 124, 149, 212, 243, 248, 255, 257, 283, 284, 289, 301, 302, 304
    Emotional regulation, 18, 33, 65, 67, 94, 105, 186, 193, 208, 225, 243, 250, 252, 256, 273, 284
    Release to regulate, 198
    Resist to regulate, 105
    Reist to release to regulate, 242, 282, 284, 294, 296, 302, 304
    Self-regulation, 22, 103, 132, 283
Relationships, 7, 40, 55, 56, 57, 64, 65, 69, 71, 90, 93, 95, 96, 104, 113, 114, 118, 119, 123, 127, 131, 132, 144–148, 151–152, 162, 196, 197, 202, 224, 251, 252, 288, 298, 300, 301, 303
    Relational healing, 126
    Relationship repair, 26, 47, 180, 257, 260, 267, 301, 303
    Relationship Set Point, 144–146
    Relationship with our parents/caregivers 6, 15, 23–61, 69, 94, 102, 116, 156–158, 185–200, 273, 307
    Relationship with yourself, 115, 118–119, 123, 162
Reparenting, 159, 161, 162, 167, 187, 188–189, 190–191,194–199, 202, 206, 210, 212, 218, 222, 226, 229, 232, 238, 279
    Reparenting and parenting 180–183
Resentment, 6, 57, 166, 266, 267, 269, 272, 287
Resilience, 26, 56, 67, 91, 185, 200, 202, 220, 244, 254, 255, 273
    Shame resilience, 118, 265
Resistance, 15, 38, 105–106, 149, 191, 198, 209, 271, 281, 294, 299, 305, 306

Resist without shame, 242, 244
    See resist to release to regulate
Respect, 7, 31–33, 37–38, 44, 69, 73, 75, 83, 89, 94, 100, 103, 162, 177, 242, 251, 287, 288, 289
    Disrespect, 72–73, 99, 100, 104, 105, 149, 242, 247, 299, 304, 306
Rest, 56, 63, 134, 162, 170, 187, 196, 199, 214–219, 220–222, 227, 230, 231, 232, 233, 269, 309

Sadness, 6, 32, 38, 64, 76, 77, 183, 198, 199, 200, 207, 210, 276
Safety, 8, 11, 16–19, 20, 21, 23, 25–26, 28, 29, 31, 33, 45–46, 49, 51, 54, 58, 59, 63, 65, 67, 89, 92, 93, 99, 100, 101, 103, 110, 111, 116, 117, 121, 126, 129, 134, 135, 139, 142, 145, 146, 147, 150, 154, 155, 161, 162, 168, 173, 178, 179, 188, 195, 201, 204, 206, 207, 212, 213, 215, 216, 218, 219, 220, 222, 224, 227, 228, 231, 232, 233, 236, 237, 240, 242, 246, 254, 257, 260, 262, 266, 267, 283, 288, 301, 303, 305
    Emotional safety, 16, 18, 24, 35–36, 165, 166,186, 199, 200, 203, 209, 210, 223, 226, 244, 271, 272, 273, 274, 280, 295, 297, 299, 307
    Environmental safety, 27, 186
    Physical safety, 186
    Relational safety, 26, 95, 113, 186, 205, 261
    Safe people/relationships, 119, 123, 130, 131, 132,144, 149, 151–152,189, 205, 269
    Safe spaces, 118, 130, 132, 211, 249, 269, 281
    Feeling unsafe, 15, 17, 46, 52, 64, 69, 77, 86, 87, 91, 102, 123, 124, 125, 137, 138, 144, 153, 156, 187, 192, 200, 211, 223, 245, 247
School, 55
Self-awareness, 225
Self-doubt, 26, 69, 220, 227, 272, 287
Self-harm, 235–236
Self-sabotage, 55, 145
Selflessness, 32, 57, 84, 109, 170

Index

Selfishness, 32, 82, 84–85, 194, 251, 267
Shame, 11, 16, 18, 19, 29, 35–41, 45–47, 52, 55–56, 58, 81, 83–85, 88–89, 91, 93–96, 106, 109, 113–116, 119, 128–129, 133–136, 142, 144, 152–153, 159, 161, 163, 165–166, 170, 172, 173, 178, 179, 181–183, 185, 186, 187, 189, 190, 191, 193, 194, 195, 198, 199, 208, 211, 212, 215, 222, 227, 228, 232, 234, 235, 236, 237, 238, 242, 245, 246, 248, 249, 250, 251, 253, 254, 255, 256, 271, 272, 275, 276, 278, 280, 286, 287, 291, 293, 297, 299, 305, 307
  Internalized shame, 7
  Relational Shame Trauma, 6, 22, 33–34, 37, 51, 60, 64, 68, 70–71, 95, 99, 117–118, 122, 124, 126, 143, 213, 224, 252, 254, 269, 273, 292, 303
  Relational shame, 40, 69, 118, 120, 121, 201, 205, 266, 283, 289
  Shame-free boundary, 216
  Shame-laced discipline 23, 28, 33, 38, 65, 66–68, 72, 99, 182, 257, 306
  Shame-prone self-talk, 261–262, 265
  Shame spiral, 133, 196, 209, 216, 239, 257–258, 265, 266, 267, 277, 290
Shapeshifting, 5, 9, 31, 59, 63, 120, 123, 213, 309
Shift Your Focus, 245–246, 259
Shut down, 4, 15, 16–18, 20, 37, 25, 46, 55, 59, 69, 76, 100, 104, 106,153, 154, 163, 178, 181, 200, 208, 214, 241, 242, 245, 246, 248, 250, 257, 264, 272, 274, 287, 299, 306
  Emotional shut down 19, 28, 36, 39, 45, 131, 138, 187, 188, 252, 254, 266, 273, 278, 280, 299
  Physical shut down, 17–18, 49, 64, 65, 67, 101–103, 137, 160, 177, 199, 207, 215, 231, 258
  See freeze response and dorsal vagal shut down

Siblings, 48, 53, 54, 56–57, 101
Silent treatment, 4, 23, 27, 32, 35, 41–42, 51, 66, 71, 74, 138, 145, 195, 240, 290–292
  See emotional withdrawal and withdrawal of love and affection
  Psychosomatic, 230–233
  Somatic, 21
Soothing, 34, 56–57, 115, 162, 167, 200, 234, 236, 238
  Self-soothing, 24, 186–187, 227, 230, 233, 237, 238, 239
  Hidden Self-Soothing, 189, 198, 233–239
Spanking, 15, 27, 35, 126
Splitting, 42
Stand By Them, 178, 206, 209, 244–245, 260, 262, 277, 278, 296, 299, 300
Stand By Yourself, 129–130, 166, 194, 200, 202, 279
Stomachaches, 112, 231–232, 252
Stress, 22, 53, 55, 110, 147, 149, 180, 213–214, 230, 231, 238, 247, 250, 267, 268, 280, 283, 297
  Chronic stress, 214
  Stress crash, 219
  Stress hormones, 18, 256, 268
  Stress release, 102–103, 106, 109, 200, 242, 274, 306
  Stress Cycle, 20–21, 11, 132, 151, 156, 200, 268, 298
  Stress responses, 20, 67, 165, 177
Survival, 26, 27, 49, 53, 64, 67, 90–91, 181, 214, 238, 243
  Survival mode, 16, 18, 133, 142, 211, 230, 232, 266, 290
  Survival strategies, 13, 26, 54–58, 88, 95, 131, 135, 149, 222, 234

Tantrums, 15
Therapy, 9, 123, 142, 170, 180, 181, 183, 267, 275
Time In, 290
Time Out, 66, 126, 289–290
Tough love, 37, 89, 90–91

Trauma, 29, 137, 146, 185, 285, 289
  Childhood trauma, 40, 160
  Emotional trauma, 22
  Generational trauma, 34, 40, 44, 99, 179
  Relational trauma, 37, 69–70, 72, 86, 109, 123, 142, 147, 151, 157, 161, 166, 207, 208
  Trauma release, 268
  Unhealed trauma, 117
  Unresolved trauma, 7, 35, 51, 112
Trauma responses, 9, 23, 33, 142
Triggering events, 22, 31, 46, 48, 109, 148, 154, 160, 178, 181, 185, 193, 198, 206, 208, 216, 237, 239, 240, 244, 245, 249, 254, 266, 273, 280, 284, 285, 286, 290, 291, 300, 306

Unconditional love, 58, 91, 122, 129, 146
Unconditional Positive Regard (UPR), 168
Unspoken rules, 31, 33, 72–84, 109, 116

Validation, 52, 59, 128, 130, 131, 132, 167, 202, 211, 212, 232, 237, 246, 269, 281, 297
  External validation, 75, 91, 227

Withdrawal of love and affection, 4, 15, 23, 25, 27, 28, 32, 41, 52, 66, 71, 74, 95, 101, 146, 150, 167, 186, 195, 204, 241, 252, 257, 289, 301
Worth, 34, 37, 38, 58, 67, 70, 72, 73, 75, 77, 80, 84, 90, 91, 92, 95, 96, 109, 122, 124, 128, 129–137, 141, 150, 170, 171, 182, 186, 196–197, 214, 215, 217, 218, 220, 221, 222, 229, 248, 251, 257, 262, 287, 296, 301, 307
  Feeling unworthy, 33, 38, 63, 64, 117, 118, 123, 127, 129, 135, 153, 162, 196, 230, 251, 253, 269, 288, 307
  Inherent worth, 8, 121, 144, 166, 178, 211, 229
  Self-worth, 26, 28, 37, 55, 66, 67, 91, 113, 161, 227, 261, 288, 305
  A parent's worth, 31, 37, 51, 74, 75, 250–251